MARKETING

Second Edition

Pearson Education

We work with leading authors to develop the strongest educational materials in marketing, bringing cutting-edge thinking and best learning practice to a global market.

Under a range of well-known imprints, including Financial Times Prentice Hall, we craft high quality print and electronic publications which help readers to understand and apply their content, whether studying or at work.

To find out more about the complete range of our publishing please visit us on the World Wide Web at: www.pearsoneduc.com

MARKETING
IN THE
DIGITAL AGE

Second Edition

JOHN O'CONNOR
EAMONN GALVIN

FINANCIAL TIMES
Prentice Hall

An imprint of **Pearson Education**

Harlow, England · London · New York · Reading, Massachusetts · San Francisco
Toronto · Don Mills, Ontario · Sydney · Tokyo · Singapore · Hong Kong · Seoul
Taipei · Cape Town · Madrid · Mexico City · Amsterdam · Munich · Paris · Milan

Pearson Education Limited
Edinburgh Gate
Harlow
Essex CM20 2JE
England

and Associated Companies around the world.

Visit us on the World Wide Web at:
www.pearsoneduc.com

First published 1997
Second Edition 2001

ISBN 0 273 64195 6

British Library Cataloguing-in-Publication Data
A catalogue record for this book can be obtained from the British Library

Library of Congress Cataloging-in-Publication Data
O'Connor, John, 1960-
    Marketing in the digital age / John O'Connor, Eamonn Galvin.-- 2nd ed.
        p. cm.
    Rev. ed. of: Marketing and information technology : the strategy, application and
implementation of IT in marketing / John O'Connor, Eamonn Galvin. 1997.
    Includes bibliographical references and index.
    ISBN 0-273-64195-6 (pbk.)
    1. Internet marketing. I. Galvin, Eamonn. II. O'Connor, John, 1960- Marketing and
information technology. III. Title.
    HF5415.1265 .O25 2000
    658.8'4--dc21
                                                                    00-050299

10 9 8 7 6 5 4 3 2 1
05 04 03 02 01

Typeset by 43
Printed and bound in Great Britain by
TJ International Ltd, Padstow, Cornwall

CONTENTS

PREFACE

Since the first edition of this book was published in 1997 we have been in the middle of a revolution. The Internet and technologies such as the mobile phone have grown exponentially and dramatically changed the way we practice marketing. In 1997 we demonstrated how marketing and information technology were inextricably linked. Those links have grown to the extent that we can now say that any marketing person who does not understand the role of information technology will become an endangered species. The furious rate of change and competition is rapidly weeding out those adverse to technology.

The content of this new edition has been updated to reflect the changes of the last few years. We have added a new structure, which should make it easier to navigate the book. Each chapter has been updated with the changes brought about by the Internet and e-Business. We have also added a number of new case studies and you will now find many URL addresses to web sites. These changes were necessary to bring this edition up to date. We think of this book as a roadmap that will help you navigate the different areas of marketing rather than as a final destination. It can be used to orient yourselves on the basics before launching onto the web to search for the most up to date information. While the last few years have seen dramatic changes we believe the rate of change will continue in the near future. It is an exciting time for anyone involved in marketing and information technology. We trust this book provides a great launch pad for the exciting journey ahead.

Our thanks

We owe our thanks again to the team at Pearson Education, Mary Lince and Liz Sproat, for making the second edition a reality. A special thanks goes to the reviewers and practiners who have contributed their comments and ideas to this edition. At HotOrigin John would like to thank David Dalton and the team for providing such an exciting work environment. At GE Eamonn would like to thank Gary Reiner, Jan DeWitte, Simon Cooper, Declan Daly, Nitin Mittal, the Corporate Inititiatives Group team and the e-Business leaders in each GE business for providing so many new insights on marketing and e-Business. Also to Tom for taking all of this into practice.

As always we would like to invite you to comment on this book. Send your comments, good, bad and indifferent, to;

john.oconnor@hotorigin.com
egalvin@indigo.ie

Enjoy!

John O'Connor
Eamonn Galvin

September 2000

ACKNOWLEDGEMENTS

We are grateful to the following for permission to use copyright material:

Harvard Business School Publishing for Exhibit 1.1 from *The innovator's dilemma: when new technologies cause great firms to fail* by Clayton Christensen 1997; The Financial Times Limited for Exhibit 1.3 from 'New-generation animal magic', © *Financial Times*, 21 July, 1999, Exhibit 1.4 from 'Chips with everything', © *Financial Times*, 21, 22 November, 1998, Case Study 1 from 'Airlines promote paperless trail of electronic tickets', © *Financial Times*, 12 August, 1999, Exhibit 2.2 from 'DVLA tries out online renewals', © *Financial Times*, 25 September, 1996, Exhibit 2.3 from Exchanging data: web-based EDI World network of 2,500 suppliers', © *Financial Times*, 2 September, 1998, Exhibit 3.2 from 'Online supermarket forces big rivals to check out prices', © *Financial Times*, 10 August, 1999, Exhibit 3.3 from 'Interactive TV put to the test', © *Financial Times*, 6 December, 1995, Exhibit 4.2 from 'Scandinavians wake up to a bright new image', © *Financial Times*, 19 November, 1998, Exhibit 4.3 from 'Customers in sharper focus', © *Financial Times*, 2 September, 1998, Exhibit 4.4 from 'Swift facts for stockbrokers', © *Financial Times*, 5 November, 1997, Exhibit 4.9 from 'Key role for IT in the marketing mix', © *Financial Times*, 2 September, 1998, Exhibit 5.4 from 'Customers compart-mentalised', © *Financial Times*, 1 March, 1995, Case Study adapted from 'A system for keeping air passengers happy', © *Financial Times*, 1 March, 1995, Exhibit 7.2 from 'A helpdesk for Europe', © *Financial Times*, 6 March, 1996, Case Study from 'Knowing when to be of service', © *Financial Times*, 12 February, 1998, Exhibit 9.1 from 'When green means go for it', © *Financial Times*, 10 October, 1996, Exhibit 9.3 from 'On-line machines that take the worry out of wash day', © *Financial Times*, 1 October, 1998, Exhibit 9.4 from 'Increasingly crucial role', © *Financial Times*, 10 June, 1996, Exhibit 9.6 from 'The virtual world of robotic production', © *Financial Times*, 2 June, 1999, Case Study adapted from 'Blade runner', © *Financial Times*, 23 July, 1996, Exhibit 10.1 from 'Citibank offers cheap loans', © *Financial Times*, 17 July, 1999, Exhibit 11.4 from 'Strength of sales offers radical change to industry', © *Financial Times*, 5 May, 1999, Exhibit 11.5 from 'Cashing in on the hole-in-the-wall', © *Financial Times*, 21 July, 1999, Exhibit 11.6 from 'Working with mixed pallets', © *Financial Times*, 1 December, 1998, Exhibit 12.6 from 'Net ads fail the soap test', © *Financial Times*, 28 August, 1998, Exhibit 13.1 from 'How a 12,000−strong sales force builds better links with clients', © *Financial Times*, 7 April, 1999, Exhibit 13.2 from 'Store Planning: Window on the world', © *Financial Times*, 3 September, 1997, Exhibit 13.3 from 'Keeping track of customers', © *Financial Times*, 5 November, 1997, Exhibit 13.5 from 'Why so many companies are embracing the CRM trend', © *Financial Times*, 3 February, 1999, Exhibit 14.2 from 'Turning their heads', © *Financial Times*, 22 September, 1998, Exhibit 14.3 from 'A leader among PC makers', © *Financial Times*, 3 June, 1998 and 'Fishing gear maker floats a helpful idea', © *Financial Times*, 3 February, 1999, Case Study from 'Can somebody come to the line, please?', © *Financial Times*, 3 February, 1999, Exhibit 15.1 from 'Prudential woos youth with high-tech, high-interest deal', © *Financial Times*, 6 October, 1998 and 'Banks scramble to follow Egg's lead' © *Financial Times*, 14 August, 1999, Exhibit 15.4 from 'Companies can tap into a growing range of services', © *Financial Times*, 4 August, 1999, Exhibit 15.5 from 'Sales teams need convincing too', © *Financial Times*, 2 September, 1998 and Case Study from 'Advantages slip through a crack in the barcode', © *Financial Times*, 1 September, 1998; The Economist Newspaper Limited for adapted extracts from the articles 'Battle of the brand' in *The Economist* 13 June 1998, 'Flying in Circles' in *The Economist* 17 July 1999 (Exhibit 1.6), 'Bar-coding the poor' in *The Economist* 25.1.97 (Exhibit 2.1), 'Data Wars' in *The Economist* 22 July 1995 (Exhibit 4.6), 'Fire and Forget?' in *The Economist* 20 April 1996 (Exhibit 5.8), 'Hi ho, hi ho, down the data mine we go' in *The Economist* 13 August 1997 (Exhibit 7.3), 'Mail chauvinist' in *The Economist* 7 February 1998 (Exhibit 7.4), 'Market makers' in *The Economist* 14 March 1998 (Exhibit 8.5), 'The Microsoft of toyland' in *The Economist* 21 November1998 (Exhibit 9.2), 'It was my idea' in *The Economist* 15 August 1998 (Exhibit 10.3), and 'Japan's Bell Curve' in *The Economist* 3 October 1998 (Exhibit 11.2), all © The Economist Newspaper Limited, London 1995, 1996, 1997, 1998, 1999; News International Syndication for adapted extracts from the articles 'Web of competition traps bookseller' © David Sumner Smith/Times Newspapers Limited, 25 July 1999 (Case Study, Chapter 2) and 'Bulmer bridges the gap — Data Warehousing' by Rodney Hobson in *The Times* 5 June 1996 © Times Newspapers Limited 1996 (Exhibit 5.5); Centaur Communications Ltd for Exhibit 4.5 from the article 'Streets ahead' in *Marketing Week* 17 May 1996; Peter Chisnall for Exhibit 4.8 adapted from *Marketing Research*, 5th Edition, 1997 published by McGraw Hill Publishing Co. Maidenhead; CACI Limited for Exhibit 5.2 adapted from the CACI Web site www.caci.co.uk; Claritas UK for Exhibit 5.3 adapted from www.claritas.co.uk; A. Kransdorff for Exhibit 5.9 from 'Keep know-how in the company', *Financial Times*, 31 July, 1996, © A. Kransdorff, 'Corporate Amnesia'; The Dialog Corporation for Exhibit 5.10 adapted from www.dialog.com; Computer Weekly for Exhibit 5.11 adapted from the article 'SBC Warburg speeds up research with intranet' in *Computer Weekly* 6 June 1996; Whurr Publishers Ltd for Exhibit 8.4 adapted from 'Relationship management: Generating Business in the diverse markets of Europe' by S. Pearson in *European Business Journal*, Volume 6, Number 4, 1994; The author, Thorsten Nilson for Exhibit 12.5 adapted from *Chaos marketing: how to win in a turbulent world*; Vector Communications for Exhibit 14.1 adapted from a Vocalis advertisement, 1996.

Table 2.1 from 'Italians urged to learn to love IT', © *Financial Times*, 20 July, 1999; Figure 10.1 from *The Marketing Revolution*, copyright © 1991 by Kevin J. Clancy and Robert S. Shulman, reprinted by permission of HarperCollins Publishers, Inc. (Clancy, K.J. and Shulman, R.S. 1991); Table 15.1 from 'Change in sentiment over IT outsourcing', 1998, © *Financial Times*, 4 August, 1999; Table 5.2 from the CACI Web site, copyright © CACI Ltd, 1999; Figure 13.3 from *Datamation* (1 May 1995), copyright © EarthWeb Inc. www.earthweb.com, 1995; Table 14.1 from the Industrial Development Authority of Ireland Web site, www.ida.ie, 1999.

Whilst every effort has been made to trace the owners of copyright material, in a few cases this has proved impossible and we take this opportunity to offer our apologies to any copyright holders whose rights we may have unwittingly infringed.

THE MARKETING REVOLUTION

Part I of this book deals with the changing nature of marketing. Although the marketing function has been successful up to now, a number of structural changes within industry and society are challenging the way that marketing should be conducted today. The greatest structural change of all is the arrival of the digital age and it is in the face of this electronic and information revolution that marketing managers must find their future.

Part I contains three chapters:

1   Marketing's challenge

2   The arrival of the digital age

3   How can marketing respond?

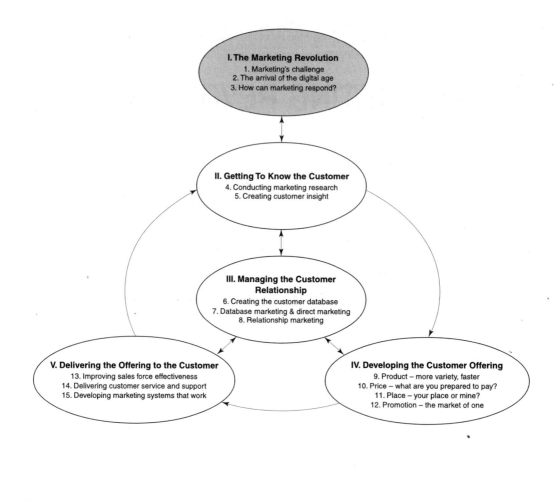

I. The Marketing Revolution
1. Marketing's challenge
2. The arrival of the digital age
3. How can marketing respond?

II. Getting To Know the Customer
4. Conducting marketing research
5. Creating customer insight

III. Managing the Customer Relationship
6. Creating the customer database
7. Database marketing & direct marketing
8. Relationship marketing

V. Delivering the Offering to the Customer
13. Improving sales force effectiveness
14. Delivering customer service and support
15. Developing marketing systems that work

IV. Developing the Customer Offering
9. Product – more variety, faster
10. Price – what are you prepared to pay?
11. Place – your place or mine?
12. Promotion – the market of one

1

MARKETING'S CHALLENGE

SUMMARY

A 1998 article in *The Economist* magazine sums it up nicely:

'Marketing has become a complex art. Technology and trade have increased the potential for global brands. The fragmentation of audiences and rising costs of television and print advertising are making other media attractive. And direct marketing and the Internet are rewriting all the marketing rules.'[1]

Over the last 30 years marketing has developed into a well-defined discipline with accepted frameworks and models. In the 1950s it embraced the new technology of television and developed mass marketing techniques that are the cornerstone of many of today's well-known brands such as Coca-Cola, McDonald's and Sony. It has developed effective models of consumer behaviour and we have seen the development of the role of the brand manager as the key implementor of the marketing concept. By and large, marketing's role in identifying and meeting customers' needs has served companies very well.

However, the last decade of the twentieth century saw changes that are causing a major redefinition of the role and concept of marketing:

☐ Customers have become more sophisticated and demanding.

☐ The way products are developed and brands are managed has changed radically.

☐ Distribution channels have become 'virtualised'.

☐ Payment systems have also become 'virtualised'.

☐ Markets have become increasingly global.

In the face of these challenges the traditional marketing organisation will have to change. Some have referred to this as 'marketing's mid-life crisis'.

MORE SOPHISTICATED AND DEMANDING CUSTOMERS

Changing consumer lifestyles

Today customers are more demanding, less loyal and less willing to forgive companies whose products and services do not meet their high standards. Customer loyalty programmes and relationship marketing are responses to customers who have become progressively more disloyal and more likely to switch products. The main trends in customers' lifestyles and attitudes include the following:

- *Cash rich, time poor.* Many people have more disposable income today but find themselves with less time to do the things they can now afford. Such people are looking for convenience and speed and are comfortable doing business over the phone and the Internet.
- *Increased leisure time.* Other consumers are moving to a 35-hour week while maintaining or increasing their levels of disposable income. These changes are reflected in the growing popularity of eating out, use of health and fitness clubs, and other leisure activities.
- *Increased technology ownership.* Consumers are eagerly adopting new technologies such as mobile phones, personal digital assistants (PDAs), digital video disc (DVD) players, digital televisions and, of course, home computers. Older age groups, particularly retired people, are also eagerly embracing the Internet.

Changes in the way products and services are marketed, which we will examine in the following pages, are a response to this fundamental change in customer sophistication. Customers are demanding better products and quicker introduction of new features — hence the proliferation of products and the shortening of product life cycles. The demand for greater flexibility in the purchase of goods and services is leading to a proliferation of distribution channels and customers. One of the drivers for global brands is the fact that customers seek out similar goods, values and standards of service as they travel abroad.

CHANGES IN PRODUCT MANAGEMENT

▪ Shortened product life cycles

Over the past decade many companies have both cut the average time to bring a product to market and shortened the corresponding life cycle of the product. One computer manufacturing company decreased its product development cycle by two-thirds between 1967 and 1990. Pharmaceutical companies such as Eli Lilly are attempting to halve the time it takes to test a new drug. These trends are not confined to products in the high-tech or pharmaceutical industries. The same can be seen in the automobile industry, the consumer goods industry — in fact, in almost every industry. The impact on the marketing function has been dramatic, with demand for more and more revenues in shorter and shorter timescales. The success in the UK of the citrus drink Sunny Delight shows how good marketing and the appropriate use of technology can help. Procter & Gamble planned the UK launch of Sunny Delight for April 1998. It tested the product extensively during the previous 12 months, and involved the retailers in early promotional campaigns, by employing data from loyalty card schemes to select young, low-income families. It sent out mailshots to these families offering discounts on the product. Sunny Delight may not last long enough to become one of the great soft drink brands but the combination of sophisticated test marketing and targeted direct mail helped the drink to jump straight into Britain's league table of top brands within 16 months of its launch, with annual sales of almost £160m.[2]

The trend is most pronounced in Internet companies. First-e, the first European Internet bank, was launched a mere 12 months after the idea was first conceived.[3]

■ 'Disruptive' technologies

Perhaps more important than the reduction in product life cycles is what Christensen (1997)[4] refers to as *disruptive* technologies – new products that quickly cannibalise sales of existing products and render those products obsolete. Exhibit 1.1 examines how Seagate Technology failed to manage the impact of one disruptive technology, the hard disk drive. These technologies cause great difficulties for traditional marketing organisations, as they require significant resources to develop at a time when the market for the product is still immature or even non-existent.

Exhibit 1.1

HARD DRIVE AT SEAGATE

Seagate Technology used to be a world leader in disk drive technology in the PC industry. When engineers at Seagate showed prototypes of new 3.5-inch disk drives to the marketing personnel, they asked whether a market for the smaller, less expensive drives existed. The marketing organisation, using its habitual procedure for testing the market appeal for new drives, showed the prototypes to leading customers, asking them for an evaluation. One customer, IBM, showed no interest in Seagate's disruptive technology because they were looking for higher-capacity drives. In any case, they had already had a slot for the larger drives designed into their computers. Seagate's marketers drew up pessimistic sales forecasts and senior managers shelved the project, just as the 3.5-inch drive was becoming firmly established in the laptop market. In this case, Seagate made a conscious decision not to pursue the disruptive technology. In other cases, engineers and marketers starved the disruptive technology of the resources necessary for a successful launch.

Source: Christensen (1997).

■ Product proliferation and brand extensions

If marketing departments have been pressurised into bringing newer products to market more quickly, they have also been exposed to higher launch costs and greater risks of failure. In response, many fast-moving consumer goods companies (FMCG) have chosen to extend existing brands. The result has been an explosion of brand extensions and new variations on existing brands.

In the UK instant coffee market, Nestlé's brands now include Nescafé, Gold Blend, Blend 37, Alta Rica, Cap Colombie, Nescafé Decaffeinated, Gold Blend Decaffeinated, Alta Rica Decaffeinated, Fine Blend, Nescafé Cappuccino, Unsweetened Cappuccino and Espresso – a fine combination of product proliferation and brand extension. Although it may seem a bewildering array of products, it is one of the reasons why Nestlé holds more than 50 per cent of the UK's £500 million instant coffee market. The toothpaste market provides a good example of both product proliferation and brand extension (*see* Exhibit 1.2).

Exhibit 1.2

KEEP SMILING – IT'S GOOD FOR YOU

Manufacturers are offering toothpastes with a variety of benefits – from tartar control to whitening – to keep consumers smiling. 'The marketplace has changed a lot in a short space of time,' says Jack Haber, general manager at Colgate-Palmolive. 'Toothpaste was just toothpaste. Now there is much more diversity as consumers fine-tune their needs.' Colgate Baking Soda & Peroxide was launched in 1995, followed in 1996 by Colgate Whitening with Baking Soda & Peroxide, and by Colgate Tartar Control Plus Whitening in 1997. 'It's no longer just about fighting cavities, but also about teeth that are healthy and look good.'

Source: Soap-Cosmetic-Chemical Specialties (September 1997).[5]

However, there is growing evidence that consumers are no longer willing to put up with an ever-increasing number of products when the level of differentiation is minimal. Even in the mid-1990s there was some evidence of consumer irritation and bewilderment among UK consumers in the face of:

- 1,000 new consumer products reaching supermarket shelves every month;
- over 3,000 food and drink launches per annum, including more than 300 yoghurt launches and more than 375 launches of new sauces and pickles;
- more than 100 washing powder products, with each of the leading brands available in up to 15 variants, including colour wash and standard, biological or non-bio, powder or liquid, low temperature or suds and a variety of pack sizes and refills.[6]

In the FMCG market in particular, manufacturers are losing control to retailers that are finding it easier to promote own-label products in an environment where brand extensions have begun to compromise the quality of the original brand.

THE 'VIRTUALISATION' OF DISTRIBUTION CHANNELS

■ The growth of telephone sales and service

Today, sales and service are increasingly conducted through a number of different channels or, in some instances, through virtual channels only. During the 1990s First Direct grew rapidly in the UK as an innovative telephone bank, even though it still allowed customers to use the branches of its parent, Midland Bank (now HSBC). Dell and Gateway 2000 are just two US manufacturers of personal computers that sell directly to customers by telephone. These changes are the result of an increasing willingness on the part of consumers to use the telephone to buy goods and services. The vast majority of companies today use the telephone as an integral part of their sales and service operations and have migrated significant proportions of their business to this channel.

▓ The rise of the Internet

The Internet is rapidly catching up with the telephone as a mainstream channel for sales and service. By mid-1999 Dell Computers was selling $18 million worth of equipment to customers every day, over the Internet.[7] And there are many more examples to show that consumers are comfortable with sales and service through this relatively new delivery channel. Consider the success of Egg,[8] a new banking organisation launched in the UK in late 1998, offering a limited number of services via telephone and Internet. Within eight months it had signed up more than half a million customers. Across the globe a number of new Internet-only organisations established themselves with tremendous success. The Internet bookseller Amazon[9] launched an attack on the staid world of bookselling and quickly gained market share against its main 'physical' rivals such as Barnes & Noble who were forced to launch their own Internet-based services in response.[10]

Even countries like Japan, where the Internet was not expected to take off as rapidly as elsewhere, are succumbing to Internet fever (*see* Exhibit 1.3).

Exhibit 1.3

PLAYTIME

It is 11pm and Akari Fujimoto is touring an amusement park. She does some shopping and leaves with a few items for her room. An unusual night on the town for a Tokyo resident? It might be, except that Mrs Fujimoto embarks on such virtual expeditions daily. She is one of hundreds of thousands of Japanese who subscribe to PostPet, a Web site where 'animated pets' deliver e-mail messages to the customer.

The program, designed by Sony Communications Network, was an instant success when it was launched in 1997. But in the past six months sales of the second-generation software, at 339,000 units, are more than double those of the first program. The Japanese PostPet site gets 27 million hits a month. The success of PostPet, a next-generation Tamagochi, the enormously popular handheld pet, has come without advertising. It challenges predictions that the Internet will be slow to catch on in Japan.

Source: Financial Times (21 July 1999).

▓ Other channels

The telephone and Internet are not the only new channels in play at present. Automated teller machines (ATMs) have become hugely popular with the public, not only for withdrawing cash, but for the provision of other services as well. In the near future other channels will also gain acceptance. Digital television and the interactive nature of the service will also allow companies to sell and to serve over this medium. Mobile telephones are being Internet-enabled too, allowing them to support a range of commercial activities.

The virtualisation of products and services and the swift acceptance of electronic commerce are recurring themes throughout this book.

THE 'VIRTUALISATION' OF PAYMENTS

▦ Plastic cards

Regardless of where the sale takes place – in the virtual or the physical world – another form of virtualisation has also taken off, namely the virtualisation of the payment process. Plastic cards, typically of the magnetic stripe variety, have become common-place and allow the cardholder to perform a variety of different functions, including:

- withdrawing money from an automated teller machine (ATM card)
- paying for goods in a store or supermarket (credit or debit card)
- acting as a means of identification for gaining entry into secure buildings (identity card)
- accumulating points on a loyalty scheme (loyalty card).

In the 1980s the most common type of virtual payment was the credit card transaction. By the end of the 1990s the debit card had also gained widespread acceptance. For example, the Switch debit brand in the UK has 16 million cardholders and is accepted in 280,000 retail outlets, including most of the top retailers and supermarkets, petrol companies and major national chains. Even retailers that traditionally did not accept cards other than their own, such as Marks & Spencer, broke their rules and now accept Switch.[11] Debit cards now account for approximately 50 per cent of non-cash payments in the UK and have replaced much of the payment business previously carried out using personal cheques. Many financial institutions are withdrawing the cheque guarantee card and migrating their customers to debit cards.

▦ Smart cards

The newest variant of the plastic card is the smart card, which is one of the latest applications of chip miniaturisation. A microprocessor is embedded on to a piece of plastic that gives it an astonishing increase in functionality over the capabilities of credit and debit cards. A variation of the smart card is already used in many countries in the form of public telephone cards. In the UK, the oil company Shell has had a smart card initiative in operation for a number of years. Customers use their Shell SMART card to collect electronic points when they purchase petrol. For every £6 spent on petrol or services, the customer receives one SMART point. The points are stored in the smart card's memory and can be redeemed for free cinema tickets, air miles, tapes and CDs. Alternatively, the points can be donated to charity.

▦ Electronic cash

A wide variety of electronic cash initiatives exist, known by a variety of names including electronic purses and electronic wallets. Electronic purses are stored-value cards that hold cash in an electronic form. The card is typically a smart card and more than 1 billion had been issued worldwide by the end of 1998 under a variety of different brands, including:

▓ *Mondex*,[12] a smart card technology company owned by MasterCard International and a consortium of 28 major companies across the globe.
▓ *Visa Cash*, the card-based electronic wallet sponsored by VISA International.[13] By the end of 1998 there were 25 million Visa Cash cards in issue in 18 countries around the world.
▓ *Proton*, the only 'small country' electronic wallet scheme left. Originally launched by the Belgian bank Banksys, it is now supported by American Express and VISA International.
▓ *GeldKarte*, the nationwide stored-value system operated by a German central banking agency.

Despite the less-than-enthusiastic take-up of electronic purses (*see* Exhibit 1.4), many electronic money initiatives are in operation across the world. Take-up has been much stronger in Europe than in the USA. For example, French VISA cards have carried microchips since the 1980s.

Exhibit 1.4

THE FUTURE OF 'GRUBBY NOTES AND COINS'

Visions of a cashless society were dented in November 1998 when VISA and MasterCard, which stand to gain most from the end of what they call 'grubby notes and coins', abandoned their high-profile New York trial of electronic money. The finish of the year-long test in Manhattan's glitzy Upper West Side followed the ending of a similar experiment in which digital cash was carried on a card in buses and telephone boxes in Swindon, west of London.

Electronic money is here, but hardly anybody is eager to use it. Even the people of Hong Kong and Singapore – notorious technophiles and shoppers – seem unenthusiastic, despite the fact that smart or 'stored-value' cards are already in use for everything from parking meters in Hong Kong to road-pricing in Singapore. In Hong Kong, Mondex claims 8,000 merchants accept its cards. That still seems too few, too many of whom are selling things like clothes, for which standard-issue credit or debit cards are just as good. Groceries offer better prospects, but the total volume of cashless transactions in Hong Kong is still estimated at less than $10m a year – just $30 for each user.

Source: Financial Times (21/22 November 1998) and *The Economist* (21 November 1998).

▓ PC-based electronic cash

PC-based electronic wallets are designed for making payments over the Internet. They are likely to appeal to retailers who want to institute customer loyalty programmes as well as companies that want payment for Internet content they now give away for free. Although the early entrants into the market have experienced difficulties (*see* Exhibit 1.5), it is inevitable that this market will eventually grow.

Exhibit 1.5

MICROPAYMENTS; MICROIMPACT

Four of the leading micropayment systems at the beginning of 1998 were:

- *DigiCash*. DigiCash,[14] a Dutch firm founded in 1990, was one of the earliest companies to create a software-based payments system called eCash that allows users to 'withdraw' digital coins from their bank accounts, store them in a 'purse' on their PC, and use them to buy low-cost items over the Internet. Despite licensing its technology to a number of European banks, it filed for bankruptcy in late 1998 after failing to make headway in the USA.
- *First Virtual*. First Virtual Holdings[15] developed an e-mail-based system that enabled users to make secure on-line purchases using a Virtual PIN (personal identification number) linked to a credit card account. After losing nearly $30 million since its inception in 1994, First Virtual decided in early 1998 to leave the electronic cash market.
- *CyberCash*. CyberCash[16] launched its CyberCoin micropayment service in 1996 for transactions between 25 cents and $10. In the UK, Barclays Bank has licensed the software for its BarclayCoin[17] application.[18] However, CyberCash had accumulated losses of more than $60m on sales of less than $5m in 1998.
- *MilliCent*. MilliCent is the Internet micropayment system designed by computer company Digital Equipment Corp.[19] Like CyberCash's CyberCoin, MilliCent enables users to make micropayments for items such as individual songs, newspaper and magazine articles, or software programs downloaded from the Web.

THE INCREASING GLOBALISATION OF MARKETS

■ Creating global brands

As the world becomes a global village, companies are looking to extend their markets beyond their immediate geographic boundaries. And yet there is still considerable room for truly global brands to be created. Of the top 100 brands in the FMCG market in Europe, the USA and Japan, only seven brands are common to all three countries. In most European countries, many of the 'Top 10' FMCG products are still relatively unknown outside their own national boundaries, suggesting that there is still significant potential for the creation of global brands.

■ Creating global organisations

Mergers and acquisitions have continued unabated in the late 1990s in support of many companies' desire to create global reach. The first six months of 1999 saw cross-border deals worth over $400 billion, a 61 per cent increase over the same period in 1998. Consider the following 'mega-mergers' that took place in 1999:

- *Vodaphone*, whose $69 billion takeover of AirTouch Communications created the world's largest mobile telephone company

▧ *Zeneca*, the pharmaceutical company that took over its Swedish rival Astra in a deal worth more than $50 billion to create one of the world's largest drug companies

▧ *Deutsche Bank*, which bought Crédit Lyonnais's Belgian unit for nearly $600 million, a relatively small deal in itself, but evidence that pan-European banks can be created in what has traditionally been a notoriously national marketplace.

In addition, other global alliances are forming. For example, in the airline industry (*see* Exhibit 1.6), most of the major and many of the minor airlines have allied themselves into one of four major alliances that accounted for nearly half of the total world traffic market in 1998.[20]

▧ *Oneworld* (with 18 per cent of the total), comprises American Airlines, British Airways, Canadian Airlines, Cathay Pacific, Qantas, Iberia, Finnair and Lan Chile.

▧ *Star* (17 per cent), comprises United Airlines, Lufthansa, SAS, Thai Airways, Air Canada, Varig, Ansett and ANZ.

▧ *Delta* (12 per cent) has Delta Air Lines, Air France, Austrian Airlines, Swissair and Sabena.

▧ *KLM/NW* (11 per cent) has KLM, Northwest Airlines, Alitalia, Continental Airlines, America West Airlines.

Exhibit 1.6

FLYING IN CIRCLES

You are booked on the cheapest business flight from London to Seoul. You are going via Paris to pick up an Air France direct flight. On the way to Heathrow you discover that the flight from Paris is actually operated by its alliance partner, Korea Airlines, though the flight code said 'AF'. Instead of travelling with an airline you choose, you are about to board a plane with a carrier whose safety record has been sullied by crashes and near-misses. Welcome to code-sharing, the practice that shapes the route networks of most of the world's 500 airline alliances.

Air France and several other international airlines recently decided to suspend their code-sharing with the Korean carrier, on account of its poor safety record. Yet, despite the dangers of putting your brands in someone else's hands, alliances have grown tenfold in the 1990s, as airlines seek to sell tickets to a wider range of destinations without actually flying to more. Partners in an alliance sell each other's flights and even book blocks of seats on each other's aircraft. By combining networks, airlines can feed extra traffic on to their trunk routes and reap economies of scale.

Source: The Economist (17 July 1999).

MARKETING'S MID-LIFE CRISIS

▧ The case for change

In response to the challenges outlined above, marketing will have to change. Marketing managers must understand how these challenges and the arrival of the digital age have changed the ways in which marketing activities must be conducted. In Chapter 2 we will assess the impact that the digital age will have on the marketing function, and in Chapter 3 we will discuss how marketing can respond to these challenges.

Case study

TICKETLESS TRAVEL

Richard Holloway, a London-based public relations consultant and frequent business traveller, admits to a sense of insecurity with ticketless travel. 'It's a great idea when it works but it gives me a certain sense of unease not to have a paper ticket as proof of my right to travel.' Electronic ticketing – so-called ticketless travel – has been slow to take off in Europe but has transformed the way people buy airline tickets in the USA and Japan. The International Transport Association (IATA), which represents airlines worldwide, is now hoping to expand e-ticket sales worldwide. It is pioneering with IBM, the computer manufacturer, a network capable of linking the e-ticket systems of different airlines. This would allow a passenger on a journey with more than one airline to be issued with a single e-ticket, something virtually impossible today. Under e-ticketing, travellers pay by credit card over the telephone when they book and are usually issued with a receipt by phone or fax. They slot the credit card into an automated ticket machine at the airport that issues a boarding pass. IATA believes that by 2010 the majority of airline tickets in the world will be e-tickets and that in the US 80 per cent of tickets will be electronic. The benefits to the airlines are clear. A conventional paper ticket costs $8 to process compared with between $1–2 for an electronic ticket.

'E-ticketing allows passengers more flexibility and saves them considerable time on travel planning and booking,' says Lufthansa, one of the few European airlines to have introduced the system. 'They can book flights at the last minute; there is no waiting for tickets to be issued and no need either to pick them up.' United Airlines, one of the first to introduce the system on its domestic routes, says more than 50 per cent of tickets on those flights are now e-tickets. In the USA, about one-third of domestic tickets are ticketless.

But many business travellers and travel agents have mixed views. 'It is great if you don't have luggage but otherwise you still have to queue up to check in,' says David Giles, managing director of Amersham Travel and chairman of the Guild of Business Travel Agents' air working party. 'A lot of clients still prefer to have the security of having a ticket in their hands.' In Europe only 20 per cent of flights are domestic compared to 80 per cent in the USA. International flights require more documentation to satisfy security and customs procedures, and in Europe the onus is on travel agents to notify travellers of their rights under the Warsaw Convention. 'Since we have to send a fax to passengers, we might as well send them the ticket, adding that seeking refunds from airlines for flights that are not taken are harder to retrieve, partly because the absence of a ticket makes passengers forget to tell the travel agent. E-ticketing is certainly of benefit to the airlines but not necessarily the travel agent,' he said. However, Dave Young, information services manager at Hogg Robinson, the business travel agent, believes that e-ticketing could lead to reduced costs to travel agents if it were more widespread. 'We do want the rules on the Warsaw Convention to be changed so that we don't have to fax and e-mail it to clients. The big problem though is changing from one airline to another, which is a nightmare at the moment.'

Source: 'Airlines promote paperless trail of electronic tickets', by Scheherazade Daneshkhu, *Financial Times* (12 August 1999).

Questions

1 How is e-ticketing an example of marketing in the digital age, and what particular marketing issues does it pose to airlines and travel agents?

2 Why have European consumers been so slow to adopt e-ticketing, compared to their US or Japanese counterparts? Do you believe the arguments put forward by David Giles?

3 If IATA's projections for ticketless travel are true, what is likely to happen to traditional European travel agents?

4 Check out Lufthansa's Web site. Is Lufthansa likely to be one of the European winners in the digital age, or will it be one of the traditional companies that fails to make the transition?

ASSIGNMENT QUESTIONS

1 What are the major challenges facing marketing today?

2 Discuss the major changes in distribution channels over the past ten years. What are the trends for the future?

3 Assess the advantages and disadvantages of different payment mechanisms over the next ten years.

4 What are the challenges faced in creating global brands?

References

[1] The Economist (1998). 'Battle of the brand', *The Economist*, 13 June.

[2] Hollinger, P. (1999). 'Delightful debut of a strange fruit', *Financial Times*, 14 August.

[3] www.first-e.com

[4] Christensen, C.M. (1997). *The innovator's dilemma: when new technologies cause great firms to fail*. Boston: Harvard Business School Press.

[5] Kintish, L. (1997). 'Brushing up on success', *Soap-Cosmetics-Chemical Specialities*, Vol. 73, No. 9, September.

[6] Matthews, V. (1995). 'Not so much choice please', *Financial Times*, 30 November.

[7] www.dell.com

[8] www.egg.co.uk

[9] www.amazon.com

[10] www.barnesandnoble.com

[11] Carrington, St J., Langguth, P.W. and Steiner, T.S. (1997). *Banking revolution: salvation or slaughter*. London: FT Pitman Publishing.

[12] www.mondex.com

[13] www.visa.com

[14] www.digicash.com

[15] www.fv.com

[16] www.cybercash.com

[17] www.barclaycoin.co.uk

[18] Electronic Payments International (1998). 'BarclayCoin to offer e-money on an international basis', *Electronic Payments International*, June.

[19] www.millicent.digital.com

[20] The Economist (1999). 'Flying in circles', *The Economist*, 17 July.

2

THE ARRIVAL OF THE DIGITAL AGE

SUMMARY

One of marketing's greatest challenges is the arrival of the digital age. Electronic commerce, or eCommerce, has been growing rapidly in the USA over a relatively short number of years and business and marketing managers in European and Asia-Pacific regions are now beginning to realise that digital transactions are changing the ways business is conducted. As the digital age matures, marketing managers will have to understand and accept the following realities:

☐ The digital revolution has happened and the pace of change is accelerating.

☐ Governments are embracing the information society.

☐ Internet-based commerce is already a reality and the supporting infrastructure is being developed to further enhance it.

☐ Every aspect of business is being impacted by the Internet and the benefits of first-mover advantage should not be underestimated.

THE DIGITAL REVOLUTION

The rise of the Internet

In the early 1990s very few people had heard of the Internet; at the beginning of the new millennium there are literally millions of Web sites in place. While many of these can be described as 'brochure-ware', an increasing number have full transactional capabilities that support commercial payments. But, in many ways, this is only the beginning, as the level of Internet penetration is still quite low in many countries outside the USA. IDC, a research company, predicts that in the four years from 1997 to 2001 the percentage of Web users in western Europe will rise from a mere 4 per cent of the population to 15 per cent, a figure that will still be significantly less than half of the USA penetration rates (*see* Figure 2.1).

There is still significant potential for greater Internet penetration in many countries, and newer access mechanisms to the Internet, such as digital television and mobile phones, will increase its reach.

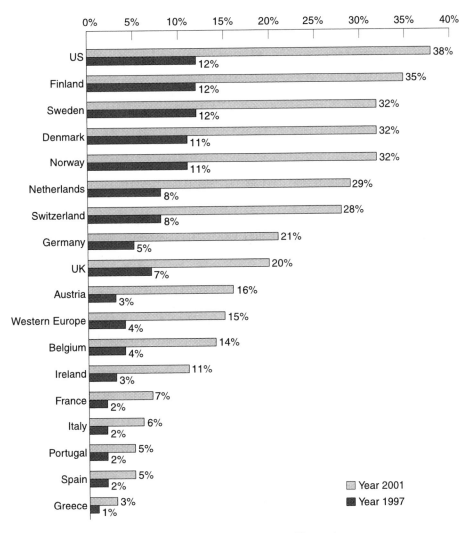

Fig 2.1   Web users as % of population (USA and western Europe)

GOVERNMENT AND THE INFORMATION SOCIETY

▨ The drivers of GDP growth

In early 1995 the members of the Group of Seven (G7) leading industrial countries met in Brussels to respond to the growth of the information society and the information superhighway on which it would depend.[1] By 1999 most EU countries had established initiatives to promote awareness and encourage the development of information technology (IT) skills.

The Italian government, in particular, has been concerned about the lack of speed with which its people have embraced the information age. In 1999 Giuliani Amato, the country's Treasury minister, unveiled a package of proposals aimed at boosting the use

Table 2.1 IT league table

	Web sites ('000s)	Personal computers (m)	Spending on IT (as a proportion of GDP, %)
US	33,387	113	3.6
Japan	1,719	27	2.9
UK	1,692	15	2.4
Germany	1,375	18	2.4
France	571	11	2.3
Italy	371	7	1.5

Source: Italian Treasury, reported in the *Financial Times* (20 July 1999).

of information technology in the Italian economy, warning that the failure of companies to invest in and use IT was an increasing barrier to economic growth.[2] As Table 2.1 shows, the sixth largest economy in the world was not investing heavily enough in IT and the Internet. The Italian government clearly felt that this was one of the reasons why Italy's annual growth rate in the ten years to 1998 averaged a mere 1.4 per cent.

Outside the USA and EU, Asian countries have been moving even faster to support the creation of an information society. Singapore, which launched a National IT Plan as far back as 1985, has enjoyed consistently high GDP (gross domestic product) growth and is the south-east Asian country with the highest standard of living behind Japan. The objective of these initiatives is to capitalise on the opportunities of the digital revolution that is sweeping the world.

▨ Government eCommerce

Apart from promoting the growth of eCommerce, governments are also embracing the Internet for their own use. For example, many governments have either implemented, or are planning to implement, payment of social security and other welfare benefits via the Internet. This type of payment is known as electronic benefit transfer (EBT) and is seen by many governments as a means to boost the introduction of electronic cash into society. EBT has already been introduced in many countries (*see* Exhibit 2.1).

Exhibit 2.1

THE DIGITAL PENSION

As Finland goes, so goes Namibia – at least when it comes to pensions. The two countries are among the pioneers of electronic pension provision, in which recipients draw their retirement cash by inserting a government-issued card into an ATM cash dispenser. This method of transferring cash from governments to people, known in the trade as *electronic benefit transfer* (EBT), looks likely to make order books and welfare cheques obsolete. More efficient and fraud-proof than paper, EBT systems are part of the welfare state of the future. Bits of northern Italy and three provinces in South Africa have already put EBT schemes in place for paying pensions; Mexico is experimenting with one that monitors the supply of subsidised milk and tortillas to some two million poor families.

Source: The Economist (25 January 1997).[3]

BUSINESS AND eCOMMERCE

▓ Electronic data interchange (EDI)

EDI is an electronic data transfer mechanism used in a wide range of business transactions. It is usually associated with the automation of the 'billing cycle' where invoices and purchase orders are generated and sent automatically from one company to another. The primary benefit for organisations that implement EDI is reduced transaction costs. USA sources claim that EDI can cut the average cost of processing a purchase order from $150 to $25.[4] One clothing retailer, working with the jeans manufacturer Levi Strauss, has automated the entire ordering and billing process for producing custom-made jeans.[5] Custom Clothing of Massachusetts has set up a system where customers' measurements are sent electronically to the fabric cutter every evening. By the following afternoon the jeans are made up and sent to the store, or directly to the customer. Invoicing, billing and the entire distribution process have been simplified and automated. Given that three-quarters of the total cost of producing a pair of jeans relate to these activities, the system has clear benefits. However, there are only 30–40,000 US organisations that use EDI, and another 15–20,000 outside of the USA. This represents a very small percentage of commercial organisations, as EDI is only being employed by the world's larger companies such as Glaxo, Marks & Spencer, Courtaulds, ICI and Cowie (*see* Exhibit 2.2). For smaller companies, the benefits of implementing EDI are often outweighed by the costs and difficulties of implementation. However, from a marketing perspective, EDI locks in the supplier with the customer, making it more difficult to break the relationship. It also increases the likelihood that suppliers will gain a greater share of the customer's business.

Exhibit 2.2

ELECTRONIC TAX DISCS

Car-fleet operators like Cowie Interleasing expect to make substantial cost and staff savings from an electronic data interchange (EDI) system for issuing tax discs by the government's Driver and Vehicle Licensing Agency (DVLA). The scheme will replace the cumbersome paper-based system and could eventually cover more than 500,000 cars. The electronic system dispenses with the present costly and time-consuming process that involves the DVLA sending out a postal reminder that the tax disc is due for renewal on each car – even where fleets of up to 50,000 cars are run by one operator, as is the case with the biggest leasing companies. Instead, each month the DVLA will send a reminder to each fleet operator by EDI with the operator responding also by EDI with a list of the vehicles it wishes to relicense. The total tax bill is paid electronically by direct debit and the DVLA prints out the tax discs as a batch and sends them either to the operator or to a collection point.

Source: Financial Times (25 September 1996).

■ The growth of Internet-based commerce

Nowadays traditional EDI is being replaced by Web-based EDI in which secure messages are being passed over the Internet. This is an important shift, as many smaller organisations were previously deterred by the cost and complexity of traditional EDI (*see* Exhibit 2.3).

Exhibit 2.3

EXTRA BENEFITS FROM XTRA TRADE

Small companies can now trade on-line using Internet-based services such as Kewill's Xtra Trade. One of the companies using Xtra Trade is the long-established UK department store Bentalls, which is now working in collaboration with rival store groups Allders and Selfridges on an awareness and education programme to encourage small and medium enterprises, which make up 80 per cent of Bentalls' supplier base, to trade with them via the Xtra Trade service. Sarah Roper, operations director for Bentalls, cites three reasons why Web-based EDI will build up its electronic trading community:

- *Low cost* – the connection fee is only £21 per month compared to a traditional EDI system that might cost suppliers £10,000 or more to build;
- *Increased accuracy* – the comprehensive range of messaging options allows suppliers to build standard electronic catalogues, reducing the amount of data processing required and increasing the accuracy of information transmitted between buyer and supplier;
- *Less duplication* – Web-based EDI implies open standards. In other words, the suppliers do not have to build a number of different systems in order to trade with different buyers.

Source: Financial Times (1998).

Internet-based commerce, or eCommerce, is more flexible, more interactive, and in theory open to any enterprise on the network, large or small, that wants to participate. Not only that, but all the indications are that Internet-based commerce will grow significantly in coming years. Many small to medium sized companies are taking their first steps across the electronic trading barrier and many large retailers are happy to support their suppliers in taking the plunge. For instance:

■ *Kingcup Mushrooms.* Kingcup Mushrooms, a small UK firm with only 30 employees, has become the unlikely pioneer of a technique that links traditional EDI with the World Wide Web to trade with the major retailer Tesco. Tesco uses an EDI service on the Internet for submitting orders, and Kingcup has access to the same service for picking up the orders and for submitting invoices. The EDI service that Kingcup uses to send invoices to Tesco costs around £1 per invoice (incoming messages are free) – considerably cheaper than by registered post, and significantly faster. Tesco and Safeway also work with their suppliers in other ways. They will broadcast sales data, allowing suppliers to see the instant impact of promotions. This gives suppliers more opportunity to respond and reduce the risk of out-of-stock items and disappointed customers.

▓ *Nuovo Pignone.* In Italy, Florence-based Nuovo Pignone manufactures turbines, compressors and other heavy machinery. The company, a subsidiary of General Electric, sources 70 to 80 per cent of its supplies from 300 companies but has a total of 2,500 suppliers scattered all over the world and ranging upwards in size from two-person machine shops. Formerly Nuovo Pignone had a traditional EDI network for trading with its large suppliers but no electronic links with the 2,000 smaller ones. Since moving to a new Internet-based trading system the lower costs and complexities have encouraged many of the smaller suppliers to join the company's Internet trading community while larger suppliers still have the option of using traditional EDI to trade with Nuovo Pignone.

The eCommerce revolution is not just confined to the USA and Europe. In China and other Asian countries the Internet is also taking off, mainly as a result of government promotion (*see* Exhibit 2.4).

Exhibit 2.4

ASIA ONLINE

America has Jeff Bezos; China has Jack Ma Yun. Both are clever entrepreneurs who have grown rich by being the first to exploit the Internet's potential. But there the similarities end. In 1995, around the time that Mr Bezos was setting up Amazon.com, Mr Ma was sending his first e-mail message during a trip to Washington to negotiate a deal for a provincial highway (of the asphalt kind). He got three responses and was so impressed that he bought a PC with some winnings from Las Vegas, signed up with a Web-hosting service, and returned to China to build up an Internet business. China would not get its first commercial Internet connection for a few more months. By the time Mr Ma's sites, ChinaPages and ChinaMarket, had their first few thousand visitors, Mr Bezos was well on his way to becoming a billionaire.

Asia is not America, especially when it comes to eCommerce. However, countries in the region are racing to wire themselves up, with such projects as Singapore's 'wired island', Malaysia's multimedia super-corridor and Hong Kong's planned 'cyberport'. In China, 1999 has been declared the 'year of getting on the Internet' and all ministries are creating Web sites. Asian governments have been the main promoters of Asian eCommerce. When China's trade ministry asked Mr Ma to set up ChinaMarket, 4,500 companies joined before he ran a single advertisement. There may not be anything headline grabbing about most e-business in Asia – an e-mail here, a Web site there – but an eCommerce revolution is nevertheless underway.

Source: The Economist (17 April 1999).[6]

▓ Rapid eCommerce growth

Consider some of the more general eCommerce trends:[7]

▓ *Business-to-consumer eCommerce is taking off.* Although it is difficult to gauge exactly the level of purchases that Internet users are making, most estimates suggest that consumers were purchasing approximately $35 billion per annum over the Internet by the end of 1999.

▥ *Business-to-business eCommerce is already a major market*. The business-to-business market is already a much bigger eCommerce market than its business-to-consumer counterpart. General Electric alone purchases over $1 billion of goods from its suppliers each year over the Internet. Most of Dell Computers' Internet sales are to business, rather than personal, customers. The business-to-business market is likely to continue to represent about 70 per cent of the eCommerce market into the future.

▥ *Further significant growth is also predicted*. Most projections place the total value of eCommerce transactions worldwide well in excess of $1 trillion by the year 2002.

▥ Growth of the supporting infrastructure

The continued growth of the Internet and eCommerce will be underpinned by a number of developments in the technical infrastructure:

▥ *Access to the Internet is becoming more pervasive*. The growth of the Internet was a result of the development of a friendly PC interface, known as a 'browser', which made it easy to navigate the Internet. Access to the Internet through other mechanisms such as mobile phones and digital television will increase the acceptance of the Internet as a means of doing business. The continued penetration of PCs into homes will also drive the market.

▥ *The communications infrastructure is evolving*. Digital exchanges, fibre-optic networks and other high-speed transmissions technologies will increase the speed of Internet communications and further stimulate the eCommerce market.

▥ *Growth in other service industries is facilitating eCommerce*. There has also been growth in the number of Internet Service Providers (ISPs) such as America Online (AOL) and BT that can provide businesses with access to the Internet. Combined with a host of companies that specialise in the development of Web sites, this makes it easier than ever for companies and individuals to go online.

▥ *Security is a major issue but steps are being taken to improve it*. Although there are still major concerns about the security of transactions conducted over a public medium such as the Internet, developments in encryption (the encoding of data to keep it confidential) and security technology will make the Internet safer and increase consumer confidence in this new medium. Security standards such as SET and SSL are already commonplace.

THE IMPLICATIONS FOR BUSINESSES

▥ Destruction of the old order

The digital revolution is likely to result in the destruction of the old order of doing business. New business rules are already being written by companies like Amazon.com, eBay, AOL and others. The implications for businesses are:

▥ *'Old' businesses and business supply chains will be destroyed*. Traditionally businesses have been organised into industries and industries into 'supply chains', a division of labour between different organisations that turns raw materials into products. As technologies enable organisations and individuals to connect with each other in new ways, old supply-chain relationships will be destroyed.

▓ *New, knowledge-based goods and services will be created.* Firms will supplement physical outputs with new electronic 'knowledge products'. For pharmaceutical companies, this means offering on-line medical advice as well as drugs. Such companies are evaluating how to deliver the right information effectively from their vast knowledge of drugs to medical staff when a treatment is being made.

▓ *Some organisations will die.* Businesses that fail to embrace the information age will die and be replaced by nimbler, information-rich competitors. Successful organisations will develop approaches to gathering, storing and disseminating knowledge both between and within organisations.

▓ *New global networks will be created.* Global networks will be created of people and organisations who can communicate but who do not know each other. In this environment buyers will look to brand names they can trust, and having a strong brand identity that consumers know will be increasingly important in a crowded advertising marketplace.

▓ The importance of first-mover advantage

In the eCommerce age, huge advantages can accrue to those who are first movers. For example:

▓ *Amazon.com versus 'The Rest'.* In 1995 Barnes & Noble was one of the premier book retailers in the USA. Amazon.com had just been established by Jeff Bezos, a former investment banker with an idea that there was a market for books to be sold over the Internet. Amazon gave its customers access to several million titles, often at a lower cost. However, Amazon's real advantage was not just access to countless books, but access to book reviews, discussion forums, and Eyes, the e-mail service that automatically notifies customers of books that might be of interest to them. Two years later Barnes & Noble launched its own on-line service and in early 1998 the European publishing giant Bertelsmann announced that it was planning to launch its own global electronic bookstore called Books Online. However, it became clear to both Bertelsmann and Barnes & Noble that neither of their ventures was likely to be as successful as Amazon, which had quickly established itself as the market leader. Bertelsmann and Barnes & Noble decided to merge in order to compete against the upstart. By early 1999 Amazon had solidified its position as market leader and had moved into several new business areas including CDs and on-line auctions, as well as purchasing a 40 per cent share in Drugstore.com, an on-line pharmacy.

▓ *Sky versus BSB.* Rupert Murdoch's Sky Corporation launched a satellite pay-TV service in the UK on 5 February 1989, a full 14 months ahead of its main rival BSB, which had missed its original target launch date by nine months. The lost time was critical. Despite having deeper pockets than Sky, BSB failed to build a customer base quickly enough to overtake Sky. By late summer 1990 Sky had 750,000 satellite subscribers against BSB's 110,000. By November that year financial problems and mounting losses forced both companies to merge, but it was the management of Sky that survived in the newly merged entity called British Sky Broadcasting – virtually all of BSB's 580 employees were fired or left of their own accord. By 1992 BSkyB was generating its first profits and when the company was floated two years later it had a valuation of £4.4 billion.

First-mover status has been very important to Internet-based companies in particular. While many virtual companies generate no profits, they have managed to attract extremely high market capitalisations. When iVillage.com, a popular Web site for US women, was floated in early 1999 its share price rose to over $100 per share, valuing the company at more than $300 million, despite the fact that it generated losses of more than $40 million the previous year. Amazon.com's market value at the same point in time was around $30 billion, also despite the fact that it had never generated profits. However, the market expectations are that these Internet-based companies will be bought out, at high prices, by larger organisations intent on buying their way into cyberspace. Hence the large market valuations. Being second or third into the market often confers the status of also-ran.

Case study

MARY'S BIG IDEA

Over the next two years Ireland faces one of its greatest economic challenges. Either it believes in what must, at the moment, seem only a vague possibility and remakes itself – at considerable expense – into a digital powerhouse, or it maintains its present, so-far successful course of attracting inward investment and occasionally incubating indigenous companies. The problem is that the future is clearly digital, at a scale that even the experts are only beginning to realise. Not to opt for the transformation is to risk closing down the state's hard-won prosperity. Technology companies like Dell, Compaq, Gateway 2000 and Intel are already the high-performance petrol fuelling the economic boom in Ireland – the so-called 'Celtic tiger'. Dell Computers recently announced the creation of 1,700 new jobs, bringing their Irish workforce to nearly 6,000 and making it one of the biggest employers in the state.

Ireland has had great success throughout the mid- and late 1990s in attracting a multitude of foreign companies to set up their European (and even global) operations there. US-owned IT companies in Ireland included IBM, Intel, Dell, Oracle Microsoft, Novell, Lotus and Compaq. Over 30 per cent of investment by US IT companies goes to Ireland. This has resulted in Ireland becoming the second largest software exporting country after the USA, with about 40 per cent of packaged software and 60 per cent of business applications sold in Europe coming out of Ireland. By creating the environment, the Republic should attract the next-generation companies looking for a European base. Build it, and they will come. Fail to provide the sophisticated, ultra-fast Internet networks they will demand in the very near future, and they will move somewhere else. Not just the technology companies – all businesses will be looking for such environments.

Perhaps no one in the higher ranks of government demonstrates an understanding of this as well as Minister of Public Enterprise Mary O'Rourke. For Ms O'Rourke moving the state forward into a high-technology future is, as she calls it, 'a big idea' that has become a personal, not just a political, issue. 'It's kind of a mission now,' she says. 'Well, mission might be a bit strong. I'm kind of evangelical about it now; I am. And when I came in here, I wasn't a bit. I think it developed because I saw the potential. I'm very good for the big pictures, you know. Not for the micro kind of things. I can sort of leap on and see where people would arrive at. I saw where this could mean so much for Ireland.' The minister speaks in rapid free association – start with electronic commerce and suddenly you're hearing about the voyage of St Brendan. But mostly there's a fervour about the possibilities for the Republic if the state can be catapulted into becoming an eCommerce centre. To that end a series of seemingly low-key but pivotal decisions were made by the minister over the summer. Piece by piece, the environment needed for a digital transformation is being established.

First, Eircom's monopoly was ended and the telecoms market liberalised. According to the minister, a competitive market is urgently needed to force the growth of high-capacity, high-speed data networks. Once the market was opened, 'I said, now we could do a whole lot of work; many, many other things,' says the minister. One of those things is a flat-rate Internet access – instead of paying phone charges for time online, Internet users would pay a monthly fee for unlimited use. 'What's the point in having wonderful global technology if people can't use it? That doesn't benefit mankind,' she says.

The department's next move was to issue a framework document outlining the government's position on encryption and digital signatures (electronic techniques for authenticating that an Internet user is the person he or she is claiming to be). Not exactly burning issues for most people but absolutely crucial for encouraging eCommerce. Along with the encryption document, the department announced the formulation of a high-profile Advisory Committee on Telecommunications, filled with top international Internet and telecommunications experts, as well as home-grown talent. There are also plans for a high-speed telecommunications 'corridor' between Northern Ireland and the Republic, she says, and for tax incentives for venture capitalists to invest in new companies. 'You have to be ahead all the time,' Mary O'Rourke says. 'There's no point in keeping pace with whatever's happening in other countries. You have to dream, think and articulate what isn't even believable in this industry.'

Ireland, however, is by no means unique in such thinking. Other economies are saying exactly the same but appear to be more advanced with their plans to create a digital economy. In the UK, for example, Peter Mandelson, when Trade and Industry Secretary, said that he intended to ensure that up to 25 per cent of British government transactions would be made online by the end of the current government's term; while more than three and a half million Canadians filed their taxes online last year. The Scandinavian countries have already taken a substantial lead in the advent of Internet-related commerce and some 60 per cent of Finnish homes, for example, have Internet access, while in the suburbs of Stockholm it is not uncommon to order one's groceries over the Internet for same-day delivery. It remains to be seen how effectively Ireland can differentiate itself and become a hub for the emerging digital economy.

Based on: 'State faces huge economic challenge', by Karlin Lillington, *Irish Times* (4 September 1998); 'Ireland's digital economy: the long road ahead' by John Kennedy, *Business & Finance* (5 November 1998); promotional material from the Irish Development Authority (IDA); 'The European call centre market: from volume to value', The Yankee Group (September 1997).

Questions

1 How can countries like Ireland differentiate themselves as a hub for eCommerce?

2 What additional steps should Mary O'Rourke take to ensure that the 'Celtic tiger' economy continues to be successful?

3 Compare the attempts that the following three European countries have made to position themselves in the new digital world: Ireland, Finland and the Netherlands.

4 Could Singapore's attempts to develop a digital economy turn it into the leading Asian 'tiger' in the future? Or will Hong Kong or Malaysia beat them to it?

ASSIGNMENT QUESTIONS

1 How has the eCommerce age changed the way in which businesses are run today?

2 Check out the current levels of Internet penetration, the number of on-line users, and the general take-up of eCommerce at Web sites like www.nua.net or www.cyberatlas.com

3 To what extent have businesses already embraced the information revolution?

4 What are the key benefits and risks of using electronic commerce?

References

[1] Black, G. (1996). 'Complications delay birth', *Financial Times*, 3 July.

[2] Blitz, J. (1999). 'Italians urged to learn to love IT', *Financial Times*, 20 July.

[3] The Economist (1997). 'Bar-coding the poor', *The Economist*, 25 January.

[4] Verity, J.W. (1996). 'Invoice? What's an invoice?', *Business Week*, 10 June.

[5] McLeod, M. (1996). 'Wired for business', *Sunday Business ComputerAge*, 26 May.

[6] The Economist (1999). 'Asia online', *The Economist*, 17 April.

[7] O'Connor, J. and Galvin, E. (1998). *Creating Value through eCommerce*. London: Financial Times Management Briefings.

3

HOW CAN MARKETING RESPOND?

SUMMARY

Given the challenges that marketing faces, and the changes that are taking place in the digital age, a basic response for marketing managers is to understand and learn about the potential of the digital revolution. In particular, marketing managers should understand the possibilities and opportunities of eCommerce. More specifically, marketing managers should:

☐ adopt a new marketing framework for the digital age

☐ understand and embrace the marketing potential of the Internet

☐ avoid some of the common pitfalls of the Internet

☐ plan for the advent of digital television and interactive services.

A NEW MARKETING MODEL FOR THE DIGITAL AGE

The buyer-driven world

The digital age puts the power into the hands of the buyer rather than the seller. It empowers the buyer with information and allows consumers to decide for themselves what, where and when they should buy. Car insurance is routinely purchased over the telephone, after ringing around to find the best price. Car buyers can check and compare car prices over the Internet before they enter the showroom. With Internet auctions, buyers set the price, not the sellers. In the USA, many patients will search the Internet for advice on their symptoms before they enter their GP's surgery – a feature that shifts the balance of power significantly away from the GP.

This is a lesson that marketers must learn. The world has changed – and the marketing function needs to change as well.

Technology-enabled marketing

Throughout this book we will explore the impact that information technology and the Internet will have on the marketing function. Customer segmentation is moving into a new information-rich era based on behaviour rather than the traditional demographic methods. Sales promotions are becoming more targeted as a result of more, and better, information. Distribution channels are multiplying and intermediaries are coming under increasing threat as manufacturers market their products directly to the customer. Companies will be forced to adopt different marketing models in order to create an

Table 3.1 Traditional versus technology-enabled marketing methods

Marketing area	Traditional	Technology-enabled marketing	Marketing implication
Pricing	Seller-driven	Buyer-driven	Internet/Digital TV
Segmentation	Geo-demographic	Psychographic	Customer database
Advertising	Broadcast	Interactive	Internet/Digital TV
Promotions	Mass	Tailored	Customer database
Sales management	Data with sales	Data shared	Marketing information systems
Distribution channels	Intermediaries	Direct	Multi-channel
Customer ownership	Company	Network	Alliances
Product	Constrained	Buyer-driven	Marketing information systems

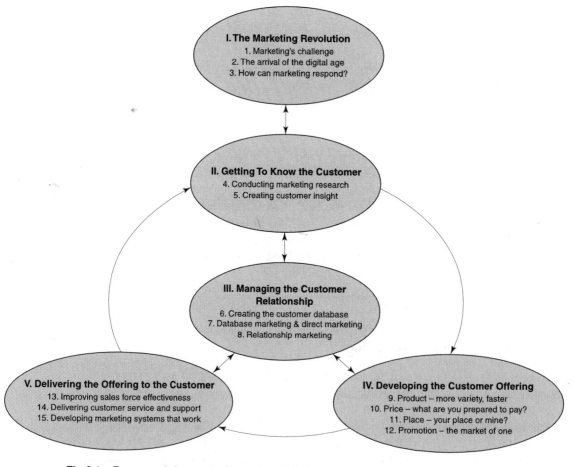

Fig 3.1   Framework for marketing in the digital age

effective response to these changes. Some of the responses required, and the implications for marketing, are summarised in Table 3.1.

▓ Using a dynamic marketing framework

In the remainder of this book, we examine some of the specific ways in which marketing must change. In doing this, we will follow the framework for:

▓ getting to know the customer more intimately than we have in the past, and creating new insights into the customer base;
▓ managing the relationship with the customer through more effective use of customer information and customer database technology;
▓ developing the customer offering, using information technology and the Internet to enhance the product, price, place and promotion elements of the offering;
▓ delivering the offering to the customer, again using IT and the Internet to support effective sales and service delivery.

The framework shown in Figure 3.1 is shown at the beginning of each part of the book, on pages 2, 38, 74, 110 and 168.

THE MARKETING POTENTIAL OF THE INTERNET

The January 1999 edition of *Business Marketing* outlined the top trends in business marketing for that year. The common theme in both 1999 and the previous year, was that of eCommerce. Those trends where information technology plays a crucial role are shown in italics in Table 3.2.

▓ Advertising on the Internet

The multimedia capabilities of the Web allow companies to present their products in a much more colourful and graphical format than a standard advertisement. In addition,

Table 3.2 Top US marketing trends (1998 and 1999)

	Top marketing trends (1998)	Top marketing trends (1999)
1	*On-line customisation*	Integrated marketing communications
2	*Electronic commerce*	*Maturing eCommerce*
3	*Web-design maturation*	*Increased Web-marketing savvy*
4	Globalisation	Corporate branding efforts
5	*Loyalty marketing*	Trade press brand extensions
6	*Database integration*	Return on investment
7	Consumerisation	*Data mining*
8	Emotion in advertising	*Enterprise relationship automation*
9	*Shifting research trends*	*Direct marketing emphasis*
10	Brand emphasis	Greater trade show accountability

Adapted from: Business Marketing (1 January 1999).[1]

a recent survey from the USA by researchers AC Nielsen found that the type of person who browses through Web pages is likely to be from the higher socio-economic groups and more attractive to advertisers.[2] Advertising can also be carried out, somewhat strangely, via radio on the Web. For example, Virgin's Web site allows users to listen to Virgin Radio, the first European radio station to broadcast live on the Internet.[3]

Unilever, the Anglo-Dutch group that spends £3.6 billion a year on advertising and marketing brands, has launched more than 40 Web sites worldwide advertising brands including Ragú, Persil, Mentadent, Fabergé cosmetics, Birds Eye frozen foods and a spread called I Can't Believe It's Not Butter. The Ragú Web site, launched in 1995 as one of the first consumer food product Internet sites, now draws tens of thousands of visitors each day, attracted by recipes, tips and Italian language lessons.

There are three methods of advertising over the Internet:

■ *Creating your own Web site.* Although potential customers must be attracted to visit your Web site in the first place, the Web can be a cheap means of getting an advertising message across to a large number of people. Small businesses can advertise to a potential market of millions for less than the cost of a single-page advertisement in most magazines.

■ *Links from other Web sites.* With literally millions of Web sites on the Internet, most companies will not have the pulling power to attract large numbers of visitors, unless those visitors are referred from another site that gets a significant amount of traffic. Such referrals are made by clicking on links from related sites. Popular portal sites such as Yahoo! and AOL can generate significant revenues for setting up these links from their Web pages.

■ *Paying for banner advertising on other Web sites.* Most interesting Web sites will try to generate revenues by charging other companies to advertise on their site. Advertising is typically done using 'banners' but advertising agencies in the USA estimate that just 1 per cent of Internet users actually click on these banners.[4]

■ Public relations and investor relations

The Web is being used for a variety of public relations functions such as the posting of notices on new products and the distribution of press releases. Most companies that distribute press releases on the Web will archive these releases and other promotional articles so that users can access them easily again. There are other innovative examples of using the Internet for public relations, such as Guinness's extraordinary hit rate on its Web site by allowing visitors to download a PC screensaver, based on a very successful television advertising campaign.

Increasingly popular is the use of the Web for investor relations, using company sites to post information of interest to existing or potential investors. For example, a small mining company like the Perseverance Corporation[5] in Australia can distribute financial statements, annual reports and brokers' reports by posting them on its Web site.

■ Customer service

The Web can allow companies to gather better information about their customers, and to strengthen their relationship with them (*see* Exhibit 3.1). For example, details of new products or updates to existing services can be communicated to customers by e-mail, with an invitation to get more information by visiting the company's Web site. Some companies specifically ask Web visitors to leave their name and e-mail address so that these communications links can be established. General Motors allows customers to design their own car on the Internet.[6] Other companies such as the German software company SAP and Microsoft are using the Web as a means of providing on-line customer service and helpdesk support.[7] For example, SAP has a free on-line database of past problems with its software and solutions that customers can search to see if they can find a match with their own problems.

Exhibit 3.1

PINPOINT THE PARCEL

In the brief annals of doing business on the Internet, Federal Express's customer Web site has become a legendary success story. The package delivery giant, which moves more than 3 million items to 211 countries every day, put up a server on the World Wide Web that gave customers a direct window into FedEx's package-tracking database. More than 150,000 users are registered with the site and they can now query and receive package status information for up to 25 shipments simultaneously. In doing so, FedEx clocks up cost savings estimated in the tens of millions of dollars every year.

Source: Federal Express Web site (1999).[8]

Direct sales

Despite some lingering concerns about security, the Web is being used more and more for on-line ordering. Allied Dunbar became the first UK insurance company to put interactive quotations on the Internet in 1995.[9] Computer hardware and software, books, music and vacation/travel-related items are the biggest sellers on the Web, but any product that already has a good image or brand name can be sold over the Internet, with the exception of those items that need to be physically tried such as fashion clothing.[10] US investment broker Fidelity claims that 1 in 20 of its new clients comes to the firm through the Internet.[11]

More recently, retailers have moved into the digital age and have started offering on-line supermarket facilities to their customers. Although the trend started in the USA, there are good examples from outside North America where on-line supermarkets have taken market share from their traditional counterparts (*see* Exhibit 3.2).

Exhibit 3.2

ADMART THROWS DOWN THE GAUNTLET　　　　FT

Jimmy Lai is no stranger to shaking up the established order. The maverick tycoon has already taken on mainland leaders and Hong Kong's newspaper cartel. Now he is attacking another cosy Hong Kong industry: the supermarkets, where two chains command a virtual monopoly. Mr Lai's AdMart, an Internet and phone-based discount retailer, set up shop in June with a modest array of product lines and even more modest prices. The result has been Coca-Cola selling for HK$1.45 (19 US cents) a can, watermelon at HK$1 a pound ... and huge demand for the products.

The supermarket industry is dominated by Park 'N' Shop and Wellcome, arms of two of the territory's biggest conglomerates, Hutchison Whampoa and Jardine Matheson. The two are believed to control some 70 per cent of the market which, according to government statistics, accounts for annual spending of around HK$1.4 billion. This dominance has caused grumbles in the past but, despite strong objections from the Consumer Council and the Democratic Party, these calls have fallen on deaf ears in government and cartels remain in property, utilities and retail, among others.

But the supermarket experience shows that where government fails, technology and the entrepreneurial spirit can take up the baton. Shortly after AdMart began operations, it was fielding 4,000 calls a day from customers and taking thousands of orders over the Internet. These exceeded expectations so much that the telephone system could not cope and the rather amateur attempts at eCommerce (orders had to be retyped in from the Web to the ordering system) buckled. AdMart has yet to prove it can overcome technical glitches but the gauntlet has been thrown down.

Source: Financial Times (10 August 1999).[12]

MARKETING TIPS AND PITFALLS

■ Marketing tips for the Web

Marketing and advertising on the Web are clearly very different to traditional promotional activities. In 1995 the US technology magazine *Datamation* published a list of business tips[13] for companies marketing on the Web, which still provides a good summary of many of the messages given in previous pages.

- ■ *Make sure your site is scalable.* Don't think in terms of Web pages you simply add and delete. You're committing to a database-driven information store and it is important to link existing databases to the Web and efficiently use existing information.
- ■ *Make your search engine and database structure are flexible and intuitive.* They must be capable of holding all of your content and still give users quick access to what they want.
- ■ *Content is king, so update it often.* Graphics attract, but their primary objective is to add value to your customer's on-line experience by delivering value-added content. Product info, news updates and even reference material and documentation are good places to start. Give both customers and browsers reasons to keep coming back. Ideas include special sales offers, premiums, contests, or even just news updates.
- ■ *Don't just sell to customers and target the content to your users' specific needs.* Don't think of the Web as only a place to advertise or promote your company. If you provide valuable information and resources, customers will keep coming back. (Hint: you'll need more than a picture of your CEO and a recorded message.) Find out what your customers want by having them register on your site. Get their names, addresses and some information about their jobs and interests.

- *Location, location, location: traffic drives sales.* If your own site isn't generating enough traffic, consider linking it to those of trade associations, standards committees or other places that people have already discovered. Some companies have grouped together to make a mall-like marketplace on the Web.
- *Create a sense of community.* Give users a stake in your site. Provide a venue where they can express their ideas.
- *Get help if all this security and browser technology is not your cup of tea.* Don't be afraid to stick to your core competencies and offload the Web work to a service bureau or consultants who specialise not just in Web development but also in your specific business.

▦ Potential pitfalls of the Internet

Despite its undoubted potential, marketers should also be aware of the pitfalls of the Internet as a marketing medium. These include:

- *Poor targeting capabilities.* The potential audience may be large but the customer has to search out the company's Web site in order to view the advertising message. As more and more companies advertise on the Internet the problem of standing out amid all the clutter poses major challenges to organisations.
- *Cost.* As mentioned above, many home pages offer little more than an electronic version of a newspaper or magazine advertisement. It can cost a considerable amount of money to develop a home page that offers greater functionality and that will stand out among the tens of thousands of others. This in turn will lead to problems of measurement and cost effectiveness.
- *Incompatible marketing messages.* Web sites are often created by the IT department rather than the marketing department. This is not necessarily a problem as long as both departments are in touch with each other. Unfortunately, the marketing message that ends up in cyberspace may not necessarily complement the marketing message that is being put out by the rest of the organisation.
- *Communications speed.* Realistically, multimedia communications need a bandwidth of at least 2 million bits per second, yet current modem technology has a typical bandwidth of only 56 kilobits per second. Even as modem technology improves, the capacity of existing copper telephone lines will still prevent higher speeds from being used. The use of higher bandwidth technologies such as ISDN and ADSL will improve communications speed.

THE ARRIVAL OF DIGITAL TELEVISION AND INTERACTIVE SERVICES

▦ Digital television and advertising

In the UK, television viewing was traditionally divided between the BBC and independent companies such as the ITV franchisees, and more recently Channel 4 and Channel 5. Because the BBC stations have been financed by a national television licence and not by advertising, marketing managers bought advertising time on ITV and, to a lesser extent, Channel 4. However, the television world changed significantly in the late 1990s as BSkyB captured a quarter of UK homes with satellite television. Then the 1998 launch of digital television in the UK heralded a new era of hundreds of channels, increasing consumer choice but correspondingly decreasing the advertising reach through any single channel. Not necessarily bad news for advertisers, however – smaller television audiences are accompanied by lower advertising costs for getting a marketing message to a group of customers in a much more focused fashion than was previously possible.

▨ The potential for digital interactive services

Digital television offers more than an increase in the number of channels. It also offers the possibilities of interactive services (*see* Exhibit 3.3).

Exhibit 3.3

THE DIGITAL HOME AND THE BATTLE FOR THE LIVING ROOM

Imagine a parent being able to summon their teenage daughter to dinner by crashing her computer instead of screaming at the ceiling. And imagine that same teenage girl ordering dinner directly from her PC by using it to contact the family's networked refrigerator. The networked digital home could give the problems of dysfunctional (and not-so-dysfunctional) families around the world a whole new twist. And (inevitably) a professional conference has emerged to chart the technology's emergence every step of the way. *Upside* magazine brought together leaders in technology, entertainment and content at the first annual Digital Living Room conference (http://www.digitallivingroom.com) in June 1998. Executives from diverse companies – including Intel, Columbia Pictures, Kodak and LEGO toys – spent three days tinkering with gadgets and learning about each other's visions of the digital home. The gathering revolved around some specific questions:

- What does the digital home look like?
- Who is the digital consumer?
- If the home is wired and teeming with flashing screens, what changes will occur in the way we live and entertain ourselves?

In the UK, many large corporations – telephone and cable companies, publishers and broadcasters, film makers and software developers among them – also have a financial interest in creating an interactive TV market. They are squaring up for what some commentators have called 'the battle for the living room'. Huge investment is being poured into the UK's technology infrastructure to support interactive TV, but the commercial side of the strategy is still hazy.

Source: www.digitallivingroom.com and *Financial Times* (6 December 1995)

The interactive services made possible by digital television include:

- *Video-on-demand.* An interactive facility such as video-on-demand would provide customers with instantaneous access to a particular movie, simply by choosing from a menu on the television screen. A cheaper and easier service to deliver is 'near-video-on-demand'. This is not a true interactive service but a variation of the 'pay-per-view' services that are already offered by many cable companies. Near video-on-demand involves showing the same movie on different channels, but starting 15 or so minutes apart.

▩ *Home shopping services*. Most people are already familiar with the concept of home shopping through the shopping channels that are available from some cable television services. However, the home shopping service that is currently offered is a very inflexible one. The viewer can only react to a particular advertisement by phoning a number that is displayed on the screen. The home shopping that can be offered via interactive television services offers greater opportunities for the viewer, and for the marketer. By scrolling through on-line catalogues, interactive television will allow viewers to request more information on products and order the product they require. The interactive nature of the services that are supported by digital television will give a major boost to television shopping.

▩ *Home banking services*. Home banking via PC and Internet is already popular. Denmark's Lan & Spar Bank became Scandinavia's first financial services company to offer a home banking service to its customers in 1994. Within two years, 10 per cent of its customer base were using the service.[14] By 1999, most of the major European banks had launched a PC-based home banking service, while in the USA, 7.5 million people bank online.[15] Home banking using digital television as the delivery medium promises to be more user-friendly but, as yet, is far less advanced than its Internet-based counterpart. Several UK banks are planning launches and banks such as NatWest are also launching a banking service via mobile phone.[16]

▩ The potential for home shopping via digital television

The market for home shopping services already exists. UK retailers like J. Sainsbury believe that up to 20 per cent of their customers would shop remotely if given the choice. Other major retailing organisations are reorganising their entire warehousing and delivery operations to support home shopping services:

▩ Delhaize's Caddy Home service offers approximately 3,500 products and uses centralised distribution centres to service its customers in Brussels and Antwerp;

▩ Albert Heijn, the Netherlands' leading grocery retailer, uses a combination of dedicated warehouses and stores for fulfilling home shopping orders.[17]

Current home shopping services on television are not interactive. They typically consist of dedicated shopping channels that display and promote a single product, and provide a telephone number for the viewers to call to place their orders. In the future, digital shopping channels will allow viewers to browse through a wide variety of items, obtain significantly more information on the product or service, and order directly through the television set itself.

In the USA, television shopping is currently dominated by QVC and Home Shopping Network, which between them reach more than 100 million homes. However, it still only accounts for 1 per cent of total retail sales in the USA. QVC[18] is the newcomer, having started in the USA in 1987, but has been the more aggressive, launching a tele-shopping channel in Europe[19] through the broadcaster BSkyB. Its initial entry was less than successful, mainly because it could only get 3 million subscribers to the service as opposed to the 10 million it needed. It was also hampered by the rival *infomercial*, the themed programmes broadcast on existing pan-European satellite channels such as NBC Super Channel and Eurosport. However, the percentage of subscribers who actually bought goods from the channel was the same as in the USA – 8 per cent – indicating that European consumers are prepared to purchase through this medium.

Case study

THE *GOOD BOOK GUIDE*

ECommerce poses a huge challenge for established companies that have built traditional routes to their markets. They cannot beat the on-line groups, so they have to join them. But as the *Good Book Guide* has found, this can severely damage their profits. Like many firms hit by the explosion in on-line business, the *Good Book Guide*, a British mail-order bookseller, finds itself between a rock and a hard place. ECommerce rivals such as Amazon.com, which sells discounted books over the Web, have eroded the *Good Book Guide*'s customer base, reduced sales volumes and pushed the direct marketing business into loss. The London company must find a way to compete with the on-line booksellers that threaten its future. But in common with legions of established firms trying to map out a strategy for the Internet, the *Good Book Guide* is finding out that the amorphous mass of eCommerce resists definition by conventional business models.

'The on-line marketplace changes by the week,' says John Braithwaite, son of the *Good Book Guide*'s founder who seven months ago was appointed to the new post of Internet Marketing Manager. 'It is clear that we've got to start using eCommerce quickly, but the costs and benefits remain a fog.'

What is certain is that urgent action is needed. The *Good Book Guide* has been aware of the threat from on-line booksellers since 1995. 'We spotted it early,' says Peter Braithwaite, John's father. 'But we didn't want to be pioneers in the field because we couldn't see where the profits would come from.' Even now, it is unclear what contribution on-line business will make to profits.

The company set up a Web site in 1997. John Braithwaite admits it was nothing more than an order-placing facility for existing subscribers to the *Good Book Guide*. 'It was only this year that we recognised we had to have a serious presence on the Web,' he says. But going online seriously has been costly. About £350,000 has been invested in new IT systems over the past three years. Two full-time programmers have been added to the 60 staff. This year, £230,000 is being spent to develop a Web site that permits orders to be fed straight through to the company's delivery systems. To begin with, the *Good Book Guide* plans to handle the despatch of all orders rather than passing them on to distributors and wholesalers. 'We don't want any doubt as to whether they have sent an order,' says John Braithwaite. 'Later we will move on to feeding some orders directly to publishers.'

Key decisions must also be taken on how to make the Web site stand out from the others. Apart from global players such as Amazon, there is a growing number of other British on-line booksellers. 'Simply having an attractive Web site won't be enough,' says Vivienne Wordley, the company's business development director. 'We need to generate incremental business to recoup the investment.' She believes most of the *Good Book Guide*'s sales will be online in three to five years.

Selling through a free medium is a big departure from the way the company's business has been run. The numbers subscribing to the *Good Book Guide* peaked four years ago, with 40,000 worldwide paying up to £33 a year for 12 issues of the 36-page catalogue. The subscription rate has now fallen to 35,000 and revenue from subscription sales has dropped from a peak of £900,000. Subscription income remains the *Good Book Guide*'s second-biggest revenue stream, accounting for 14 per cent of sales this year. Sales of books, tapes and CD-ROMs to the company's subscribers generates 43 per cent of income. Perhaps the most significant secondary revenue stream, however, is book sales to special customers. Although fewer than 300 in number, they account for 7 per cent of the sales income. Each has a personal account manager through whom they receive help and advice on purchases. Special customers include educational establishments, businesses and reading groups. Each typically spends more than £1,000 a year. They also depend on the account managers for research and recommendations. 'When they contact us, they know they are dealing with booklovers,' says Wordley. 'Our customers know we are not just flogging products.'

Subscriber loyalty has been high but the loss of sales to on-line traders has proved worrying. Not only have they eaten into the customer base, they have also spurred a growing expectation of substantial discounts. Some, like Amazon, have attracted sufficient capital to be able to invest aggressively in building market share through discounting even though they have yet to make a profit. 'We lack the resources to run at a loss for an extended period,' says Wordley. 'Heavy discounting is a nasty game to get into and we simply cannot afford to compete on price alone. The change to on-line book sales brings many risks,' says Wordley. 'Our new Web site could undermine our *Good Book Guide*. Customers may use our reviews and then buy elsewhere. And take-up levels are completely unknown.'

Based on: 'Web of competition traps bookseller', David Sumner Smith, *Sunday Times*, 25 July 1999.

Questions

1 If Peter Braithwaite could rewind the clock back to 1997 when the company's first Web site was established, what actions should he have taken differently?

2 Does the *Good Book Guide* have a future, in the face of competition from Amazon and other on-line booksellers?

3 If so, what should John Braithwaite's marketing strategy for the *Good Book Guide* be now?

4 How does the *Good Book Guide* Web site (www.gbgonline.com) compare to that of Amazon (www.amazon.co.uk) or other British-based on-line booksellers?

ASSIGNMENT QUESTIONS

1 Compare traditional marketing methods with those that are enabled by technology.

2 Discuss the impact of the Internet on marketing.

3 What are the pitfalls that must be avoided when establishing a presence on the Web? Can you name any Internet sites that have failed to avoid these pitfalls?

4 What marketing advantages does digital television have over traditional analogue television?

References

[1] Freeman, L. (1999). 'Technology influences top ten trends for 1999', *Business Marketing*, 1 January.

[2] www.nielsen.com/home/press/uk (1996). 'AC Nielsen study sheds new light on purchasing behaviour of Internet users', 9 May.

[3] Vadon, R. (1996). 'A radio renaissance worldwide', *Financial Times*, 8 July.

[4] Griffith, V. (1996). 'New look banners', *Financial Times*, 8 August.

[5] www.starnet.com.au/persever

[6] www.gm.com

[7] Shillingford, J. (1996). 'Online support helps cut costs', *Sunday Business ComputerAge*, 7 July.

[8] www.fedex.com

[9] Kelly, S. (1996). 'Ringing in the changes', *Computer Weekly*, 30 May.

[10] Richardson, M.A. (1996). *How the Internet is Affecting Business*. Datapro Information Services, July.

[11] McGookin, S. (1996). ' "Direct Age" is dawning', *Financial Times*, 10 June.

[12] Lucas, L. (1999). 'Online supermarket forces big rivals to check out prices', *Financial Times*, 10 August.

[13] McCarthy, V. (1995). 'Ten top business tips for your Web project', *Datamation*, 1 December.

[14] MacConville, D. (1996). 'Danes ahead on home banking', *Direct Delivery International*, March.

[15] The Economist (1999). 'Late developers', *The Economist*, 10 April.

[16] Winnett, R. (1999). 'NatWest to launch mobile-phone banking', *Sunday Times*, 25 July.

[17] Younger, R. (1998). 'New structures will be required', *Financial Times*, 1 December.

[18] www.qvc.com

[19] www.qvcuk.com

GETTING TO KNOW THE CUSTOMER

Part II of this book deals with getting to know and understand your customers: who they are, what they want, and how they wish to be served. This customer insight is created by analysing and mining the information that has been gathered from both external marketing research and internal customer information from the company's own systems.

Part II contains two chapters:

4   Conducting marketing research

5   Creating customer insight.

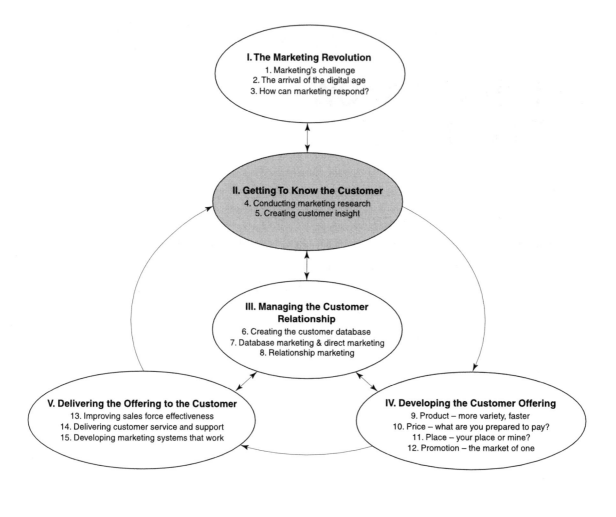

I. The Marketing Revolution
1. Marketing's challenge
2. The arrival of the digital age
3. How can marketing respond?

II. Getting To Know the Customer
4. Conducting marketing research
5. Creating customer insight

III. Managing the Customer Relationship
6. Creating the customer database
7. Database marketing & direct marketing
8. Relationship marketing

V. Delivering the Offering to the Customer
13. Improving sales force effectiveness
14. Delivering customer service and support
15. Developing marketing systems that work

IV. Developing the Customer Offering
9. Product – more variety, faster
10. Price – what are you prepared to pay?
11. Place – your place or mine?
12. Promotion – the market of one

4

CONDUCTING MARKETING RESEARCH

SUMMARY

Marketing research used to be dominated by companies that employed large teams of field researchers equipped with clipboards and pens, who were set loose on the general public to conduct face-to-face interviews. Not any more. Information technology, the Internet and software applications are revolutionising the process by which modern marketing research is conducted. If we examine the marketing research process (*see* Figure 4.1), we see that IT has particular relevance in the collection and analysis of market research data.

In this chapter, we will examine:

☐ how IT can be employed to support primary data collection

☐ how IT and the Internet have changed the way secondary market research is conducted

☐ the use of IT in the analysis of market research data, and

☐ the use of IT in specific market research applications, including continuous marketing research and advertising research.

THE USE OF IT IN PRIMARY DATA COLLECTION

Three methods of primary data collection

Primary research, or field research, is of critical importance when developing a new product or service, and in determining if that product or service will be accepted and bought by particular categories of consumer. Because of its importance and, quite often, its complexity, primary data collection is typically managed as a discrete project and usually outsourced to specialist marketing research companies, most of whom have

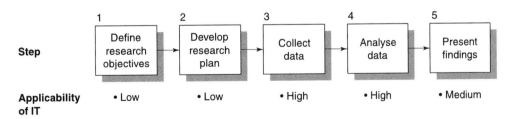

Fig 4.1 Applicability of IT during different stages of marketing research

invested large sums of money in automating the data collection process. Primary data is collected through:

▦ surveying techniques
▦ observation techniques
▦ experimentation.

Technology-enabled surveying

Surveying is the most widely used means of collecting primary market research data. Technology is having an impact on the three main contact methods:

▦ personal interviewing
▦ telephone interviewing
▦ mail.

Personal interviewing has traditionally been the dominant means of conducting interviews and has typically accounted for the majority of interviewing expenditure. However, the past decade has seen a dramatic increase in the use of the telephone in market research, for reasons of speed, flexibility and cost. As telecommunications markets around the world are deregulated the cost of telephone interviewing continues to drop. The extent to which the telephone is used differs significantly from country to country. For example, the high penetration of telephone-based surveys in the Nordic countries (*see* Figure 4.2) is a reflection of cultural acceptance of the telephone, the

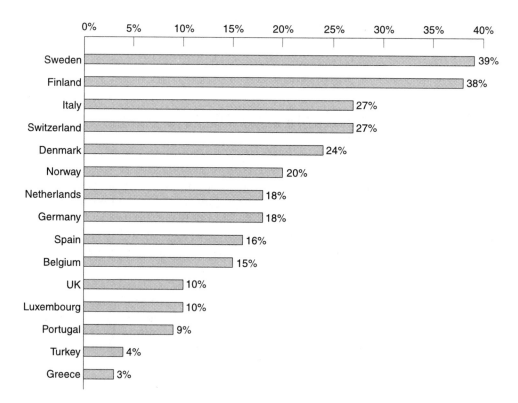

Fig 4.2 Telephone-based market research expenditure as a % of total expenditure

difficulties of conducting personal interviews across a large geographical area, and the relatively low telecommunications costs.

Two computer-assisted techniques have been making major inroads into observation and interviewing in recent years:

▪ *Computer-assisted personal interviewing (CAPI).* CAPI is a computer-aided interviewing technique that allows the interviewer to follow a script where the sequence of questions is determined by the answers that the interviewee gives (and that are entered into the computer in real-time). As each response is given and entered into the PC by the interviewer, the next question is determined by the previous response and is immediately flashed on to the interviewer's PC screen. CAPI can be employed in the field or at central market research stations. In some instances interviewees will complete self-assessment questionnaires without the aid of interviewers, cutting the cost per response dramatically.

▪ *Computer-assisted telephone interviewing (CATI).* CATI is the telephone-based equivalent to CAPI. It originated in the USA in the 1960s but has undergone significant advances in the intervening years and is now commonplace in telephone-based market research companies. Like computer-assisted personal interviewing, CATI is becoming more capital intensive and some of the major research companies have set up subsidiaries that specialise in the computer-based survey technique.[1] MORI's On-Line Telephone Surveys, established in 1988, is one of the UK's largest CATI specialists with 80 interviewer stations.[2] In Sweden, which boasts the highest proportion of telephone-based surveying in Europe, research firms like SKOP, Gallup and SIFO can conduct telephone-based surveys and report the findings in a matter of hours (*see* Exhibit 4.1). SIFO's 700 part-time interviewers and 200 CATI stations make it the largest and most sophisticated CATI specialist in Sweden.[3]

Exhibit 4.1

SOCIALIST SWEDES SURVEYED BY SKOP AND SIFO

The Swedish Prime Minister, Mr Göran Persson, remained narrowly ahead of the opposition leader Mr Carl Bildt in the popularity stakes yesterday, two days before the general election. A survey by market researchers SKOP found 44 per cent of 822 Swedes questioned on 16th and 17th September 1998 preferred Mr Persson, leader of the ruling Social Democrats, as prime minister while 43 per cent opted for Mr Bildt. A Gallup survey of 556 people on Thursday suggested 30 per cent of Swedes preferred Mr Persson while 29 per cent favoured Bildt. The results were a sharp contrast from a year ago when Mr Bildt was riding high as he returned to Swedish politics after two successful years as an international peace mediator in Bosnia. In August 1997, 64 per cent of Swedes viewed Mr Bildt, leader of the conservative Moderate Party and former prime minister from 1991–94, as the preferred premier. Mr Persson lagged far behind with 31 per cent support.

Neither of Sweden's main two parties, the Social Democrats and the Moderates, is set to win a majority in tomorrow's poll, rating 36.8 and 24.8 per cent respectively, according to a SIFO telephone poll yesterday. They will have to scramble for the support of some of the five smaller parties.

Source: The Irish Times (19 September 1998).[4]

Technology-enabled observation

Observation is regarded as the classical method of research and can be carried out in one of three main ways:[5]

- ▩ *Audits*, which include shop audits as practised by market research companies such as AC Nielsen and Taylor Nelson Sofres, as well as research of traffic patterns and volumes at shopping centres, stores or poster sites.
- ▩ *Recording devices*, including a wide variety of counting meters as well as devices that identify reactions to different types of advertisements such as psycho-galvanometers, for tracking minute changes in perspiration rates, and tachistoscopes, for measuring pupil dilation.
- ▩ *Watching buyer behaviour*, a category of research that includes a number of observation techniques from hidden video cameras to 'mystery shoppers'.

Traditionally, IT played little or no role in observation techniques. This was particularly true of audits and watching buyer behaviour, where research was typically conducted by researchers with clipboards and pens. Nowadays, auditing has become more sophisticated and IT plays a much greater role in this type of research. An example of an airline that has employed video recording for market research purposes is given in Exhibit 4.2. Similarly, market research companies like Taylor Nelson Sofres use sophisticated scanning devices to measure both grocery purchases and television audience measurement.[6]

Exhibit 4.2

VIDEO-TAPES FROM THE MILE-HIGH CLUB

Starting in 1996, SAS Airlines began intensive research, not only into what its passengers wanted but how they behaved. 'These were anthropological studies,' says Jan Olson, SAS's vice-president for products and services. To find out what its customers wanted, SAS carried out extensive market research which included video-taping customer behaviour. 'We video-taped them in arrivals, at check-in and on-board. We informed customers on a particular flight we would be studying them. We collected 1,500 hours of video-tape.' SAS calls the tapes 'probably the most comprehensive database of customer observations ever compiled in the airline industry'.

And what did the tapes reveal? 'That we weren't making the journey very easy for our customers,' Mr Olson says. The airline made several changes in the way it handled passengers to make their journeys easier: providing access to a café at the departure gate before boarding short-haul flights, introducing a holder for spectacles in the seat pocket of the aircraft, providing power points in new aircraft for personal computers, and even putting windows in the toilets to provide a view out of the aircraft. Mr Olson says these features were introduced not only because customers asked for them, but because the videos showed that they wanted greater control over their environment. When watching the videos, SAS researchers noticed that when the passengers boarded the aircraft they marked out an office-type space for themselves. 'The customers started to cocoon themselves. They put their briefcases down, they put their coats down, as if to say: *Leave me this space*. You don't get that kind of information from focus groups.'

Source: Financial Times (19 November 1998).[7]

Technology-enabled experimentation

Experiment, or simulation, is the third generic method of collecting primary market research data and is commonly used in new product development and testing. Simulation methods include:

- *computer simulation*, which simulates the way consumers might behave in real life and now includes new techniques such as virtual reality;
- *sensory evaluation*, including blind 'taste tests', which is used to test the psycho-physical properties of products;
- *test marketing*, which we will examine in more detail later in this chapter.

THE USE OF IT IN SECONDARY DATA COLLECTION

▓ Internal data sources

Secondary research, or *desk research*, makes use of previously conducted marketing research. It can involve the reuse of information gathered from newspapers, research publications or census surveys, and is often carried out on an ad hoc basis using both internal records and an increasingly wide variety of external data sources.

Internal records are an invaluable source of price lists, inventory levels, receivables and payables, as well as a variety of customer information. Internal sales figures are routinely analysed by both sales and marketing managers to provide a perspective on trends in product sales, distribution channels and customers. Internal data sources are also becoming more information-rich as the cost of holding information decreases, providing marketing managers with perhaps the most valuable source of information for market research purposes. Exhibit 4.3 gives some idea of the amount of customer and product data that is held by today's large retailers, and how this data is being used for marketing purposes.

> ### Exhibit 4.3
>
> **SHOPPING FOR MARKET RESEARCH DATA**
>
> The use of advanced IT tools for demographic analysis of customers has brought significant benefits to retailers. Comprehensive databases of customers' shopping habits have enabled retailers to make sure they stock the right products and get them on the shelves at the right time. Not only can stock levels be optimised, but customers buy more of what they really want. But now that most big retailers use some form of demographic analysis, knowledge about groups of customers is no longer enough: 'We must be able to get down to individual customers and be able to serve them more precisely,' says Mike Winch, IT director at Safeway supermarkets in the UK.
>
> With a database covering over 8m customers, this is no easy task. Safeway is the third largest supermarket chain in Britain with annual sales of £7bn. It employs 70,000 people at more than 400 stores across the UK. 'We have changed the way we manage our business from looking at products to looking at customers. We need to know about every item in their shopping basket – and that means using very advanced IT systems both to collect data from the point of sales and to analyse it,' Mr Winch says.
>
> *Source: Financial Times* (2 September 1998).[9]

■ External data sources

While internal sources provide the richest source of customer information, external data can also yield valuable information on consumer markets and trends. In the UK, typical external sources include:

■ *government sources*, including the Office of National Statistics (ONS), the Business Statistics Office (BSO) and HMSO, which publishes a wide range of market reports;

■ *national press*, such as the *Financial Times*, *The Economist*, *The Times*;

■ *trade associations, chambers of commerce and trade magazines*, including *The Grocer*, *Motor Trader*, *The Publican*, *Marketing Week* and *Campaign*;

■ *market research companies*, such as Mintel, KeyNote, ICC Business Ratio Reports, ADMAP, Media Expenditure Analysis (MEAL), Economist Intelligence Unit, Euromonitor, Datamonitor and a variety of Financial Times services including FT Extel and FT Profile;

■ *yearbooks and trade directories*, such as *Kelly's Directory of Manufacturers and Merchants*, *Kompass* and *BRAD* (British Rate and Data).

Similar sources are available in other countries. For example, the Central Bureau voor de Statistiek provides government statistics in the Netherlands while Kompass and Euromonitor operate throughout Europe.

CD-ROM has become a very popular medium for disseminating market research from these sources. Market research companies such as Mintel, Euromonitor, KeyNote and Datamonitor are all seeking new audiences through this medium rather than relying on a third party on-line service provider to act as the distribution channel for their market research.[9]

■ The trend towards commercial on-line services

Increasingly, market research companies are providing their information in on-line format, both on CD-ROM and increasingly through Internet-based information services from third-party information providers such as DataStar or the Financial Times. Many large companies will use at least one of these commercial on-line services for accessing general news information or research on more specialised subjects. There are at least 9,000 commercial databases available worldwide, containing over 6 billion records and covering information on business, technical and scientific information, company reports, broker reports, newspaper and journal articles and patent documents.[10] The advantages of commercial on-line services include:

■ *Variety*. Many on-line services provide a 'supermarket' service whereby many different services can be accessed by subscribing to a single supplier.

■ *Up-to-date information*. Many databases are updated on at least a daily basis and a large number even more frequently.

■ *Cost efficiency*. Although commercial on-line services charge either an up-front or monthly/quarterly fee, or charge on an actual usage basis, they can provide an extremely cost-efficient means of accessing a wide variety of information.

■ *Accessibility of information*. Most databases can be accessed 24 hours a day, 7 days a week.

Table 4.1 Selected commercial on-line service providers

Service	Description
DataStar	Large 'supermarket' host providing access to 350 databases of business and technical articles including European company information, news on eastern and western Europe, as well as biomedical, pharmaceutical and healthcare information. Owned by the Dialog Corporation.
Dialog Corporation[11] (now Bright Station)	Large supermarket host with wide range of US and international data, including worldwide company information, US government news, patent and trademark information and industry-specific data. Created in 1997 from the merger of MAID plc and Knight-Ridder.
Dow Jones Reuters Business Interactive[12]	Joint venture set up in 1999 between Dow Jones and Reuters. Provides business and financial information to professional customers via the Internet.
FT Profile[13]	News and business information service run by Financial Times Electronic Publishing (part of the Pearson Group). Offers a range of news, company, industry, market and country information.
Lexis-Nexis[14]	Acquired by Reed-Elsevier in 1995, this US-based service provides access to approx. 10,000 databases of legal, business, government and academic information.
Profound	Business information service for end-users and information specialists. Owned by the Dialog Corporation.
Questel-Orbit[15]	Scientific, technical and intellectual property service owned by France Telecom. Specialises in patent, trademark, scientific, technical and chemical information.

Some of the major on-line service providers that can be accessed in Europe and the services they provide are illustrated in Table 4.1.

To demonstrate the range of these on-line services, consider the scale of offerings from FT Profile:

▓ *News.* FT Profile provides access to publications such as the *Financial Times, International Herald Tribune, Les Echoes, Frankfurter Allgemeine Zeitung* and the *South China Morning Post,* as well as to numerous global news databases such as Asia Intelligence Wire.

▓ *Countries.* Profiles and analyses on every country and region of the world can be found on FT Profile, ranging from political issues and country risk intelligence to foreign trade, economic policy, transport, visa regulations and hotel listings.

▓ *Companies.* FT Profile offers an extensive collection of detailed information about companies and their activities. This includes company news, credit ratings, corporate issues, products, company rankings and sales turnover as well as access to millions of company reports and over 100,000 stockbroker reports on thousands of companies worldwide.

▓ *Industries.* Industry coverage on FT Profile ranges from company and industry news, statistics and trends to research and development, newsletters and tender opportunities. Trade press and business publications are included from across the globe, including *Marketing Week, Lloyd's List, Cable Satellite and TV News* and *Japan Textile Week.*

▥ *Markets*. FT Profile provides comprehensive market coverage including such activities as trends, advertising spend, brand activity and emerging markets, as well as research reports on consumer products, services and industries across the world. These include over 200 international trade titles covering the advertising and marketing industry, such as *Campaign, Marketing Week,* and *Asian Advertising and Marketing.*

▥ The rise of the Internet

The Internet has become a growing source of accessing and disseminating marketing research information. Nowadays companies place their financial results on their Internet sites and many will have a specific 'investor relations' page dedicated to the provision of company information to Internet users. However, for most marketing research situations, a commercial on-line service is likely to provide a more comprehensive service. Already the Internet has become the medium of choice for accessing the many commercial on-line services that are currently available. For example, marketers can access DataStar's databases on the Internet through DataStar Web service. Similarly, Questel-Orbit's Internet-based service is QWeb.

Internal versions of the Internet, known as an *intranet*, have also become common-place in the collation and dissemination of internally generated market research around organisations. Financial research, in particular, is routinely shared across divisions in large banks and insurance companies, using intranet technology (*see* Exhibit 4.4).

Exhibit 4.4

SWIFT RESEARCH FOR STOCKBROKERS

NatWest Markets, voted number one in UK broking research in Reuters' 1997 survey, is putting all its research on to an in-house intranet. On the intranet (or private 'Internet') analysts and sales people at the company will be able to find research produced in the company's offices around the world. The system is being rolled out to 220 sales people and analysts in Europe. It will then be introduced to staff in other parts of the world.
Source: Financial Times (5 November 1997).[16]

USING IT TO ANALYSE INFORMATION

▥ Providing faster statistical analysis

Statistics, or quantitative methods, have been used for many years in the analysis of marketing research data. However, the increasing power and decreasing costs of personal computers have more recently placed many of the more sophisticated statistical tools in the hands of marketing managers. The subject of statistics is beyond the scope of this text but the main categories, and some of their applications, are:

▨ *Multivariate methods*, which attempt to analyse the relationships between different marketing variables. Sub-categories include factor analysis, cluster analysis and multi-dimensional scaling techniques such as conjoint analysis, a consumer research technique for finding correlations between variables. For example, conjoint analysis was used by Novotel to examine the trade-offs that consumers make when they compare different aspects of hotel accommodation, such as size of room or bed versus type of television.[17]

▨ *Regression techniques*, including multiple regression, are often used in customer segmentation and sales forecasting.

▨ *Artificial intelligence*, including expert systems and neural networks, is used for market pricing and media planning.

▨ *Statistical decision theory*, sometimes referred to as stochastic methods, is used to optimise sales forces and call centre staffing, and for optimising pricing decisions.

▨ Analytical tools

A variety of analytical tools are available to conduct statistical analysis, including:

▨ *Spreadsheets and other decision support systems (DSS)*. The most commonly used market research analysis tool is the humble spreadsheet. Spreadsheet software packages such as Excel and Lotus 1-2-3 have become the standard mechanism by which all marketing managers perform basic analysis.

▨ *Geographic information systems (GIS)*. These are decision support systems used for visualising and analysing geographical data (*see* below).

▨ *Data mining and neural networks*. For more sophisticated analysis, several other decision support systems are available, including data mining and neural networks.

▨ Geographic information systems

GIS are computer systems that store, retrieve, display and manipulate geographically based information. In the past they were expensive and cumbersome systems that were rarely used outside the central planning departments of companies. Nowadays they have moved closer to the sharp end of the business and bring a wide range of various marketing data to the fingertips of the marketing manager. The main characteristic that distinguishes GIS from other systems is the ability to point and click on a particular area of the PC screen to obtain a range of information that has been assembled for that particular geographic feature. Typically, GIS allow at least four, but frequently many more, different layers of information to be overlaid in the same picture:

▨ maps and other geographically based information
▨ geo-demographic information from census information and electoral registers
▨ internal information on customers
▨ other internal market information such as sales force territories, store catchment areas, newspaper, television and other media boundaries.

Additional layers of information can also be added. More sophisticated GIS include global positioning system (GPS) satellite receiver information. For example, taxi companies or haulage organisations can attach GPS transmitters to their vehicles, allowing each vehicle to be tracked and shown on a PC screen. Nowadays advanced GIS systems have GPS connectivity bundled into their products, either as a basic feature or an additional service.

GIS have a variety of uses in marketing research. For example, Levi Strauss uses a GIS to analyse sales and shipments by area and to make predictions on future sales, market potential and customer trends. The supermarket chain Tesco uses it for analysing changes in population, income and road and rail locations, so that it can plan the locations of its large stores more effectively; and Woolworth's also has a system for analysing local demand (*see* Exhibit 4.5).

Exhibit 4.5

GAINING LOCAL INSIGHTS

Kingfisher chain Woolworth's uses a GIS for market analysis. Using CACI's InSite system, the company recently segmented its portfolio of 779 stores into 'city centre', 'heartland', and 'local' stores, each group with a different fascia. According to Chris Garthwaite, stores marketing manager for Woolworth's, the system 'is a very effective tool in understanding our local market, enabling us to respond to opportunities within key areas. It has been especially useful in understanding and responding to competitors' activity'. Since adopting the InSite system in 1987, Woolworth's has steadily built up the functions and data it uses. Local population characteristics and estimated expenditure have been aggregated to store catchment level using a shopping centre gravity model supplied by The Retail Dimension, and distance and drive-time from CACI. Counts on workers within two kilometres of each store from the 1991 census have been added to give an insight into daytime demand and the potential for lunchtime 'stepping out' products. Competitor data on 140,000 multiple retail branches is included, giving fascia name, holding company details, principal category of operation, in or out-of-town location, nearest shopping centre and distance, and whether it is an anchor store or not. In addition to evaluating new store opportunities and targeting local promotions, Garthwaite says that the chain can analyse how many Kingfisher stores face competition for music and video sales, for example.

Source: Marketing Week (17 May 1996).[18]

In conjunction with geo-demographic and psychographic information, GIS can help companies target their marketing efforts more effectively. For example, they can graphically illustrate that, on average, people in Merseyside spend one-fifth more on toys, prams and other children's products than do those elsewhere in the UK. Similarly, they can show that people in Surrey are 20 per cent less likely to visit pubs regularly and only half as likely to visit wine bars as the average British citizen.[19]

CONTINUOUS MARKETING RESEARCH

How continuous research is conducted

Continuous marketing research is a means of discovering marketing trends by taking a series of samples over an extended period of time. Chisnall (1997)[20] identifies three primary means of conducting continuous marketing research:

■ *Consumer purchase panels*, which are the commonly used panels, allow market research companies to track consumer purchases and usage. The widespread use of handheld electronic scanners to capture bar-code data has revolutionised the recording, gathering and dissemination of purchase panel data. Electronic data capture and transfer allow purchase data to be collected daily, providing market research companies with almost instantaneous feedback on consumers' responses to marketing initiatives.

■ *Telephone panels*, based on regular telephone interviews with a panel of members, are also commonly used to gather market data in both consumer and industrial markets. Central telephone interviewing facilities using CATI are common nowadays.

■ *Store audits* provide purchase information from retail outlets. Because sales figures from the factory do not accurately reflect consumer demand, the store audit is an important mechanism for tracking sales promotions, forward stocks and prices as well as actual purchases. Information can be gathered using handheld bar-code scanners but the trend is to obtain information directly from the electronic point of sale (EPoS) equipment at the checkout desk.

Although not always categorised under the heading of continuous market research, *omnibus surveys* consist of a series of short questions from different clients who share the costs of the survey. Leading providers of omnibus surveys include BMRB in the UK, and Gallup and NOP throughout Europe. Again, the trends are for more of these omnibus surveys to be carried out by telephone. One notable European omnibus survey is CAPIBUS Europe, which surveys 5,000 adults per week across the UK, France, Italy and Spain. As the name implies, the omnibus uses computer-assisted personal interviewing to deliver results in less than four weeks.

■ Continuous market research – the international dimension

Few continuous market research companies operate on a global basis. Two companies that do are AC Nielsen[21] and IRI[22] (*see* Exhibit 4.6).

Exhibit 4.6

DATA WARS

Forget such long-standing feuds as Coke v Pepsi or Procter & Gamble v Unilever. For the past few years the fiercest battle in the marketing world has been fought between AC Nielsen and Information Resources Inc. (IRI), two rival suppliers of market data on the sale of consumer goods, both based in Chicago. AC Nielsen and IRI have poached each other's clients and staff almost as fast as they have piled up losses. Talk to either, and it is not long before they start denigrating their fellow firm.

The main business that IRI and AC Nielsen (along with most of the other big established firms such as France's Sofres and Germany's GfK) specialise in is 'continuous' research – ie using data from shops and permanent panels of customers to calculate what products are sold where, and to whom. The business, which used to throng with clipboard-carrying researchers, is now dominated by point-of-sale scanners and computer databases. To keep up, both AC Nielsen and IRI have had to make huge investments in information technology, whose cost they have not always been able to pass on to their clients.

▶

Last year alone, says Mr Cotsakos, president of AC Nielsen, they invested more than $300m in acquisitions and technology. It has equipped a panel of 40,000 households in America with self-scanning equipment to keep an electronic record of their purchases. Nielsen Media Research is now exploring ways of tracking customer use on the Internet. The group has also ploughed money into building a global operation: the 94 countries that it covers today compare with only 25 in 1990. Last year, it paid almost $150m for Surveys Research Group (SRG), an Asian research firm based in Hong Kong.

Source: The Economist (22 July 1995).[23]

Across Europe, countries are not researched as a single market. Many large agencies such as IRI and GfK cover only a few countries. The European Society for Opinion and Marketing Research (ESOMAR)[24] is also attempting to harmonise the way research is carried out across Europe. For example, in Germany, the definition of an 'adult' is 18 or over while in other countries it is as low as 12, making it difficult to conduct meaningful Europe-wide marketing research.

If we examine how Taylor Nelson Sofres conducts continuous market research into public opinions, we realise that European market research is still conducted on national lines rather than on a pan-European basis (*see* Exhibit 4.7). However, it is also clear that the cost and sophistication of continuous market research is driving research companies like Taylor Nelson Sofres to consolidate the research market across Europe.

Exhibit 4.7

POLITICAL RESEARCH ACROSS EUROPE

Political research is one of Taylor Nelson Sofres' specialities. Many of our companies have been given the vote of public confidence by local political parties, TV and radio companies, unions and the written press when it comes to monitoring public opinion, measuring trends and gauging attitudes and carrying out estimation polls during elections:

- *Belgium – Dimarso.* Dimarso launched its political research activities in 1963 and today is the leader in Northern Belgium in this sector.
- *Denmark – Gallup A/S.* Gallup A/S is one of the oldest (60 years) and best-known market research institutes in Denmark. 96% of Danes equate Gallup with opinion polling and market research.
- *France – Sofres.* Sofres is now the leading political and opinion pollster in France. Over 130 surveys are conducted yearly covering a wide range of subjects influencing the population's opinion.
- *Germany – Emnid.* Emnid started its polling activities as early as 1945, and enjoys an excellent reputation in political research in Germany, with long-standing relationships with the cable TV company NTV and with the magazine *Der Spiegel*.
- *Italy – Abacus.* Abacus's political research activities really took off in 1992 with the national elections. In 1996, a weekly TV programme called Moby Dick on Italia Uno was launched and has contributed largely to Abacus's reputation for political research in Italy.
- *United Kingdom – Harris.* Harris Research first worked for the Conservative Party in 1966 and now has a panel of 150 MPs which is consulted 6–7 times a year, giving direct access to parliamentary opinion across a wide range of issues.

Source: Taylor Nelson Sofres Web site (1999).

▓ Test marketing

Given the high failure rate among new product launches, it is important to conduct test marketing in a rigorous fashion. Test marketing is standard practice among consumer product manufacturers but has not reached the same level of sophistication in industrial markets or financial services. Many banks and insurance companies still fail to carry out adequate test marketing before they launch new financial products. Although test marketing has become more accepted and sophisticated, it does suffer from some drawbacks. It is regarded by some companies as slow and expensive but, more importantly, it can provide competitors with advance warning of new product launches. Newer approaches to test marketing attempt to address these deficiencies:

▓ *Simulated test marketing (STM)* is seen as an attractive alternative to formal test marketing. It involves the use of computers to manage and monitor the results of a product test in a simulated environment that will not alert competitors to a new product launch. Early STMs involved providing consumers with advertising material and free samples to be tested at home, followed by telephone interviews to gauge consumer reaction to the product. The responses were scored and analysed by computer to assess the likelihood of success. The latest advances in STM use a technique known as virtual reality.

▓ *Scanner-based test marketing* is not really a new approach but does recognise the value of bar-code scanning as a means of providing quick feedback to manufacturers. The growth of EPoS and bar-coding in retail stores allows new products to be evaluated very quickly – an important consideration when the success or failure of new fast-moving consumer goods products is determined nowadays in a matter of weeks and months, rather than years.

ADVERTISING RESEARCH

▓ Advertising research categories

Advertising research is used to evaluate the effectiveness of advertising as a means of communication and persuasion, and can be categorised under three broad headings:

▓ *Advertising content research* is used at two stages in advertising: *pre-publication*, where individuals or groups are invited to view 'mock-up' advertisements and tested on their degree of recall of specific aspects of the advertisements, and *post-publication*, where unaided (spontaneous) recall and aided (prompted) recall of advertisements are also measured.

▓ *Advertising effectiveness research* aims to evaluate the degree of success achieved by advertising through different media. Tracking studies are typically used to identify the effectiveness of marketing research.

▓ *Advertising media research*, which attempts to improve the efficiency of advertising by analysing the media available for promoting products and services. Aspects of advertising media research include press readership measurement, television and radio audience measurement, as well as cinema and poster research measurement.

More recently, marketing research companies have been attempting to get to grips with measuring the effectiveness, or reach, of Internet advertising.

▦ Television audience research

In the UK, the Broadcasters' Audience Research Board (BARB) dominates much of the television advertising media research. BARB commissions both quantitative audience research for measuring audience size, and qualitative research for measuring audience reaction. Across Europe, television audience research methods are becoming more automated, harmonised and standardised. Nowadays, most measurement is conducted using electronic systems known as 'peoplemeters' which record the television viewing habits of sample households. Peoplemeters were first introduced in the USA by AC Nielsen in 1987. Panel members press a key on a keypad when they leave the television room and stop watching television but the peoplemeter does the rest by monitoring and recording the television station being watched (*see* Exhibit 4.8).

Exhibit 4.8

EUROPEAN PEOPLEMETERS

In 1995, 20 'peoplemeters' were in use in 18 different countries to measure television advertising. These included all West European countries with populations of 1 million or more, and also Hungary in Eastern Europe. Apart from Belgium and Portugal, each country is served by one peoplemeter panel. Two significant peoplemeter systems are *Telecontrol* developed by SRG of Switzerland and *AGB* which is organised by the various national companies which were, at one time, bought by Robert Maxwell. After his death they were broken up into separate ownership. The AGB Italia group has interests in Italy, Portugal, Greece, Turkey and Hungary while Sofres, the other principal research group in Europe, owns or has substantial holdings in the Portuguese, Spanish and south Belgian operations. Norwegian audience research, covering both radio and television, is organised by Norsk Rikskingkasting and includes thrice-weekly telephone surveys of 200 people, randomly selected over the age of nine years. *Telecontrol* V1 meters are operated by the research company MMI. In Denmark, the Gallup TV service also operates *Telecontrol* V1 meters while in Sweden, Eurometers are used in a television audience research service operated by Nielsen.

Source: Chisnall (1997).

Peoplemeters still rely on individuals to record accurately the times that they leave the room or stop watching the television so some margin for error exists in the audience data collected by these devices. However, the replacement of paper-based diaries with electronic measurement has made a significant impact on the quality and accuracy of television audience measurement.

▦ Radio audience research

Given the greater number of radio stations available to listeners, radio audience research is more complex than television audience research. RAJAR (Radio Joint Audience

Research) is the trade association for commercial radio stations in the UK. It gathers audience data from a panel of 150,000 respondents who use seven-day paper-based diaries to record the stations that they listen to. Interestingly, despite the variety of commercial radio stations available in major cities such as London, listeners typically listen to fewer than three stations a week. Radio research has not yet embraced the electronic meters used in television research, mainly for reasons of cost, despite the fact that such meters have been used in the USA, in conjunction with paper diaries, for many years.

OTHER RESEARCH APPLICATIONS

■ Public relations research

As Exhibit 4.9 shows, the measurement of the effectiveness of PR is an imprecise science, typically involving the measurement of the number of words or column inches that are generated as a result of a press release or similar public relations initiative. IT is beginning to make inroads in this area of marketing as well, although the technology is still relatively immature. Much of the so-called 'text mining' technology is based on neural network technology that allows words, the structure of sentences and inflections to be analysed to determine the degree of satisfaction that customers or commentators have with a particular product or service. Apart from automating the task of assessing hundreds of separate articles, a greater consistency is achieved through the use of information technology – when analysed manually, different analysts can take different interpretations of the words in a press article.

Exhibit 4.9

THE POWER OF PR

Words in print have been analysed since Caxton invented the press. In fifteenth century Sweden, the appearance of the heretical *Books of Zion* led to an assessment of their religious orthodoxy in probably the earliest attempt at media evaluation upon which the lives of the publishers turned. Yet even in today's world of media sophistication, the means of assessing the value to a company of news pieces, articles and features, often rises little above the measurement of column inches or the size of a headline. 'Given the increasing amounts of money that is spent on this kind of public relations, which runs into billions worldwide, it is remarkable that PR companies remain so crude in the justification and targeting of the spend,' comments Adam Briggs, senior lecturer at the London Guildhall University. But the question is *how*?

   Part of the answer is found in leading edge information technology. PR is nothing if not the management of human reactions, though this is all about intangibles such as 'the feel' of an article or comment. IBM's text mining solution provides one example of how technology is now beginning to cope with analysis at this level. Electricité de France, the large utility group, has used IBM's solution to study public perception of its electrical car and nuclear power development programmes in press reports.

Source: Financial Times (2 September 1998).[25]

1 Describe how IT can support the gathering of primary marketing research data.

2 Browse the Internet sites of AC Nielsen (www.acnielsen.com) and IRI (www.infores.com) and compare the services that each provides.

3 Examine the trend towards commercial on-line services in the UK by examining those that are provided by a service such as FT Profile (www.ftep.ft.com).

4 Sweden and Finland spend almost 40 per cent of their market research budget on telephone-based surveying while the equivalent figure for Ireland, Greece and Turkey is less than 5 per cent. Why?

5 Explore the Taylor Nelson Sofres Web site (www.tnagb.com) to find out how continuous market research companies are consolidating across Europe.

References

1 Gofton, K. (1997). 'Playing the numbers game', *Marketing Technique*, 17 July.

2 www.olts.co.uk

3 www.sifo.se

4 Irish Times (1998). 'Persson stays ahead as Swedes go to the polls', *The Irish Times*, 19 September.

5 Chisnall, P. (1997). *Marketing Research, 5th Edition*. London: McGraw Hill.

6 Gofton, K. (1997). 'Fingers on the pulse', *Marketing Technique*, 17 July.

7 Bray, Roger (1998). 'Scandinavians wake up to a bright new image', *Financial Times*, 19 November.

8 Manchester, P. (1998). 'Customers in sharper focus', *Financial Times*, 2 September.

9 IWR (1996). 'Market research firms bypass online', *Information World Review*, July/August.

10 Poynder, R. (1996). 'Searching questions', *Sunday Business ComputerAge*, 14 July.

11 www.dialog.co.uk

12 www.reuters.com

13 www.ftep.ft.com

14 www.lexis-nexis.com

15 www.questel.orbit.com

16 Shillingford, J. (1997). 'Swift facts for stockbrokers', *Financial Times*, 5 November.

17 Wittink, D.R., Vriens, M. and Burhenne, W. (1994). 'Commercial use of conjoint analysis in Europe: results and critical reflection', *International Journal of Research in Marketing*, Vol. 11, No. 1.

18 Reed, D. (1996). 'Streets ahead', *Marketing Week*, 17 May.

19 Marsh, P. (1996). 'Picked out by programs', *Financial Times*, 24 May.

20 Chisnall, P. (1997). *Marketing Research, 5th Edition*. London: McGraw Hill.

21 www.acnielsen.com

22 www.infores.com

23 The Economist (1995). 'Data wars', *The Economist*, 22 July.

24 www.esomar.nl

25 Vernon, M. (1998). 'Key role for IT in the marketing mix', *Financial Times*, 2 September.

5

CREATING CUSTOMER INSIGHT

SUMMARY

One of the most talked-about topics in marketing today is customer insight. Also referred to as *business intelligence*, it is the capability that companies need to create a sense of what their customers want and need, and adapt their products and services to those changing customer needs. In order to create and sustain customer insight, organisations must:

☐ generate deeper insights through customer segmentation

☐ apply new approaches to segmentation using information technology

☐ gather data on customer purchases, transactions and habits, and 'warehouse' that data so that it can be analysed by marketing managers

☐ use data mining techniques to find hidden insights that can be used for marketing purposes, and finally

☐ create a knowledge organisation to share customer insights throughout the organisation.

INCREASING SOPHISTICATION OF CUSTOMER SEGMENTATION

Traditional approaches to customer segmentation

Segmentation involves identifying sizeable groups of customers with similar buying needs and characteristics. By identifying and understanding the major segments in any market, organisations can develop more appropriate product and service offerings targeted at particular groups (*see* Exhibit 5.1). All decisions on the marketing mix are then made with the specific customer segment in mind, in contrast to a mass-marketing approach where all customers are treated in a similar fashion. A good segmentation approach should fit the four key requirements of being measurable, accessible, substantial and actionable.

Exhibit 5.1

HAVING A GO AT CUSTOMER SEGMENTATION

For many years, a multinational fertiliser company had exhibited at a major exhibition that was attended by farmers from all over South Africa and supported by most of the multinationals interested in the agricultural market sector. The company felt that it had to

▶

attend as all its main competitors would be there and so their hospitality tent was duly stocked with the necessary quantity and quality of lager for its Afrikaner clients. The utmost care was taken to ensure its tent was the last stop for its thirsty guests at the end of the day.

However, the company questioned the return it was getting from the exhibition and eventually decided to modify its approach. The next year, it organised the erection of a rifle range and hired a number of sub-machine guns; not surprisingly, the opportunity to use these guns was irresistible to the Afrikaners who flocked to the tent to 'have a go'. However, before they were allowed a turn, each farmer had to complete a detailed survey on his farm, fertiliser usage, spending habits, product perceptions etc. From this vital information, the company was able to identify that a number of previously unrecognisable segments existed in what had been thought of as a price-driven commodity market. Subsequently, this information helped the company to reposition a number of its existing products and to introduce some new ones with the result that it was able to achieve a 23% increase in market share.

▒ Increasing sophistication of geo-demographic segmentation

Another traditional approach is to segment customers into distinct groups based on *geographic, demographic* and *socio-economic* information (*see* Table 5.1). The term *geo-demographic* is often used to describe the type of segmentation that is carried out using these three traditional segmentation variables.

In the past two decades information technology has been harnessed very effectively to provide marketers with considerable geo-demographic information about their customers. Indeed, the combination of IT and the availability of geo-demographic data based on national census information has fuelled the tremendous growth in database marketing and direct marketing. In the UK the ACORN geo-demographic classification tool from CACI uses a wide range of data from the 1991 census and sophisticated statistical techniques to classify all inhabitants across the UK into 54 distinct types. The 54 types aggregate up to 17 groups and six major categories (*see* Table 5.2). These ACORN classifications provide a matrix of consumer characteristics that is comprehensive enough to define the potential for many marketing and planning operations.

Table 5.1 Traditional segmentation variables

Key geographic variables	Key demographic variables	Key socio-economic groupings
▒ Country	▒ Age	A (professional/senior managerial)
▒ Region	▒ Education	B (middle managers/executives)
▒ Population density (urban, rural etc.)	▒ Family	C1 (junior managers/non-manual)
▒ Administrative area	▒ Income	C2 (skilled manual)
▒ Postal code	▒ Occupation	D (semi-skilled/unskilled manual)
▒ Climate	▒ Religion	E (unemployed/state dependent)
	▒ Sex	

Table 5.2 UK ACORN categories and groups

ACORN categories	ACORN groups	Approximate socio-economic equivalent
A Thriving	1. Wealthy achievers, suburban areas	ABC1
	2. Affluent greys, rural communities	ABC2D
	3. Prosperous pensioners, retirement areas	ABC1
B Expanding	4. Affluent executives, family areas	ABC1
	5. Well-off workers, family areas	ABC1C2
C Rising	6. Affluent urbanites, town and city areas	ABC1
	7. Prosperous professionals, metropolitan areas	ABC1
	8. Better-off executives, inner-city areas	ABC1
D Settling	9. Comfortable middle-agers, mature home-owning areas	ABC1
	10. Skilled workers, home-owning areas	C1C2DE
E Aspiring	11. New home-owners, mature communities	C2DE
	12. White-collar workers, better-off multi-ethnic areas	C1
F Striving	13. Older people, less prosperous areas	C2DE
	14. Council estate residents, better-off homes	C2DE
	15. Council estate residents, high unemployment	C2DE
	16. Council estate residents, greatest hardship	DE
	17. People in multi-ethnic, low-income areas	DE

Source: CACI Web site (1999) © CACI Ltd.[1]

Geo-demographic segmentation based on census data provides an aggregate picture of the characteristics of people living in a particular district. The smallest grouping used in such segmentation is a postcode, which contains approximately 15 households. The term ACORN provides a good indication of how the segmentation works – it stands for 'a classification of residential neighbourhoods'. Systems such as ACORN are based on the premise that individuals are more similar to their neighbours than they are to people living several streets away.

Companies can also use classification systems such as ACORN and Mosaic to profile their own customers into distinct segments. From a given list of names and addresses (from the company's own customer database, for example), information services organisations can identify the major segments or profiles within the database that will enhance the company's ability to target and cross-sell to customers (*see* Exhibit 5.2).

Exhibit 5.2

DRAWING BLOOD IN SCOTLAND

Among the non-corporate users of geographically based marketing information supplied by specialised software groups is the Scottish National Blood Transfusion Service (SNBTS). SNBTS has five regional transfusion centres that collect blood from 300,000 donors annually. SNBTS needs 40,000 new donors per year – that's 770 per week – so it turned to the information specialists CACI when it wanted to find the answers to three questions:

■ Which types of people have a high propensity to give blood?

■ Where are these types of people located in each of the five SNBTS regions?
■ How do we plan and set targets for developing the performance of each of the five regions?

CACI profiled the SNBTS database of donors using the Scottish*ACORN population classification, for each of the five regions. Only the donors' postcodes were used for the analysis to ensure confidentiality. In general terms, the profiling established that the overall SNBTS donor profile is fairly affluent, with Scottish*ACORN groups A (affluent consumers with large houses), B (prosperous home owners) and D (private tenements and flats) being particularly prominent.

Source: CACI Web site (1999) © CACI Ltd.

USING NEW APPROACHES TO CUSTOMER SEGMENTATION

The move from macro-segmentation to micro-segmentation

Even with the availability of good geo-demographic information, the marketing manager still faces the problem that the smallest neighbourhood unit that a system like ACORN can define consists of about 15 households. Two customers in the same segment (or even two people who live next door to each other) are likely to have different tastes, attitudes and purchasing behaviour. In addition, reliance on data from a national census that is carried out once every ten years has been seen as a drawback to the traditional geo-demographic segmentation approach. More importantly, geo-demographic segmentation based on census data provides an aggregate picture of the characteristics of people living in a particular district, rather than of the individual. As one commentator points out:[2]

> 'The simple geo-demographic code is like the common currency of prediction. It is useful but to drive modelled solutions, it is individual data that provides the power.'

Traditional geo-demographic approaches can be described as macro-segmentation. The individual data described above comes from micro-segmentation approaches based on behaviour and psychographic characteristics.

Gathering data on customer behaviour

Advances in information technology have enabled marketers to gather large amounts of data on customer *behaviour* and use that data to segment customers based on such variables as:

■ product usage
■ loyalty
■ purchasing patterns
■ benefits sought.

The increasing use of electronic point-of-sale information is providing companies with detailed information by individual customer. In the food retailing industry, product purchasing information gathered through EPoS systems is combined with personal information that customers provide when they sign up for loyalty schemes, giving the retailers a deep understanding of how their customers buy products from their stores and how those purchasing patterns change over time.

▦ Gathering data on customer psychographics

Key psychographic variables that are increasingly used in customer segmentation include:

▦ lifestyle
▦ attitude
▦ personality
▦ interests
▦ activities.

Although still not as widely available as socio-economic data, the amount of *lifestyle* data being gathered and used has increased dramatically in recent years. Many of the lifestyle databases in the UK have been compiled by the marketing database company Claritas.[3] For example, Claritas's Behaviourbank and Lifestyle Selector databases were compiled from responses to questionnaires that were completed by millions of consumers in return for special-offer coupons. Lifestyle segmentation typically requires the amalgamation of data from a variety of different sources.

▦ Traditional versus non-traditional approaches to segmentation

During the 1990s the increasing use of these new methods of segmenting customers sparked a fierce 'geo-demographic versus lifestyle' debate. Now, both proponents accept that the combination of both approaches offers a more complete solution than either approach on its own. For example, CACI's Lifestyle Plus and Claritas's PRIZM targeting systems (*see* Exhibit 5.3) are among a number of systems that combine the individual detail of lifestyle data with the solid foundation of census information and the statistical reliability of market research to give more targeted marketing solutions.

Exhibit 5.3

WHITE HOT GOODS

Hotpoint had invested in a bespoke point-of-sale display specifically for a new out-of-town superstore, the first for the retailer outside its traditional geographical area. The display showed Hotpoint's product portfolio across a range of price points, but sales through the store were running at 9% lower than elsewhere and a lower average price per sale was being achieved. Hotpoint and the retailer were keen to address this problem and work together to increase product sales through the store, raise the average value per sale and ensure the product range reflected the profile of customers. To achieve this, they needed to attract a more affluent customer than normal for the retailer.

Using PRIZM, Claritas's segmentation system, customer groups were identified that matched the profile of Hotpoint's existing customers. These more affluent, established

▶

families with children at home were the type the retailer needed to attract. A catchment area was created around the superstore, highlighting the location of those who matched the target profile. The retailer prepared a direct mail pack offering a free video cassette for those consumers who visited the store, and additional offers were available if they purchased a Hotpoint appliance. The offer was sent to 40,000 homes.

From past experience, the retailer anticipated a 1% response rate. The actual response was 5%, with 2,000 customers visiting the store. As a result of the joint initiative, significant sales were generated. Hotpoint products accounted for 27% of all white goods purchased at the store, with an average value 16% higher than the average achieved for white goods sold overall. The initiative is now being rolled out to ten more superstores.

Source: Claritas Web site (1999).

International segmentation data

Most of the geo-demographic and lifestyle information is gathered on a national level and multinational companies will not find it easy to collate and analyse customer data across national boundaries. However, some steps have been taken to adopt a more international approach to the subject of customer data. CCN has divided the population of Europe into ten generic categories, each with broadly similar lifestyle profiles: affluent apartment dwellers in Madrid and Heidelberg share the same health-conscious and adventurous characteristics, while those who live in old industrial communities, from Belgian coalfields to Spanish steelworks, prefer low-price and heavily branded products.[4]

WAREHOUSING CUSTOMER DATA

The data warehouse

Over the past 20 years the sources of market research and the amount of data on customers and customer transactions have increased enormously (*see* Figure 5.1). As information becomes cheaper to warehouse and as companies integrate their information systems, the trend is set to continue unabated. Benetton, the fashion retailer, is linking its point-of-sale terminals in 7,000 shops and five continents.

Throughout the 1990s many large organisations started to examine the way in which this market data was reported and used. The oversupply of data and the undersupply of good management information prompted these companies to investigate how technology could be used to provide better decision-making information. One solution is the data warehouse, a very large database that holds operational, historical and customer data and makes it available to marketing managers for decision-making and analysis. It is designed to help marketing managers make better decisions by analysing summarised snapshots of corporate performance.

The retail industry, which uses large amounts of bar-code data from checkouts to provide accurate purchasing information, provides one of the best examples of the data warehousing concept in action. Exhibit 5.4 shows an often-quoted example of how

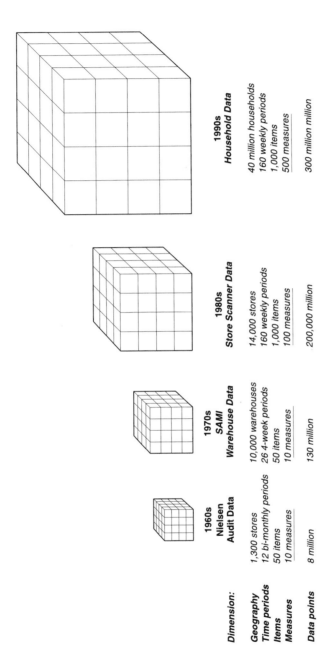

Fig 5.1 Growth of market data

Source: Andersen Consulting, 1998.

data warehouses can be used to gain interesting customer insights. In truth, companies will need greater insights than these to justify the costs of building a data warehouse. Many supermarket chains have integrated their entire ordering, stocking and replenishment systems with their checkout systems, in order to achieve benefits.

Exhibit 5.4

NAPPIES AND BEER

There is a strange story about nappies – diapers in North America – and beer that concerns the use of an 'information warehouse' by a US retailer. In trawling through some historical data and analysing it, the manager in a large US retailer noticed a distinct correlation between the sale of nappies and beer, just after work hours, which was particularly marked on a Friday. Further research confirmed the explanation: the man of the family was stopping off on his way home to pick up nappies for the baby – and a six-pack for himself. The retailer responded by merchandising nappies closer to the beer section and was rewarded by an increase in sales of both items.

Andy Smith, marketing director of database company Informix in the UK, confirms that the beer and nappies story is true. It originated with Wal-Mart, one of the largest proponents of data warehousing in the US, which uses an Informix-based data warehouse. 'The big retailers are the people driving data warehousing, because the competitive pressures are so great,' he says.

Source: Financial Times (1 March 1995).[4]

■ The effectiveness of data warehouses

Despite the high costs involved, data warehouses have proved successful in several aspects of the marketing function; notable proponents in the UK include Tesco, British Airways and Barclays Bank. At Fingerhut, the US-based marketing company, the data warehouse holds the equivalent of 3 billion pages of data on more than 30 million customer households. Fingerhut tracks up to 2,000 data elements including demographics, buying patterns and preferences, credit history and even hobbies, anniversaries and birthdays.[5] The research company Datapro cites several examples of successful data warehouse initiatives:

■ *Category management.* Data warehouses can help retail product managers gain a better understanding of consumer buying patterns and consumer response to their promotions.

■ *Claims analysis.* Insurance and healthcare firms use data warehousing applications to control costs and provide better customer service.

■ *Financial and market planning.* Many organisations gather and collate financial data from different sources in order to carry out product costing and customer-profitability analysis.

■ *Rate management.* Telecommunications companies use data warehouses in their efforts to determine the most profitable and competitive rates for cellular, local and long-distance calls.

In general, data warehouses are appropriate for companies exhibiting the following characteristics:

- an information-based approach to management
- involvement in highly competitive, rapidly changing markets
- a large, diverse customer base
- data stored in different systems.

▓ Lower-cost solutions – the data mart

Data warehousing systems are usually built to meet the specific requirements of individual organisations. They are expensive – a data warehouse set up by a UK healthcare service provider cost £1 million – and it can take several years to migrate all the customer information from the old computer systems into the warehouse. Data warehousing projects can cost up to $10 million over a five-year implementation period.

Given the high costs and long timescales involved, many companies question whether the benefits are sufficient to justify the cost. According to one UK insurance company[6] which has already invested heavily in building a data warehouse for decision-making purposes:

'We are still getting the data into our warehouse, rather than pulling it out.'

One solution is to scale down the scope and coverage, confining the activities to, say, a single department with less data and less complexity. Data warehouses that are built on a relatively small scale are termed 'data marts', while one company even refers to its mini-versions of such a warehouse as 'data sheds'![7] A data mart cannot do everything a data warehouse can, but it can be implemented at a fraction of the cost. Rather than gathering all the company's information into a single warehouse, a small, cleaned-up subset of data is held, often at a summary level. Typically a data mart is designed for a smaller number of users, which reduces the implementation costs and means that it can be built using off-the-shelf computer packages. Companies such as Bulmer in the UK have moved to a combination of data warehouses and data marts (*see* Exhibit 5.5).

Exhibit 5.5

GOING TO THE MART

HP Bulmer, the cider company, has since 1991 made a capital investment of £2 million a year in its IT system development and replacement programme. Bulmer decided to introduce a data warehouse to smooth the transition between old and new technology. Dr Martin Wynn, Bulmer's information technology director, says: 'Old and new systems are different not only in the technology they use but in the way they define things such as products, supplies and customers. As we switched over we wanted to draw data from both systems. The warehouse gave us information in a meaningful form that we could not get otherwise.

▶

Dr Wynn says: 'We can see how information changes from day to day, week to week and month to month. It helps us direct our sales effort.' Staff have been trained, with the 35 national account managers going through a two-year programme that has transformed the way they use computers. The warehouse has broken down barriers between departments, so that finance and sales staff look at the same data and understand each other's problems.

Source: Adapted from *The Times* data warehousing supplement (5 June 1996).

MINING CUSTOMER DATA

▦ The power of data mining

With the aid of a good database of information and some good analytical tools with which to query the database, companies can 'mine' for hidden information that can be used for marketing purposes. Companies that mine their data are looking for new correlations that may help them gain some insights into customer behaviour and competitive advantage in the marketplace. In insurance, for example, it has long been recognised that female drivers are a lower risk than their male counterparts and can be offered cheaper car insurance premiums. Data mining is used to find further sub-segments of female drivers with different price and risk profiles. Instead of providing a standard premium to women in the same age category, insurers can now price differently in order to retain their most profitable customers or encourage customers who are likely to be unprofitable to go elsewhere. Exhibit 5.6 provides an example of an Australian company that turned to data mining to protect market share by getting to know its customers better.

Exhibit 5.6

MINING FOR A FEW GOOD CUSTOMERS IN AUSTRALIA

Telestra, Australia's government-owned telecommunications giant, knew that full dereg-ulation of the country's telecoms market would threaten its dominant market position. The first sign of the impending struggle came in the mid-1990s with the entry of the second national carrier, Optus Telecommunications. By 1997, the upstart Optus had grabbed market share from Telestra in the long-distance and international call markets. Telestra's response was to use data mining techniques to develop behavioural models of people who wanted to switch carriers and those who were prepared to stay. Their behaviour was matched for 12 months and Telestra was able to identify the types of customers who said they would leave and did leave, and those who claimed they would remain loyal but left anyway. Telestra also began sifting through billing data to identify when and where customers had changed to a competitor's service – and then used the knowledge to gain back more than 50% of customers.

Adapted from: Economist Intelligence Unit and Andersen Consulting (1998).

▦ Creating a data mining capability

While fast computing, efficient databases and high-speed networks are important elements of the data mining infrastructure, a variety of non-technical factors must be put in place as well. These include:

- methods for identifying, locating and extracting good quality, relevant data for analysis;
- tools and techniques for identifying patterns and relationships in the data;
- statisticians and analysts to prepare the data, carry out the analysis and interpret the results;
- the presentation of relevant relationships mined from the data so that management and marketing decisions can be taken.

▦ Data mining techniques

There is currently no agreed classification scheme for data mining techniques. However, we can classify the more popular techniques into the following types:

- *Inductive reasoning*. Induction is the process of starting with individual facts and then using reasoning to reach a hypothesis or a general conclusion. In data mining inductive reasoning the facts are the database records, and the hypothesis formulation usually takes the form of a decision tree that attempts to divide or organise the data in a meaningful way. Decision trees are not suitable for all kinds of problems. Some decision tree-based tools have problems dealing with continuous sets of values, such as revenue or age, and may require that these values be grouped into ranges. For example, grouping ages 16 to 23 together may hide a significant break that might occur at age 20. Tools such as Darwin from the data mining company Thinking Machine avoid this problem by using techniques to cluster the data first.
- *Artificial neural networks*. The concept behind neural network technology is that a computer can be 'trained' to solve a problem in a similar fashion to a human brain, by recognising familiar patterns. While conventional computers have to be programmed with very specific instructions, neural computers do not require the same explicit instructions. Instead they adapt their responses based on previous problems and solutions that are given to them. The systems 'learn' from these problems and, after a sufficient 'training' period, can offer a solution to a new problem. At present the most commonly used applications of neural networks are the areas of micro-marketing, risk management and fraud detection (*see* Exhibit 5.7).
- *Data visualisation*. Data visualisation refers both to the creation of visual images of things that we are unable to see, and to a way of displaying qualitative and quantitative data at a glance.
- *Memory-based reasoning*. Memory-based reasoning is another artificial intelligence technique that is used for classification in a fashion similar to what humans may do to classify objects by comparing attributes with those of other objects recalled from memory. Tools that use memory-based reasoning classify records in a database by comparing them with similar records that have already been clustered or classified.

Exhibit 5.7

SAUSAGES AND WHITE BREAD

Retailers now have another weapon in their armoury of customer analysis techniques: neural networks. Already data warehousing technology has been deployed by many supermarkets as a means of searching through all the information gained from loyalty schemes introduced by retailers such as Tesco. By analysing the information, retailers can identify shopping trends and so better market products within a store.

In tests, the neural network software has identified patterns that retailers might not think of looking for. The system picked up the fact that people who buy sausages tend to buy white bread, for example. Armed with this information supermarkets can make customers aware of a special offer on a white loaf as they pick up their sausages.

The software can also predict individual buying habits, by searching through information gained from a store's loyalty scheme, and so identify which customers are likely to take up an offer and then continue to buy the product. With this knowledge the retailer can tailor its promotions and save money by only targeting those customers that are likely to provide a long-term gain.

CREATING A KNOWLEDGE ORGANISATION

▨ The value of a knowledge organisation

Many companies underestimate the knowledge that is held within their organisations. Recently academics have attempted to put a value on knowledge capital of pharmaceutical and chemical companies:[8]

- Merck's knowledge capital has been estimated at $48 billion, thanks to its 'knowledge-intensive' pipeline of new products. Merck has annual sales of $24 billion.
- Bristol-Myers Squibb's knowledge capital of $30 billion compares to its sales of $17 billion.
- Du Pont's knowledge capital of $26 billion compares to its sales of $40 billion.

Another reason for the focus on the value of knowledge capital is that the loss of corporate knowledge and the creation of corporate memory are finally being recognised as major management, and marketing, issues. It is a more topical subject in the USA than in Europe, but it is moving up the management agenda on this side of the Atlantic. The reason for the concern stems from the fact that managers are spending fewer years with the same company before moving on to their next job or career (*see* Exhibit 5.8).

According to Pencorp,[9] the number of UK managers who have more than six years' tenure with their current company has decreased from more than 60 per cent in the 1950s and 1960s to less than 20 per cent in the 1990s. With so few long-term employees in our organisations today, it is little wonder that senior managers are looking for new methods of capturing vital knowledge even when the original source of the knowledge has moved on to another job or another company. Exhibit 5.9 provides

Exhibit 5.8

CORPORATE ALZHEIMER'S

Having spent the 1990s in the throes of restructuring, re-engineering and downsizing, American companies are worrying about corporate amnesia. There was a time when air travellers in search of timely take-offs and sterling service would fly with Delta Air Lines. That was before Delta embarked on a cost-cutting and re-engineering programme, that has shrunk its workforce by about a sixth, or 12,000 jobs. Somewhere along the way, Delta seemed to 'forget' that service was what gave it an edge, and the loyalty of many customers. That firms should have 'memories' – and that these are strategically important – is not as whimsical as it sounds. John Challenger, executive vice-president of Challenger, Grey & Christmas, a consultancy based in Chicago, thinks that shrinking companies are at risk of 'corporate Alzheimer's'. He argues that the success of a firm depends not only on its skills and knowledge but also on its collective business experiences, successes and failures, culture, vision and numerous other intangible qualities.

Adapted from: The Economist (20 April 1996).[10]

Exhibit 5.9

LONG-TERM MEMORIES

At Kraft, food arm of Philip Morris, the US cigarette, beer and foods group, the company's oral history archive has been used to fashion a new marketing approach to an old product. Towards the end of the 1980s one of the company's brands, Cracker Barrel cheese, was not selling well. Linda Crowder, the brand's manager, used the oral tapes to delve into the brand's origins in 1953 in order to shape a new marketing strategy. By reading the transcripts of interviews, she was able to gain the insights of Med Connelly, national sales manager of cheese products from 1959 to 1962, the period when the brand's sales began to take off: 'He gave us a perspective we just couldn't get anywhere else,' she says. 'Our research gave us a sense of what the theory was when Cracker Barrel was first introduced, and what we told consumers about the brand in the beginning.'

Source: Financial Times (31 July 1996).

one example of a company that has attempted to capture this knowledge and improve its long-term memory.

The speed at which knowledge is shared around an organisation has become a key differentiating factor between the excellent organisations and the mediocre. A central role in the dissemination of knowledge around organisations is played by technologies such as intranets, extranets and groupware.

▓ Intranets and extranets

There are several enabling technologies that allow organisations to share information and knowledge more easily between employees. During the 1990s local area networks (LANs) linked PCs within the same building or on the same floor of a building.

Employees located in different buildings or different cities can be linked using a wide area network (WAN), which links several LANs together.

More recently companies have turned to intranet and extranet technology to link people electronically. While the Internet is a global public medium, there are also private versions of the Internet that can only be accessed by employees of one organisation and are protected by passwords and other security features. These *intranets* can also link to the outside world by connecting to the Internet, but they are primarily for internal use within a company. Marketing managers tend to use intranets for the following applications:

▓ publishing corporate documents such as product literature, marketing literature, annual reports, newsletters, price lists, manuals and corporate policies;
▓ providing access to searchable directories such as corporate phone books, addresses, calendars, departmental diary systems and schedules;
▓ distributing software to a wide number of users, for example issuing updates of quotation software to life assurance and pensions sales representatives;
▓ connecting large numbers of employees in various geographic locations by means of electronic mail.

When these networks are extended to the company's trading partners over secure connections they are known as *extranets*. As Exhibit 5.10 points out, these private networks based on the same technology and software as the Internet are becoming increasingly popular for sharing and disseminating information.

Exhibit 5.10

ROCHE ON ALERT – VIA EXTRANET

Hoffman-La Roche Pharmaceuticals Division is one of the world's largest pharmaceutical companies, developing, producing and marketing cost-effective drugs to combat human diseases. Roche Discovery Welwyn is one of six research centres at Pharmaceuticals Division and employs 340 scientists.

Roche decided to implement an on-line information service, delivered to the desktop of every scientist. It examined a number of options and eventually selected a customised version of DataStar Web from the Dialog Corporation. DataStar Web provides access to 350 databases using Internet technology. Roche selected DataStar Web because:

■ The product interface could be customised according to the specific requirements of Roche users.
■ Security was a key issue. Roche wanted to use a dedicated secure network (an extranet) rather than the commercial Internet.
■ Dialog Corporation offered a fixed price scheme, allowing the information department to predict costs and adhere to budget.

'Being able to access databases directly from the desktop has made the whole research process much faster and more streamlined for the users,' said Sue Jackson, Roche Discovery Welwyn's Head of Information. 'But an even more exciting change has been the introduction of the alerting system, which enables them to receive automatic updates about specific areas of research, without them having to do the running themselves.'

Source: Dialog Corporation Web site (1999).

▥ Groupware

One current debate is whether intranets and extranets will displace 'groupware', the similar but more costly proprietary systems that are not based on Internet standards. Examples of groupware include Banyan's *BeyondMail*, ICL's *Teamware*, Novell's *Groupwise* and the most popular and best-selling groupware product of all, *Lotus Notes* from Lotus Corporation (*see* Exhibit 5.11). Groupware tends to offer more features and better security than an intranet, but this is changing as the boundaries between groupware and intranets become more and more blurred. Companies such as the pharmaceutical organisation Glaxo-Wellcome, which uses both intranet and groupware technology across 27,000 desktops, will continue to use both.[11]

Exhibit 5.11

MARKET RESEARCH – BY INTRANET

Global investment bank SBC Warburg has adopted intranet technologies and Lotus Notes software to transform the way it produces research reports. Analysts in the bank's foreign exchange and economic research group produce studies and forecasts in daily, weekly, monthly and quarterly newsletters and reports. The process was paper-based three years ago when the bank set out to move to electronic methods. Alan Roberts, director of the bank's foreign exchange division in London, said the first step was defining the priorities as 'speed, quantity, and cost, in that order.' The bank also brought a coherent structure to the process. Analysts work with economic and financial market information, data from modelling and analysis, and less formal information gathered simply by being in the markets. Outputs go to the bank's traders and sales staff as well as clients. Now many customers of the research group's output can access it through Web browsers.

Source: Computer Weekly (6 June 1996).[12]

Case study

BRITISH AIRWAYS

British Airways wants to know more about its customers and their long-term needs. In that, it is similar to banks, insurance companies, retailers, health care providers and other explorers of data warehouse technology.

However, the international nature of BA's business has led to a pragmatic 'horses for courses' approach in which several solutions, hardware and software, have to work together. Mr Bill Teather, head of corporate management, confirms that BA has been working on the data warehouse projects for the last six years, although the term has only recently penetrated beyond the technical community to managers in BA.

'To meet customers' needs and to improve our own asset utilisation, we need to be able to answer all sorts of questions. Those answers feed into decisions on how we operate in the future,' explains Mr Teather. 'The data warehouse will tell us what mix of fares will be used on what routes, who flies where, for what price, and to what extent different countries and agencies are selling different mixes of the product. We look to the warehouse for detailed information about route profitability, so we can see where our aircraft are best deployed. For that, our users need good access to warehouse statistics.'

BA's first data warehouse applications were all about customer servicing and ticketing. Ms Sandy Hulbert, head of management information services for British Airways, explains: 'The big move is to try to personalise travel: it's all about knowing your customers and treating them as individuals. We are looking at who goes where, and when, but all these factors feed into long-term planning, load factors, the frequency of flights, and so on. The warehouse also records customer preferences, and the value of a customer through his or her booking history. It's all to do with trying to predict what the customer wants.'

Ms Hulbert emphasises the importance of linking applications and making data available to users regardless of barriers imposed by geography, hardware or software.

Once the data warehouse has proved its worth in strategic planning, BA plans to use the data for all sorts of different purposes, including cargo, engineering, marketing and operations, she adds. Word is already beginning to spread about the effectiveness of the data warehouse – 'luckily, the airline has taken IT to its heart, and people are very business focused. It's wonderful when management see IT as a value-added tool, not a threat; it makes us enthusiastic about what we can do.'

FT

Source: Adapted from 'A system for keeping air passengers happy', *Financial Times*, 1 March 1995.

Questions

1 How can BA's data warehouse lead to improved profitability and more personal customer service?

2 Where is the information to populate the data warehouse likely to come from?

3 Comment on BA adopting a 'horses for courses' approach to data warehouse projects.

4 Why is it important that data is available to users regardless of barriers imposed by geography, hardware or software?

5 Comment on BA's investment in IT and how it might enable the company to achieve its aim of becoming the 'world's favourite airline'.

ASSIGNMENT QUESTIONS

1 Visit Claritas's Web site (www.claritas.co.uk) and comment on how the company can help businesses segment their customers.

2 Describe and discuss the issues that companies face if they decide to undertake a data warehouse or data mining initiative.

3 Conduct a search on the Internet to find out what types of organisation provide data mining software and data warehousing solutions.

4 Why is corporate knowledge so important in the early 21st century?

References

[1] www.caci.co.uk

[2] Reed, D. (1996). 'The data game', *Marketing Week*, 3 May.

[3] www.claritas.co.uk

[4] Dempsey, M. (1995). 'Customers compartmentalised', *Financial Times*, 1 March.

[5] EIU (1998). *Managing Customer Relationships*, Economist Intelligence Unit. New York: EIU and Andersen Consulting.

[6] Gurton, A. (1996). 'Same story, different tune', *Computer Weekly*, 18 July.

[7] The Times (1996). 'Churchill Insurance', *The Times* (data warehousing supplement), 5 June.

[8] The Economist (1999). 'A price on the priceless', *The Economist*, 12 June 1999.

[9] Kransdorff, A. (1996). 'Keep know-how in the company', *Financial Times*, 31 July.

[10] The Economist (1996). 'Fire and forget?', *The Economist*, 20 April.

[11] Oldroyd, R. (1996). 'Glaxo's intranet injection', *Sunday Business ComputerAge*, 26 May.

[12] Green-Armytage, J. (1996). 'SBC Warburg speeds up research with intranet', *Computer Weekly*, 6 June.

MANAGING THE CUSTOMER RELATIONSHIP

In Part I of this book we examined how customer information could be gathered from both external market research and from internal company information systems, warehoused and mined for critical insights about customers. Part II was all about getting to know the customer more intimately. Part III expands on this theme by exploring how marketing systems and customer databases can be used to manage the relationship with the customer more effectively. It begins with an examination of how customer databases can be created and used for marketing purposes. It continues with an examination of database marketing and direct marketing, and finishes with a discussion on how true marketing-led organisations are attempting to use their customer databases to create a relationship with those customers that they value most.

Part III contains three chapters:

6 Creating the customer database

7 Database marketing and direct marketing

8 Relationship marketing.

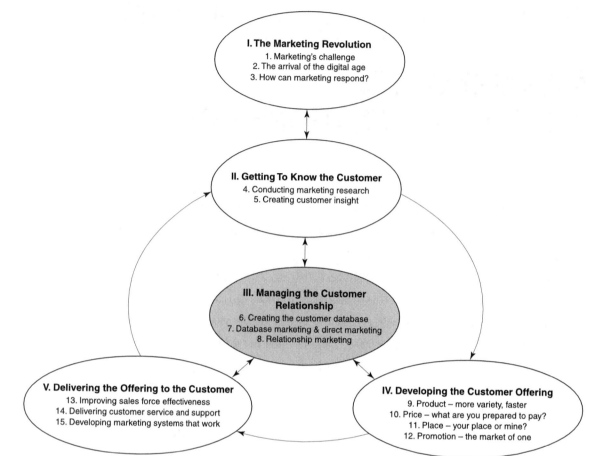

6

CREATING THE CUSTOMER DATABASE

SUMMARY

Marketing managers are constantly bombarded with customer information from many different sources. Their effectiveness in managing the customer relationship is dependent on their ability to access relevant information on customers, customer attitudes, likes and dislikes, customer purchases and transactions, and to use that information for making appropriate marketing decisions. The first step in managing the customer relationship is to gather all relevant information on those customers into a single database. In order to do this, marketing managers must:

☐ understand the nature and role of marketing information systems (MkIS);

☐ understand the central role that the customer database plays in any marketing information system;

☐ understand the steps required to build an effective customer database;

☐ treat the customer database as a strategic resource.

MARKETING INFORMATION SYSTEMS

What are marketing information systems?

Marketing information systems comprise all computer and non-computer systems that assist the marketing function to operate effectively. Good MkIS include many systems that are not generally thought of in marketing terms, for example general ledger, accounts receivable and production-planning systems. Some of the key attributes of Marshall and LaMotte's (1992)[1] definition of MkIS are as follows:

- *They do not limit the definition to computer hardware or software.* Their definition places greater emphasis on the provision of relevant information rather than on the technology itself.
- *The definition calls for organised, regular flows of relevant information.* MkIS should not be developed as isolated, ad hoc systems. They should draw data from many different sources and organise it so that useful information can be provided to marketing managers.
- *The information must be relevant to marketing decisions.* High-level marketing decision makers must be included in planning the information requirements.

▓ *Marketing managers are expected to carry out further analyses of the information provided by the system.* An integral part of any MkIS are tools that allow marketing managers to analyse and manipulate data in order to make marketing decisions.

Unfortunately, for every example of a successful implementation that is written up in the marketing journals, there is at least one other example of failure to achieve any significant benefit. In fact, Talvinen and Saarinen (1995) contend that there is little systematic empirical evidence available to prove that marketing information systems have brought about sustained benefit for the companies that have built and developed them.[2]

▓ Sources of marketing information

Four key sources of marketing information are defined by Kotler (1994):[3]

▓ *Internal records*, including current and historical sales figures, price lists, inventory levels, accounting information such as receivables and payables, as well as customer complaints.
▓ *Marketing intelligence*, from sources as diverse as trade publications, books and newspapers, competitor advertising, trade associations, company personnel who have worked for competitors, and informal briefings from sales staff.
▓ *Marketing decision support information*. For example, in a supermarket, the most valuable source of marketing information comes from the hundreds of thousands of transactions that are scanned daily at the checkouts in each store.
▓ *Marketing research*, which we discussed in Chapter 4.

In practice, this information is often held on other computer systems to which the marketing department has limited or no access. Having identified the information required for making good marketing decisions, marketing managers can construct their marketing information systems to extract product and customer information from a variety of internal and external sources.

▓ International marketing information systems

As companies become more international, it becomes increasingly important to share marketing information across national boundaries. Very often customers are becoming more international themselves and organisations have to put together multinational teams to meet their customers' needs. Benetton, for example, offers a range of 3,000 products and operates a global order-entry and distribution system that allows it to manage distribution to its 5,000 franchised stores across the world, from a warehouse in Italy. Daniels (1993)[4] compares the Portuguese and Spaniards of the fifteenth century, who had fast ships to support speedy communications, with today's global companies that require global networks and customer databases to keep them ahead of the competition. The design and implementation of cross-border systems and databases is more difficult than building a system within one set of national boundaries as it requires more effort to co-ordinate and reconcile the needs of different national marketing departments.

THE CENTRAL ROLE OF THE CUSTOMER DATABASE

▓ Customer databases

The most valuable information in a truly customer-focused organisation is its intimate knowledge of the customer base. This requires customer information to be gathered and stored in a customer database where it can be accessed by marketing managers. There are typically two uses of customer information: *operational* and *analytical*. The distinction is an important one, as we will see in the following pages when we discuss the design and development of customer databases. By *operational*, we mean the day-to-day support of the business. Examples include:

▓ a customer service representative of an electricity company accessing a customer's account details in order to answer telephone queries;

▓ a bank teller accessing a customer's current balance in order to decide whether or not to make a cash advance;

▓ a hotel receptionist keying in a customer's name to find out which room the customer has been booked into.

By *analytical*, we mean the analysis of historic and transaction data in order to create or adjust a particular product offering or promotion. For example:

▓ the selection by an electricity company of the most appropriate customers for a mailshot in order to promote and sell home heating appliances;

▓ the profitability analysis of a bank's customers;

▓ the analysis by a hotel manager of the home addresses of customers to measure the effectiveness of a particular advertising campaign.

Typically, the modern company has its customer data stored in one or more databases that are used for a variety of purposes. Figure 6.1 illustrates the central role of the customer database.

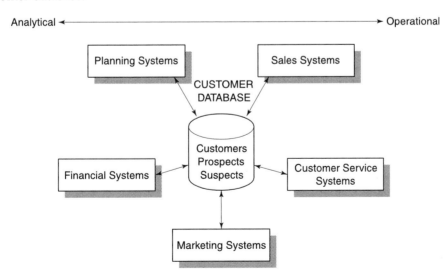

Fig 6.1   The central role of the customer database

There are a few points to note about Figure 6.1. First, a single customer database is depicted as supporting a variety of operational and analytical systems. In practice, the information in the customer database is often downloaded into separate information systems that are designed specifically for analytic purposes such as data mining. Note also that the customer database may contain information on potential, as well as existing, customers. The benefits that can be gained from investing in building a database of existing customers is illustrated by the example of Samsonite (*see* Exhibit 6.1).

Exhibit 6.1

A CONVINCING CASE FOR A CUSTOMER DATABASE

Samsonite Corp. is looking to expand its use of database marketing next year after improving its sales and return-on-investment through its use. In 1994, Samsonite sales grew 10 to 15 per cent. The company began building its customer database to better understand why customers bought Samsonite luggage, which is frequently more expensive than other luggage. The company has used the database primarily to build customer profiles which include information such as age, income, gender, colour preferences, education, credit card usage, occupation, hobbies, favourite features of a particular product, and likelihood of purchasing another Samsonite product in the next year. Using these profiles, Samsonite convinces retailers that there are enough prospects living in the neighbourhood to justify carrying certain Samsonite products.

Samsonite has about 1.5 million customers on its database, which it began building in early 1991. The company's goal is to expand the database by 300,000 names a year through its retail sales. The programme is based on the product-registration cards customers return after they purchase a piece of Samsonite luggage.

Source: DM News (16 October 1995).

Customer databases also provide the means to determine customer profitability. By analysing the characteristics of long-term profitable customers, new sources of profitable business can be identified and unprofitable segments can be avoided (*see* Exhibit 6.2). Even the ability to identify the top 10 per cent of customers in terms of profitability can be a major benefit to organisations.

Exhibit 6.2

WHISKY DRINKERS

Contrast the person who buys a bottle of whisky – no matter the brand – once a year, with a brand-loyal regular drinker. Both names might appear on the same database and may be sent the same direct mail. Eventually the cost of communicating with the first customer will outweigh the revenue they contribute to the company. The money it is costing you to maintain a fruitless relationship with that person would be better spent generating more revenue from the loyal one. Most companies faced with this situation would have the sense to cease communicating with the non-profitable customer. For some it is not that simple – profitable or not, they remain stuck in the relationship.

Source: Precision Marketing (5 February 1996).

Companies take many different approaches to deciding which customers to include in the database. The drinks company Seagram, for example, has a worldwide database policy that restricts customer information on the database to that which is both recent and relevant. Names will not get on to the database in the first place unless they pass certain criteria. Similarly, if customers stay on the database for too long without responding to any offers, they are removed.[5]

▨ Sources of customer information

Customer information can be sourced from within the company or purchased from external sources (*see* Table 6.1).

The most useful sources of customer information are often the internal systems within an organisation. Additional external information and lists can be sourced from list operators such as those shown in Table 6.2.

Table 6.1   Internal and external sources of customer data

Internal sources of data	External sources of data
Accounts/general ledger	Census data
Customer application forms	External lists of particular types of
Customer complaints	customers
Customer enquiries	Market research (specially commissioned)
Customer information files	Records from sister companies
Market research (existing)	
Merchandising statistics	
Promotional campaigns	
Service reports	
Warranty cards	

Table 6.2   Top 10 UK-based database marketing list operators

Company	Volume of names traded	Number of lists owned or exclusively managed	Date of establishment
1 Mardev/Ibis	103 million	200+	1971
2 Dudley Jenkins List Broking	100 million	140	1970
3 NDL International	87 million	3	1985
4 HLB	85 million	38	1986
5 Cheryl Nathan List Broking	75 million	43	1985
6 CDMS Marketing Services	50 million+	3	1985
7 CCN Marketing	40 million	4	1980
8 Independent Direct Marketing	30 million	39	1990
9 DunsMarketing	24 million	3	1974
10 The Mail Marketing Group	17 million	37	circa 1950

Note: Data not available from CACI, one of the largest and longest-established companies in the business.

Source: Precision Marketing (10 April 1995).

DEVELOPING THE CUSTOMER DATABASE

▩ Steps in developing a customer database

There are seven steps that should be followed in designing a customer database. As Figure 6.2 shows, the first six steps need to occur only once while the final step, maintaining the database, is an ongoing activity.

Step 1. Define the database functions

The first question to ask when deciding to build a customer database is: 'What do I want this database to do?' This may seem obvious, but it is fundamental to the success of any customer database initiative. The design of the customer database, and how data is held on it, will depend on whether the database is used primarily for operational or analytical purposes.

Operational applications have different demands, such as quick response time and access to transactional or account data. If an electricity company is to provide good customer service, the customer service representative (CSR) who takes the customer call needs to access that customer's latest account details within a matter of seconds, just by keying in the customer's name or address.

The operational system described above is probably also used to send out the monthly or quarterly bills, but may be of limited use in analysing trends, selecting customer groups for a mailshot or for analysing electricity consumption across different geographic areas. For marketing analysis a much wider set of data will be required and that data needs to be organised in a different fashion. Processing power to crunch through millions of calculations per second may be more important than fast access to individual items of information.

Thus the design and organisation of a customer database are critically dependent on its primary purpose. IT people may focus on the operational aspects of systems, which can lead to the development of marketing systems that fail to meet the expectations of the marketing and sales staff. The onus is on the marketing department to communicate clearly its requirements to the IT department.

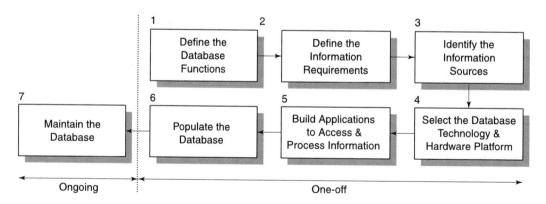

Fig 6.2   Seven steps in developing a customer database

Step 2. Define the information requirements

There are two approaches that can be taken to defining the information required. The first is to focus on a small amount of key customer information that can be used to make marketing decisions. The second approach is to capture as much information as possible and then start looking for trends within the data. This is the data mining approach, where an organisation creates a large data warehouse that is analysed to identify meaningful trends. In determining the most appropriate approach to take, the following questions should be asked:

▓ *What data do we need?* Regardless of the approach taken, there are key pieces of information that the marketing manager must have. Typically, data on customer name, address, age, profession and income are required. Other information on nationality, language spoken and personal hobbies is useful, but often of secondary importance.
▓ *Does the data support our marketing segmentation strategy?* As organisations become more sophisticated in targeting specific market segments it becomes more important to capture data to support these segmentation strategies.
▓ *How easily can the information be updated?* Keeping customer data up to date is critical. If data changes regularly and cannot be easily updated it may not be worth the cost of obtaining it.
▓ *Should the database include prospective customers?* Marketing managers must decide whether to limit the database to existing customers or extend it to include information on prospective customers.

Step 3. Identify the information sources

Having defined the information required, the next step is to identify how the information will be acquired and updated on an ongoing basis. Customer information can be sourced from within the organisation or from third parties. While the purchase of mailing lists is still a popular method of finding potential new customers, the effectiveness of using such lists for direct marketing can be poor. Unless carefully targeted, response rates can be low and the cost of generating a sale can be higher than traditional methods of advertising. Therefore the most commonly used sources of customer data are normally internal.

Step 4. Select the database technology and hardware platform

There are several different ways in which data can be held in a database. The choice of database technology and database management system depends on the uses that are intended for the database. Without getting too technical, a relational database is likely to be the preferred database solution for the vast majority of applications. The main advantages of relational databases are faster processing speeds and the flexibility to create more complex queries to determine relationships between data. The selection of a hardware platform will depend on a number of factors, including the existing hardware, the size of the database and the number and location of potential users.

Step 5. Build applications to access and process information

Once the technology has been selected the applications to utilise the information held on the customer database can be built. We will examine database marketing applications in more detail in the next chapter.

Step 6. Populate the database

The task of populating a customer database is a major exercise and poor-quality customer data is the primary reason for most database marketing failures. Much of the required information on existing customers is already held in paper or electronic format within the organisation. However, a major problem is the number of different locations where such information can be found. In many organisations, such as banks and insurance companies, the computer systems that hold the data are organised on a product, rather than a customer, basis. In other words, if Joe Bloggs has a current account, a savings account, a credit card and a pension with the same financial institution, it is entirely feasible that his details are held on four different databases. When data is centralised on to one database, it is likely that four separate entries will be made for Joe Bloggs. When a mailshot is planned it is also entirely possible for Joe Bloggs to receive four separate pieces of direct mail. Apart from the cost of unnecessary paper and postage, Joe Bloggs will not be left with a very favourable impression of the company.

Software can be purchased to assist in the 'de-duplication' of customer records so that there is only one record for each customer on the database. However, such software is not foolproof. In some instances there is no alternative to contacting large numbers of customers to obtain or confirm their details. Several creative techniques can be employed to persuade the customer to divulge such personal information. Many companies on the Internet ask their customers to provide, or update, their own information. Whichever approach is used, the exercise of populating the database will take time and require considerable resources.

Step 7. Maintain the database

Once marketing managers are satisfied with the quality of the information in the database, an ongoing maintenance activity is required to keep it up to date, otherwise its effectiveness as a marketing tool diminishes quickly. As Curtis (1996) states:

> 'the database is a living breathing thing that requires constant attention – you can't just build it and say "that's it".'

This maintenance activity is a major task. Births, deaths, marriages and changes of address can alter between 8 and 12 per cent of the information in a database in any one year. In the UK, Royal Mail has been changing an average of 5 per cent of its post codes annually.[6] It only takes a few years for the integrity of customer information in any database to degrade to a level where its usefulness becomes questionable. Incorrect or out-of-date information can drive customers away rather than enhancing the relationship (see Exhibit 6.3).

Ideally, companies should regard all contacts with a customer as an opportunity to update the customer's details on the database. For example, if a customer walks into a bank branch to open up a new account, all the relevant details should be entered on to the database at the point of contact with the customer, and any existing information that the bank may have on the customer should also be verified at the same time. In reality few organisations can claim to have up-to-date information on their customers. Consider the following case of a European bank[8] that carried out an analysis of the quality of its customer information:

Exhibit 6.3

DRIVING THE CUSTOMER AWAY

Nurturing customers correctly can lead to a long-term commitment between two parties. Information systems designed to build and uphold this relationship can, however, lead to the demise of the relationship. Some sellers fail to recognise when a customer has moved into a new phase. For example a mother whose youngest child is 10 may still be labelled a 'new mom' on a direct marketer's database and still receive catalogues on baby supplies.

To use information systems effectively and prevent loss of customers, identify perishable descriptors ('new parent', 'student', etc.) and find ways to identify when specific customers' characteristics change. Pay as much attention to systems that help listen to customers as to systems that tell customers about products.

Source: Information Week (12 June 1995).[7]

- 10 per cent of accounts in the customer database did not have a valid name
- 13 per cent did not have a full address
- 47 per cent did not have a title/sex for the customer
- 55 per cent did not have a marital status
- 72 per cent did not have a home phone number
- 75 per cent did not have a date of birth
- 77 per cent did not have an occupation
- 85 per cent did not have a record of the number of dependent children.

The percentage of customer records where all eight fields were completed was extremely low and, with complete information on only a few per cent of all customers, the effectiveness of the bank's customer database was seriously compromised.

TREATING THE CUSTOMER DATABASE AS A STRATEGIC RESOURCE

▨ The need for a change in mindset

A mindset and attitude change is required in most companies before employees treat every contact with the customer as a means of improving the level of information held on that customer. Often there is no incentive to log a customer telephone call or ask all those questions when a new customer walks in the door. More often than not major process and procedural changes are required to ensure that each customer contact can be captured without hindering or slowing down the transaction. For example, many airlines have loyalty schemes. However, when a customer arrives at the check-in counter, there may be another half a dozen people in the queue and the last thing that the check-in clerk (or the person in the queue who is already late for a flight) needs is the additional delay of accepting the loyalty card and typing the details into the system. One answer is to have a swipe-card mechanism for customers to record their own flights, or to implement a system for recording the flight when the ticket is purchased rather than when the boarding card is issued. Another is to embrace the power of the Internet and allow customers to check, and update, their own details online. It is not uncommon nowadays for companies to pay their customers to provide more detailed personal information that can be used to improve the subsequent marketing messages via the Internet.

Whatever techniques are chosen to update customer information, company employees must be encouraged to recognise the value of the customer database, and the data held on it. Such data is an important strategic asset.

Case study

BARCLAYS BANK

Barclays Bank introduced a new customer database that has dramatically improved its ability to effectively target its different customer groups. With over 2,000 branches throughout the UK and over 14 million customers, Barclays is one of the largest UK banks. Specialising in three major activities – personal banking, credit cards and financial services – its customer records were, until recently, held on three separate databases. This system presented obvious difficulties, as it was impossible to tell if, for example, a Barclaycard (credit card) customer also held a personal account with the bank. This made cross-selling to existing customers a somewhat 'hit and miss' activity, and meant that Barclays did not have a full picture of who its customers were.

Barclays decided in 1989 that it was essential to integrate the three databases into one, creating a company-wide database that would support the sales effort both at branch level and within central marketing. The bank could then implement a centralised marketing approach that could be both co-ordinated and targeted. What was needed was a new database that would hold a complete profile of each customer's relationship with Barclays and that would be accessible throughout the whole organisation. 'Since we used to have account-based databases, we knew how many accounts were held – more than 25 million, in fact – but we had no idea how many customers we had,' said Ken Pilbeam, head of operational systems management at the bank. 'Therefore, as part of our new database, we wanted to build a profile of each person, with information on every Barclays product he or she held.'

The new Customer Information System (CIS) was piloted in 1991 and later implemented nationwide, greatly enhancing how the bank holds and accesses its information, according to Pilbeam. Barclays can now look at its direct marketing activity from the customer's perspective, he said, and implement properly targeted cross-selling campaigns. 'It is now an easy task to monitor the perceptions and attitudes of our customers against the frequency and type of direct mail and telephone contact.'

Equipped now with a better understanding of the customer, Barclays claims it finds that not only are the direct marketing campaigns more cost effective through improved targeting, but they are receiving a better response. Using the new system, customers' names are now associated with the accounts they hold, allowing Barclays to sort by name for the first time. The Barclays marketing team can now be confident that when they select, for example, a Barclays loan campaign for branch customers, they are not including any existing Barclays loan customers – a phenomenon that has always caused much irritation to customers. Prior to the new database name and address de-duplication was outsourced to computer bureaux, and direct marketing was done by a product group, rather than on a company-wide basis. With the new integrated database customers no longer risk being the target of marketing efforts by two different departments at the same time, meaning that marketing is now more 'customer friendly'. Although data is held centrally, each of nearly 3,000 staff in the branches can have on-line access to the database via workstations, and can see all the bank's relationships with each of its 14 million customers. The customer database maintains customer details, displays product information, creates sales leads, records customer contacts, captures credit and insurance applications and even prints application forms.

Another benefit that the marketing department has discovered is the speed of the new system, Pilbeam said. 'Before, branch counter staff could only look up records by account number. If an account customer wanted to enquire about the status of his Barclaycard account, this would involve phone calls that were both time-consuming and irritating. Now Barclays has the database at the counter and if a customer from Aberdeen walks into a branch in the Isle of Wight his details will be available on screen.' Another useful feature of the new system at Barclays is the phonetic name and address matching. When staff deal with customers over the phone they can match by the sound of the name rather than by the exact spelling. The customer's address verifies the match. On a database of this kind it is essential that customer data is kept accurate and up to date, so the database is updated every day at Barclays' Computer Operations in Gloucester. Details of a new account opened today will be on the screen nationwide by 9 am the following day. Pilbeam said the system has allowed him and his team to become customer focused rather than product focused. 'As a result, we have improved our customer service and reduced our costs.'

Source: Adapted from *FSI* (October 1995).[9]

Questions

1 Why did Barclays build a CIS?

2 What benefits has CIS brought to the bank?

3 'We had no idea how many customers we had.' Discuss.

4 How can Barclays use the customer database to improve its relationship with customers?

5 Did Barclays follow the seven steps for developing a customer database?

ASSIGNMENT QUESTIONS

1 Describe a marketing information system.

2 Why is a customer database central to any marketing organisation?

3 Discuss the steps in developing a customer database.

4 Why is it so important to keep customer data up to date?

5 Provide an example of an Internet site that encourages, or pays, its customers to update the information held on them.

References

[1] Marshall, K.P. and LaMotte, S.W. (1992). 'Marketing information systems: a marriage of systems analysis and marketing management', *Journal of Applied Business Research*, Vol. 8, No. 3, Summer.

[2] Talvinen, J.M. and Saarinen, T. (1995). 'MkIS support for the marketing management process: perceived improvements for marketing management', *Marketing Intelligence and Planning*, Vol. 13, No. 1.

3   Kotler, P. (1994). *Marketing Management: Analysis, Planning, Implementation and Control*, 8th edition, New Jersey: Prentice-Hall.

4   Daniels, N.C. (1993). *Information Technology: The Management Challenge*. Wokingham: Addison-Wesley.

5   Curtis, J. (1996). 'Sorting out the wheat from the chaff', *Precision Marketing*, 5 February.

6   Reed, D. (1996). 'Power merge', *Marketing Week*, 12 July.

7   Information Week (1995). 'Systems designed to support customers can actually drive them away', *Information Week*, 12 June.

8   O'Connor, J. (1990). Unpublished research.

9   FSI (1995). 'A sophisticated marketing tool', *FSI*, published by Lafferty Publications.

7

DATABASE MARKETING AND DIRECT MARKETING

SUMMARY

The customer database is probably the greatest application of information technology in marketing today. Database marketing and direct marketing have developed significantly in the past few years. In order to take advantage of these developments, marketing managers need to:

☐ appreciate how database marketing has evolved;

☐ understand how database marketing adds value and how it can be used to improve marketing performance;

☐ become familiar with new direct marketing techniques, particularly those that have gained in popularity in the digital age;

☐ become more adept at managing data privacy issues.

THE EVOLUTION OF DATABASE MARKETING

▨ What is database marketing?

Database marketing can be defined in a number of different ways. The term *direct marketing* is often used instead of database marketing and, more recently, the use of such terms as *relationship marketing* and *customer relationship management* has become commonplace. However, database marketing is much more than these terms imply, and we like Shaw and Stone's (1988)[1] broad definition of database marketing as:

> 'an interactive approach to marketing, which uses individually addressable marketing media and channels (such as mail, telephone, and the sales force) to:
> ▨ *extend help to a company's target audience*
> ▨ *stimulate their demand*
> ▨ *stay close to them by recording and keeping an electronic database memory of customer, prospect and all communication and commercial contacts, to help them improve all future contacts and to ensure more realistic planning of all marketing.'*

Exhibit 7.1 provides an example of how one company uses database marketing for designing mailshots, but a closer examination shows how the database marketing system is also used to reduce marketing costs, improve the quality of communication and generally manage the interaction between the company and each individual customer.

Exhibit 7.1

HAVE I GOT A CAR LOAN FOR YOU!

First Direct's database marketing system builds customer profiles and allows the bank to identify the next products the customer is most likely to buy. 'We can predict that a particular 30-year-old family man with a mortgage is most likely to purchase a new car, so we'll target car loan information at that customer,' says Peter Simpson, First Direct's commercial director. The bank claims it has cut marketing costs by 40% as a result of lower-cost promotions yielding higher returns. The system allows First Direct to mark on the database appropriate and inappropriate customers for particular products and then target those customers in mailshots accordingly.

Source: Precision Marketing (5 February 1996).[2]

The evolution of database marketing

Database marketing has evolved from the use of unsophisticated direct-mail or telemarketing lists where all that was required for a direct-mail or telemarketing campaign was a list of addresses or telephone numbers. In the early days the large amounts of junk mail arriving at people's homes caused many consumers to switch off and ignore further mailshots. However, the route to more effective direct-marketing campaigns was through better customer information to increase the relevance of the offer and better management of the communication between the company and the customer.

Despite the practical difficulties of building a sophisticated database marketing operation, it can be argued that the database is the greatest single application of information technology within marketing. The rapidly declining costs of computer hardware and software have increased the attractiveness of database marketing, resulting in a massive shift in the last decade towards its importance and use. By some accounts,[3] the cost of storing and accessing a single customer name on a database dropped from over $7 in the USA in 1974 to less than one cent 20 years later. Nowadays companies are becoming much more precise about the type of potential customer they will mail to and the size of mailshots is reducing correspondingly, while the effectiveness of, or response rate from these mailings is increasing.

THE VALUE OF DATABASE MARKETING

How database marketing improves marketing performance

Linton (1995)[4] defines a number of ways in which database techniques allow marketing managers to improve performance:

- increased understanding of customers
- improved customer service
- greater understanding of the market
- better information on competitors
- more effective management of sales operations
- improved marketing operations
- better communication with customers.

Increased understanding of customers

Even where companies have built a customer database, it is surprising how few analyse their databases for answers to questions such as:

- How many customers do I have?
- What products are they buying?
- Which segments do those customers fit into?
- Which delivery channels do they prefer?
- Which customers can I not afford to lose?

A marketing database that allows marketing managers to understand their customers is the first step towards building long-term relationships with them.

Improved customer service

One of the most commonly used applications of database marketing is customer service, where it can be used for a wide variety of operational functions, including:

- *Enquiries.* Enquiries can be supported through marketing databases that allow access to a variety of customer, product, price and transaction information.
- *Complaints.* Complaints handling is typically supported through the use of databases that categorise, monitor and track customer problems.
- *Helpdesk facilities.* Helpdesks allow customers to phone a central telephone number for answers to commonly asked questions and solutions to commonly encountered problems (*see* Exhibit 7.2).

Exhibit 7.2

HANDY HELP FOR PETROL PROBLEMS

BP Oil, part of the UK's largest company British Petroleum, is introducing a helpdesk across Europe. The scheme has started in Germany where it will support point-of-sale and back office systems being installed at 1,300 petrol stations. Until recently, many of BP's retail systems problems were tackled with fairly cumbersome paper procedures. BP's helpdesk in Hamburg, which is staffed by 12 operators, has access to data on all earlier calls from a particular petrol station which may throw light on a problem. If they cannot resolve the matter on the spot, they can send a fax from their PC to call in expert support. The helpdesk is logging calls at a rate of 1,800 per month and, on average, a query takes two days to resolve. BP is hoping to integrate its helpdesk systems between countries so that experience of handling calls can be aggregated in an international database and solutions shared.

Source: Financial Times (6 March 1996).

In most cases these customer service applications are provided both in face-to-face situations and via a telephone service. The use of marketing databases in supporting telephone-based customer service activities is examined in more detail in Chapter 14.

Greater understanding of the market

In Chapter 4 we examined the use of information technology in marketing research. The integration of marketing research data with other information on the marketing database will allow companies to answer strategic questions such as:

▓ What direction should we take with new product development?
▓ Which new delivery channels should we be experimenting with?
▓ Which new markets should we be expanding into?

Better information on competitors

According to Linton, competitor assessment is easily overlooked and very often is not captured in a formalised way. The integration of competitor information into a marketing database, rather than in the heads of individual marketing managers, will allow the following questions to be answered with greater speed and accuracy:

▓ Who are our main competitors by product or market segment?
▓ How have their market shares changed in recent weeks/months/years?
▓ What is their pricing structure and what impact have price changes had on market share?
▓ How much are our competitors spending on promoting their products and services?

The formal analysis of competitor activity and the impact of marketing decisions taken by competitors will enable the marketing manager to make better-informed decisions and have a clearer understanding of the likely impact of those decisions.

More effective management of sales operations

Another major area of operational support that is enabled by database technology is the management of sales operations. We will provide a more extensive examination of the use of marketing databases within sales in Chapter 13, but a sample of sales activities supported through marketing databases includes:

▓ managing the performance of different sales representatives
▓ managing customer contacts and client portfolios
▓ demonstrating product features and providing quotations
▓ capturing and fulfilling customer orders.

Improved marketing campaigns

The management of marketing campaigns involves a series of steps from initial analysis and planning through to the subsequent monitoring of those campaigns. These steps are depicted in Figure 7.1, as well as the different technologies used to support each stage of a campaign.

Better communication with customers

It is sometimes forgotten that communication is a two-way process. All too often marketing managers mistake the periodic mailing of promotional material for a

Fig 7.1 Database marketing in the management of marketing campaigns

meaningful and relevant dialogue with customers. Marketing databases should be used for issuing customer communications at appropriate times, such as in the case of Heinz's 'At Home' magazine in Exhibit 7.3. Where marketing databases are used to support customer service representatives, they should also be capable of reminding CSRs of all previous customer contacts, whether that contact was by mail, telephone or in person.

Exhibit 7.3

CARZ AND BEANZ

When Land-Rover launched its new luxury Range Rover in Britain it spent nothing on mass marketing, but instead splashed out around £30 a head on mailing quirky gifts – seashells, chrysanthemums, maple leaves – to 11,000 people whom it had identified as potential buyers. It paid off: 85% of them visited showrooms to see the new model, compared with a 1–2% response rate for normal advertising.

▶

What works for a $60,000 Range Rover also works for something costing less than $1. In 1994 the British division of Heinz, an American food giant, abandoned conventional ads for individual products such as ketchup and baked beans in favour of database-driven direct marketing. By combining its existing 1 million names (gathered from people who had responded to previous offers on tinned goods) with lists of similar households bought from brokers, Heinz has built up a database of 4.6 million people to send a copy of 'At Home', a free magazine of recipes which also promotes its products. Heinz will not give figures, but says that the strategy has paid off.

Source: The Economist (23 August 1997).[5]

DIRECT MARKETING

■ The concept of direct marketing

The concept of direct marketing is simple. Instead of broadcasting a mass marketing message through television or print to a wide number of people, a customised message is instead sent on an individual, and direct, basis to a much smaller number of people who are more predisposed to listening to the message and buying the product or service. National television advertising is very expensive and many organisations are questioning its effectiveness. Where a direct sales force is used, it can cost £100−£200 for a face-to-face sales call and it may take several calls to close a sale. Direct marketing can be a more cost-effective alternative for generating a sale.

The most commonly understood form of direct marketing is *direct-mail advertising*. Two other types are *direct-response advertising* and the telephone-based version of direct marketing known as *telemarketing*. Direct marketing had its first golden age in the 1950s, in the form of mail order catalogue selling, as the post-war boom drove consumer spending. However, this golden age was coming to an end in the 1960s and 1970s as competition from television intensified.

■ The resurgence of direct marketing

In recent years direct marketing has seen a major resurgence. The forces behind its re-emergence are:

■ *Fragmentation of advertising media.* The arrival of commercial television may have heralded the decline of direct marketing in the 1960s, but commercial television itself came under fire in the 1990s from a variety of different cable and satellite channels. Advertisers began to understand what Livingston and Schober (1995)[6] refer to as the 'dishwasher powder effect' − why advertise dishwasher powder on television if 85 per cent of households do not have a dishwasher and if direct marketing can help you identify the 15 per cent who do?

■ *Increasing retailer power.* Manufacturers are now facing an increasingly tough battle for 'mindspace and shelfspace'.[7] The increasing power of retailers and the success of own brands have made it more and more difficult for manufacturers to gather information and develop relationships with their customers. An increasingly effective means of bypassing the manufacturer and gaining the 'mindspace' of the end-customer is via direct marketing.

■ *Declining brand loyalty.* The product proliferation that we discussed in Chapter 1 has done nothing for brand loyalty. Direct marketing can help win back that brand loyalty by keeping a particular product or service in the consumer's mind on a regular basis.

■ *Search for long-term customer relationships.* Not all customers are profitable. And those customers who are often only become so after the company has recouped the costs of recruiting them in the first place. Companies are beginning to understand the desirability of retaining customers and maintaining their loyalty. Regular communication, via direct marketing, can help.

This resurgence is enabled by the increased productivity and processing power of information technology. As the technology continues to develop and marketers become more skilled in using it to its maximum advantage to target key customers, it will continue to grow in importance. Already, companies like Great Universal Stores have started to apply modern direct marketing techniques to revive the stagnant old mail order businesses that once dominated direct marketing (*see* Exhibit 7.4).

Exhibit 7.4

GUS GOES SHOPPING IN FRANCE

Within as many days, Great Universal Stores (GUS), Britain's largest mail-order company, announced two takeovers. The attention-grabber was a £1.6 billion hostile bid for Argos, a British catalogue retailer. But the deal that hints at GUS's real future came a day earlier, when it bought a marketing company in France for a paltry £70 million. Both bids bear the stamp of Lord Wolfson, who became chairman of GUS 18 months ago. His task is to reinvent a company whose main business is not so much mature as geriatric. For years under Lord Wolfson's elderly cousin, GUS failed to grapple with the stagnation in its core business of agency mail order – a type of catalogue retailing in which self-employed 'agents' earn a commission by recruiting customers who pay on credit. But the formula is dated. Credit is widely available these days, customers shun weighty all-purpose catalogues, and many women who earned a bit extra as agents now have full-time jobs.

The new formula is based on more targeted direct marketing. Lord Wolfson was quick to see the potential in SG2, the data-processing arm of French bank Société Générale, of databases that contain both credit information and the buying patterns of customers. Fifteen months ago he spent $1.7 billion transforming GUS's small British customer-credit database with the acquisition of Experian, a Californian firm that has information on marketing, car buying and real estate in America. It was followed by the purchase of Direct Marketing Technology, another American firm, for $299 million. This week's French deal takes the company into continental Europe. Together, these databases give GUS detailed profiles of 780m customers in 18 countries which it can use itself, or – more often – sell to banks, other retailers and direct marketers.

Source: The Economist (7 February 1998).[8]

▧ Direct marketing in the digital age

The digital age is now also providing companies with a new and richer source of customer information with which they can target selective audiences − the Internet. Today, many Web sites will gather significant amounts of customer data in return for free information or other services. This personal information can subsequently be used by those companies, or others to whom the information is sold, for direct marketing.

However, the fact that these increasingly rich sources of customer information can and are being collated into large customer databases is the source of much concern and debate. Are consumers sufficiently well protected from companies that can abuse this information? What limitations should be put on the use of customer data? And are special rules required for the Internet?

MANAGING DATA PRIVACY ISSUES IN THE DIGITAL AGE

▧ Mounting customer concern

Consumers are becoming increasingly concerned about the amount of information that is being gathered on them and how this information is used. The UK's Data Protection Registrar received a large number of complaints from customers of Tesco after the retailer contacted them to ask their permission to target them with third-party offers, using information gathered from Tesco's loyalty card scheme.[9]

Concerns will continue to grow as the Internet, regarded by some as the world's biggest data collection agency, increases its reach. For example, small programmes known as 'cookies' are downloaded to the hard disks of computers used by Internet users. These cookies can be used to trace a surfer's path through the Internet and pass this information back to the Web site owner. Only 2 per cent of Web sites that gather customer data, either directly by requesting customers to register in order to use their site or indirectly through the use of cookies, tell their visitors what they gather and how they use it.[10] In 1999 it was also revealed that Intel's computer chips and Microsoft's software transmitted unique identification numbers whenever a PC was logged into the Internet, potentially allowing consumers' Internet activities and transactions to be tracked and monitored.

▧ Addressing data privacy concerns

The Economist, in a 1999 article,[11] provides an excellent summary of the options that have been proposed to address privacy concerns:

▧ *More laws.* The amount of data privacy legislation enacted in response to consumer concerns will increase significantly in coming years. Unfortunately, although legislation is being put in place, particularly in Europe (see below), privacy lawsuits rarely succeed.

▧ *Market solutions.* The USA has tended to rely on self-regulation and market pressures. However, a Federal Trade Commission (FTC) survey in 1998 found that self-regulation has had little impact, with a mere 2 per cent of Internet sites posting privacy policies in line with FTC recommendations.

▓ *Use of 'infomediaries'*. Infomediaries are firms such as credit card companies that become brokers of information between consumers and other companies, offering consumers privacy if they route transactions through them. The number of infomediaries is growing but it is not clear that they can provide a total solution.

▓ *Technology*. Encryption allows consumers to protect information that they send across any network such as the Internet. However, governments have access to the keys to decode the encrypted data so consumers can never feel completely secure.

▓ *Transparency*. The most radical idea is to admit that data privacy is doomed and that a clear and simple rule should be adopted that gives all citizens access to all information.

The Economist concludes that none of these options will provide adequate protection and that data privacy debates are likely to become more intense. In the meantime, a combination of legislation and self-regulation will have to suffice.

▓ Impact of data privacy legislation

In 1998 a European Union (EU) directive on data protection was adopted, obliging all member states to update their data protection legislation. Under such legislation companies will be allowed to 'process' personal data on individuals only where the people concerned have given their consent or where, for legal or contractual reasons, this 'processing' is deemed to be necessary (for example, consumer credit legislation requires financial institutions to ask certain questions of any individual applying for a loan). Personal data 'processing' is given a much wider definition in the directive than in most existing data protection legislation in operation around Europe. Individuals will also have the right to object to being targeted by direct-marketing activities. Furthermore, the directive will extend the scope of the legislation to include manually held, as well as electronically held, data on individuals.[12]

The 1998 Privacy Directive enables EU countries to ban the export of personal data to countries that fail to meet its privacy protection requirements. It also lets EU citizens sue organisations that misuse personal data. As EU member countries enact their own laws in accordance with the 1998 directive, the protection afforded to the individual will be increased, as will customers' understanding of their rights to privacy. These changes will pose particular issues for the holders and users of customer information, particularly where direct-marketing activities are concerned.

▓ Data privacy in the on-line world

The USA is further ahead in terms of Internet usage than any other country. The Gartner Group predicts that, by 2001, the USA will be squeezed into adopting more stringent data privacy regulations for the on-line user. Pressure to conform will grow as the trend toward privacy regulation gains momentum beyond the boundaries of the EU. Countries such as Brazil, Chile, Argentina and Canada, as well as several in eastern Europe, are considering or have already implemented stringent, EU-style data privacy policies. Gartner urges US companies to go ahead and make the move to stricter privacy policies in anticipation of changes in US statutes.

▨ Self-regulation guidelines for businesses

A 1999 Georgetown University survey[13] examined the privacy practices at top commercial Web sites. The survey found that, while 93 per cent of Web sites collect personal information about visitors, only two-thirds give notification of how that information will be used. Worse, less than 10 per cent comply with the privacy protection standards outlined by the Federal Trade Commission. To meet the FTC standards, a site must do five things:

▨ notify users when data is being collected
▨ give users a chance to 'opt out' of giving information about themselves
▨ give users access to their information so they can correct it
▨ provide adequate security for customer databases, and
▨ provide access to a live customer contact.

These principles are being taken on board by the progressive marketing companies (*see* Exhibit 7.5) but there is clearly a long way to go before consumer concerns are addressed by the majority of companies gathering customer information over the Internet.

Exhibit 7.5

PRIVACY AT MCGRAW-HILL

'I would like to share what works for us at The McGraw-Hill Companies. It's a policy we publish on our more than 80 company Web sites, built on four principles expressed not in legalese that makes Internet users worry about loopholes, but in plain language people can understand. Together, they're the fruits of our extensive and intensive effort to create a privacy policy that's simple enough to understand and comprehensive enough to work:

■ The first principle is NOTICE. Tell prospective customers what information you're collecting and what you're planning to do with it. When it comes to collecting information, uncertainty is the enemy. If you keep people in the dark about what's happening to their private information, they'll imagine the worst.

■ The second principle is CHOICE. Adopt a policy with a procedure by which customers can choose not to have their information shared outside your company. It's a way of saying you recognise the information they've shared with you is, in important ways, still theirs.

■ The third principle is SECURITY. Give the customer confidence that their information is safe from tampering, safe from theft, and safe from misappropriation and misuse.

■ The fourth and final principle is REVIEW AND CORRECTION. Give customers a way to see what information has been collected from them, and a means to correct any errors in that data.

These four principles make a solid privacy policy – one that's understandable, defensible and ultimately acceptable to most consumers. At least that's what we're finding at The McGraw-Hill Companies.'

Source: Harold McGraw III, quoted in *Direct Marketing* (April 1999).[14]

Most companies understand their customer sensitivities and try to address their data privacy concerns. Some have even made their own attempts to restrict the transfer of customer information outside their own organisations. Organisations such as the Red Cross, AT&T and Reader's Digest refuse to market their customer lists to other firms and others, such as the retailer Land's End, will retain all customer information and rent out only the names. One large credit reporting agency, with 120 million names in its file, has also decided to stop providing mailing lists to direct marketers.

ASSIGNMENT QUESTIONS

1 How can database marketing improve marketing performance?

2 Conduct some Internet research to find examples of companies that employ IT to improve the effectiveness of marketing campaigns.

3 What factors have driven the resurgence of direct marketing in recent years?

4 What does the Georgetown survey on Internet privacy tell you about the way that regulation is likely to develop?

5 QXL, the Internet auction house that is the subject of a case study at the end of Chapter 10, has a policy on consumer privacy. View it at www.qxl.co.uk and comment on how effective it is likely to be.

References

[1] Shaw, R. and Stone, M. (1988). *Database Marketing*. Aldershot: Gower.
[2] Curtis, J. (1996). 'Sorting out the wheat from the chaff', *Precision Marketing*, 5 February.
[3] Welch, M. (1993). 'Database marketing begins to register', *Business Marketing*, March.
[4] Linton, I. (1995). *Database Marketing: Know What Your Customer Wants*. London: Pitman.
[5] The Economist (1997). 'Hi ho, hi ho, down the data mine we go', *The Economist*, 23 August.
[6] Reed, D. (1996). 'Power merge', *Marketing Week*, 12 July.
[7] Corstjens, J. and Corstjens, M. (1995). *Store Wars: The battle for Mindspace and Shelfspace*. Chichester: John Wiley.
[8] The Economist (1998). 'Mail chauvinist', *The Economist*, 7 February.
[9] Financial Times (1997). 'Getting personal', *Financial Times*, 28 July.
[10] The Economist (1998). 'You are being targeted', *The Economist*, 27 June.
[11] The Economist (1999). 'The surveillance society', *The Economist*, 1 May.
[12] Dresner, S. (1995). *Privacy Laws and Business Newsletter*, April.
[13] www.msb.edu/faculty/culnanm/gippshome.html
[14] McGraw, H. (1999). 'Managing the privacy revolution', *Direct Marketing*, Vol. 61, Issue 12.

8

RELATIONSHIP MARKETING

SUMMARY

Relationship marketing is a term that has gained popularity in recent years. Companies are beginning to understand the value that customers, rather than products, generate for them. Consequently they are now striving to develop meaningful relationships with key customers and to manage those customer relationships more professionally and proactively than they did in the past. In order to conduct relationship marketing effectively, marketing managers must learn to:

☐ understand why relationship marketing has grown in importance in recent years and why customer loyalty and loyalty schemes have become commonplace themes in marketing;

☐ become more familiar with the key principles of customer relationship management (CRM);

☐ determine the role that information technology has to play in relationship marketing in their organisations.

THE RISE OF RELATIONSHIP MARKETING

▓ Building relationships versus conducting transactions

Relationship marketing is not a new concept. It was originally introduced by Leonard Berry[1] in 1983 when he made the distinction between *relationship* marketing based on the concept of developing a long-term relationship with a customer, and *transaction* marketing which viewed the customer in terms of one-off transactions. In the same year, Theodore Levitt exhorted companies to leave behind the culture of selling, and instead move to a marketing culture based on proactive relationships with customers.[2] So what exactly is relationship marketing? A recent definition from Gordon[3] describes it as the:

> '*ongoing process of identifying and creating new value with individual customers and then sharing the benefits from this over a lifetime of association.*'

Some of the implications of this definition have been explored and expanded upon by other commentators. These include:

▪ the need to integrate marketing, quality and service, rather than treating them as separate elements of strategy, in order to strengthen customer relationships;[4]
▪ the need for 'internal marketing' of goods and services, new technology and new processes to employees, if enduring relationships are to be created with customers;[5]

▧ the need to design and manage carefully the 'service encounter' – the period of time in which the consumer directly interacts with a service.[6]

We will examine these implications throughout this chapter. Indeed, they should be seen as key design principles in any application of information technology that we will discuss in this book.

▧ The value of customer loyalty

Relationship marketing is all about developing long-standing, meaningful relationships with customers. Long-term customers are more profitable for the following six reasons:[7]

▧ Regular customers place frequent, consistent orders and, therefore, are less costly to serve.
▧ Longer-established customers tend to buy more.
▧ Satisfied customers may sometimes pay premium prices.
▧ Retaining customers makes it difficult for competitors to enter a market or increase their market share.
▧ Satisfied customers are a source of referrals of new customers.
▧ The cost of acquiring and serving new customers can be substantial.

This concept of long-term customers generating greater profits is supported by Reichheld and Sasser (1990),[8] who analysed the actual lifetime value of customers across a number of different industries. The financial basis for these claims is relatively simple, as can be seen from Figure 8.1 below.

Reichheld and Sasser demonstrated that a 5 per cent increase in customer retention had the impact of increasing profits by 35–85 per cent, depending on the industry in question. Yet many companies still do not appear to have learned this lesson. In a more recent book, Reichheld finds that US companies lose half their customers in five years and half their employees in four.[9]

Database marketing can be used to identify particular groups of customers who warrant special attention or care (*see* Exhibit 8.1). Although this can sometimes be seen as discrimination against other customer segments, it is nevertheless an important fact

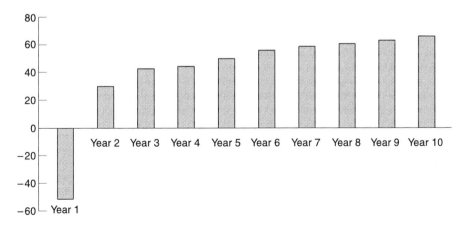

Fig 8.1   Annual profit per customer

that in certain industries most of the profits are generated by a relatively small number of customers. This is particularly true in financial services when the top 10–15 per cent of bank customers typically generate all the profits while up to half of all customers are loss making at any particular point in time.[10] As a result, many banks focus on providing a premium service to their wealthier and older customers.

Exhibit 8.1

BUILD THE DATABASE, CREATE THE RELATIONSHIP

Insurance giant Prudential is to implement a massive reorganisation of its 10 million computerised customer records in order to identify its best and worst customers. The group hopes to be able to sell more products to profitable customers and weed out those who are not providing adequate returns. The reorganisation involves bringing together customers' records in one database, principally to identify which of Prudential's products they do not hold, in the hope of increasing sales. Prudential describes the moves as 'an initiative that will help us create total relationships with our customers'. It is joining the likes of American Express, Abbey National and other financial services companies already exploiting the power of database marketing. This is based on computer analyses of customer records to identify groups of people sharing particular characteristics, such as age, wealth, occupation and other such lifestyle factors.

This phenomenon is also true in other industries. Airlines try to identify, satisfy and retain customers who are frequent fliers. The more discerning companies will have procedures in place for attempting to win back those customers worth regaining, and actively attempting to rebuild the relationship. Customer exit interviews, or telephone calls, are an effective means of finding out what went wrong and potentially winning the customer back.

▧ Customer loyalty schemes

Jones and Sasser (1995)[11] show that satisfied customers will still defect and that companies must strive to achieve 'completely satisfied customers'. They make the interesting distinction between true long-term loyalty and 'false loyalty' that is caused by factors such as:

▧ strong loyalty-promotion programmes such as frequent-flier schemes
▧ government regulations, which limit competition and reduce consumer choice
▧ high switching costs, such as penalty clauses
▧ proprietary technology, which limits alternatives.

The first example is the most interesting of all. It implies that marketing managers can delude themselves into thinking that a strong loyalty card scheme will, on its own, generate long-term customer relationships. Although loyalty schemes have been hailed as examples of relationship marketing Hart et al. (1999)[12] find little evidence to verify this contention. There is some evidence that most loyalty schemes are little more than defensive measures in markets that are mature and competitive.[13] Miller (1998) goes further and suggests that loyalty schemes are designed to make it hard for customers to leave, rather than trying to make them an advocate for a particular company, brand or product.[14]

Despite these concerns about the true purpose and value of customer loyalty schemes, their popularity, at least in the eyes of the retailers, continues unabated. UK supermarket chains continue to revamp and update their loyalty card schemes to help revive interest among shoppers (*see* Exhibit 8.2).

Exhibit 8.2

COUNTING ON THE LOYALTY OF THE 'ULTRA' CUSTOMER

Tiered and tailored loyalty cards are likely to replace retailers' basic schemes as they seek to motivate and retain high-spenders. Tesco's relaunching of its Clubcard into gold, silver and bronze customers this summer comes as no great surprise. It was four years ago last February that Britain's biggest supermarket chain started its loyalty card scheme, and now, with 14 million members and a bulging database of customer information, it makes perfect sense to use that information to refine Clubcard and reawaken interest. Naturally, Tesco is keeping its cards close to its chest, but it is likely that by June, members will be banded into three streams, with the top band the most generously rewarded in points, holiday vouchers and money-off incentives tied to stores such as B&Q.

But while British Airways' frequent-fliers' programme can exploit the cachet of business travel, it's arguable whether this strategy would work in the more democratic world of supermarkets. One trial in the US gave top customers an express checkout, but they preferred the anonymity of queuing with everybody else. In any event, the cleverer retailers such as Tesco and Boots use the card data to support regular personalised mailings (around 36 million annually by Tesco) which lets them tailor products to individuals discretely. The cleverer the card, the better the chance of using data in a constructive way. Boots uses its Advantage card in leading the way. A late starter, coming online in September 1997, and now with 10 million members, this is a smart card which means that information on the customer is carried within a chip on the card itself.

Source: Marketing (15 April 1999).[15]

▓ Building customer loyalty and improving customer retention

Relationship marketing can only happen as part of a wider, all-encompassing programme that puts the customer at the heart of the organisation and where processes are designed, or redesigned, around pleasing and delighting the customer. The critical point for marketers is that true customer loyalty does not result from the implementation of card schemes or from sales promotions. They must work out what engenders loyalty in customers if they are to discover how to improve retention figures. Most marketing managers will have to work hard at this as customers can be fickle and inherently disloyal. Marketing managers need to aspire to the levels of loyalty displayed by football fans and other customer groups that display 'true loyalty' (*see* Exhibit 8.3).

Exhibit 8.3

TRULY GREAT FOOTBALL CLUBS – MANCHESTER UTD, CHELSEA AND ENFIELD TOWN

Football fans are extraordinarily loyal. According to research, 58 per cent of males were committed to their team by the age of 11. More than half the children of parents who supported a team went on to support the same team, while a third of all fans still follow their local side. 'I think we've got the most loyal fans in the Premiership,' Chelsea's commercial manager, Carol Phaier, says. 'Our supporters are unbelievable and, as people say, a husband can change his wife, a wife can change her husband, but you never change your football team.' It helps explain how relatively modest sides have managed to exploit the relationship with their fans almost as effectively as the big boys.

For years, clubs were content merely to pursue shirt sponsorship deals, and then do nothing with the sponsor once they had signed up, points out Tony Simpson, managing director of Team Marketing, which acts as a consultant to many football clubs. 'For example, we went up to Leeds United where the shirt sponsor was Hewlett-Packard. The Leeds database showed that home computing was the third largest hobby of its supporters, and yet no connection was being made between the two bits of information. And this was based on a profile of 23,000 people. When you think what sort of marketing initiatives are based on far smaller samples, it shows just what the potential is. Manchester United mails out a glossy merchandise catalogue to a quarter of a million fans three times a year, while teams like Chelsea dispatch their own version to around 200,000 fans.'

In all, according to Team Marketing's Simpson, every single Premiership club and all but a couple of Division One operators are now using direct marketing techniques to sell to their fans. Edward Freeman, who helped develop Manchester United's entire merchandising operations, singles out three other well-managed direct marketing operations: Chelsea, Leicester and ... little Enfield Town.

Source: Campaign (31 July 1998).[16]

CUSTOMER RELATIONSHIP MANAGEMENT

▪ Customer relationship management principles

Every day companies have thousands, perhaps millions, of interactions with their customers – a concept that Jan Carlson of SAS Airlines used to refer to as 'moments of truth'. True customer relationship management is about managing all these moments of truth in a consistent fashion. Companies that are held up as good examples of CRM tend to do three things better than their competitors:

- ▪ they design the 'service encounter' with the customer correctly
- ▪ they reward the customer for the encounter
- ▪ they go further, by 'crowning' or 'delighting' the customer.

Designing the service encounter correctly

Customer databases and other IT applications enable employees to provide a satisfying and consistent service encounter for the customer, regardless of the method that the customer chooses to interact with the organisation. For example, in a bank, it is important that:

- Employees in the bank's call centre have an equal, or better, understanding of the bank's products than their counterparts in the branch network. This requires them to be given either the training or the computer systems support to explain product details to customers.
- Branch staff are committed to capturing as much customer information as they can when new accounts are opened, so that a more complete picture of the customer can be created that can be used in subsequent service encounters.
- They are also committed to updating key elements of customer information on the bank's long-standing customers, as these customers are likely to be the most profitable.
- IT managers design customer service systems so that the 'interfaces' through the branch, telephone, ATM, kiosk or Internet, are consistent and have the same 'look and feel'.
- Marketing managers view direct mail as part of an ongoing dialogue with the customer, rather than a one-off blitz to promote a specific product or service (*see* Exhibit 8.4).

Exhibit 8.4

BUILDING A RELATIONSHIP WITH DIRECT MAIL

Pepsi recognises that in many of its product categories, for example diet cola, a small segment of customers is responsible for a high proportion of consumption. (Even mass markets today obey Pareto's 80/20 rule.) Pepsi in the US has for several years developed marketing campaigns (such as 'Summer Chill-Out' in 1992) to generate the names of diet cola drinkers, including those of its arch-rival Coca-Cola. It then targets to these names motivating repeat purchase offers to increase its share of their custom. For several summers, Pepsi ran this type of activity as an isolated promotion. The consumer names generated were not used beyond the relatively short promotion time span. Recognising that it was dropping consumer relationships soon after creating them, Pepsi has more recently announced a strategic commitment to direct marketing on a continuing basis. It will create and maintain relationships with individual consumers – and with trade partners.

Similarly, in the late 1980s, American Express experienced considerable adverse feedback from its cardholders over the intensity of its sales efforts and the frequency of its mailings. It has since recognised the benefits of a communication programme which offers its members enhanced benefits and rewards for usage. American Express has recognised that the long-term value of the customer relationship outweighs any short-term sale opportunity.

Source: Pearson (1994).[17]

Rewarding the customer for the encounter

The 'fewer than ten items' checkout in a supermarket is a good example of a 'service encounter' that has been designed well. The express lane removes a bottleneck for those customers who buy only a few items but who have to queue up behind families with large trolley-loads of food. However, it is a poor example of rewarding loyalty, particularly the loyalty of those families that fill the large trolleys every week when they shop. The concept that customers should be rewarded for loyalty was the driving force behind the many loyalty card schemes that have been introduced by airlines and supermarkets. And at the heart of each of these loyalty card schemes is the customer database. Again, the key point to remember is that the database must be used to reward customers, not put them off by indiscriminate use of direct mail (*see* Exhibit 8.5).

Exhibit 8.5

HOW TO MAKE LOYAL CUSTOMERS DEFECT

There are new ways of using detailed information to target promotions. The sheer detail of the information that can be gathered about consumers is made possible by the declining cost of computer power. However, this detailed information is not always guarded by retailers, but shared across all stages in the supply chain. Ultimately such a system helps suppliers to devise precise promotions and provides the feedback needed to refine them. However, the risk is that attempts to reach the consumer will begin to seem intrusive. Susan Fournier, of Harvard Business School, has found that consumers are growing irritated and overwhelmed by the personal information being gathered about them in the name of direct marketing. One woman recently cancelled her supermarket loyalty card after she received a personalised letter reminding her that it was time she bought more tampons.

Source: The Economist (14 March 1998).[18]

The example in Exhibit 8.5 shows how easy it is to violate some of the principles of customer relationship marketing. Interestingly, the most advanced user of direct mail in Europe is Germany, a country that also has the most stringent data protection legislation governing the sale or rental of customer data.[19] With proper respect for consumer privacy, German businesses have been able to collect data from willing customers and use that data to sell more effectively and to improve customer satisfaction and loyalty.

'Delighting' and 'crowning' the customer

The only way to make sure that you are satisfying and delighting your customers is to have an intimate understanding of what they want. One means of achieving this is to invite them to become part of your organisation and to help design and refine your product offerings. Customer-focused companies have traditionally been able to do this without recourse to information technology. Market research and focus groups have provided the means of achieving this and some organisations have developed the customer contact to a fine art. Feargal Quinn, who runs an upmarket supermarket chain in Ireland called Superquinn, refers to this as 'crowning the customer'[20] — a similar concept to Jones and Sasser's concept of 'completely satisfied customers'. In Superquinn:

■ customers can cut the stalks off the broccoli they purchase because some customers thought that they should not have to pay for the part of the product that they would throw away anyway;

▓ when they weigh the broccoli, they find a magnifying glass at the scales because some elderly customers complained that the scales and labels were difficult to read;

▓ and when they pass through the checkout they find their receipts identify the amount of Irish-produced goods that make up their total bill, again because customers asked for this information.

Information technology can help to crown the customer. It can also help in inviting customers to talk to you and tell you what they really want. McKenna (1995) refers to this as 'Real-time marketing',[21] a concept that requires:

▓ replacing the broadcast mentality that has long dominated marketing with a willingness to give customers access to the company and to view their actions and feedback as integral to developing or improving products;

▓ focusing on real-time customer satisfaction, providing the support, help, guidance and information necessary to win customers' loyalty;

▓ being willing to learn how information technology is changing both customer behaviour and marketing, and to think in new ways about the role of marketing within the organisation.

Regardless of which term one prefers, the uses of database technology in crowning the customer, engaging in real-time marketing and completely satisfying the customer provide illustrations of the true meaning of the phrase 'database marketing'.

THE ROLE OF IT IN RELATIONSHIP MARKETING

▓ The power of IT to build or destroy relationships

All of this provides a very important backdrop to a discussion on the role of information technology in managing the customer relationship. It should be recognised that, to some extent, IT has actually decreased the amount of contact between many company employees and their customers. This is certainly true in banking, where automated teller machines have taken many customers, particularly the busier and more profitable ones, away from the branch and into a less personalised relationship with the bank. In other cases the downgrading of the customer service role to that of a glorified telephone operator has effectively disenfranchised many service employees.[22] For IT to be truly effective it must enable *everybody* in the organisation to service customers more effectively, reduce defection rates and increase the lifetime value of customer relationships.

As part of an integrated approach to customer relationship management, information technology has a major role to play in developing long-term relationships. The most important IT-based tool in the marketer's arsenal in this regard is the customer database. Used properly, a customer database can:

▓ allow marketers to move away from mass marketing to becoming much more targeted and focused in their approach to customers;

▓ transform direct marketing from a one-way communications vehicle into a two-way conversation with the customer;

■ support customer service representatives and sales staff to deal with customers on a much more personalised basis.

Ultimately, the customer database can lead to what Peppers and Rogers (1996) refer to as 'one-to-one marketing'.[23]

■ The role of IT in customer service and sales

Information technology can be applied in a variety of ways to support customer service and sales operations. Some of the more common applications, which we will examine in more detail in Chapters 13 and 14, include:

■ *Sales force automation.* In recent years a wide range of software solutions have come on to the market aimed at improving the effectiveness of the traditional sales force. The software, which is typically held on a laptop computer, is often sophisticated enough to link the salesperson with the company's main computer systems, allowing the salesperson access to customer and sales data.
■ *Telephone call centres.* Most people are now very familiar with the telephone call centre as a means of serving customers. The most recent variation of the telephone call centre is the 'customer contact centre', which is where a centralised operation provides a much wider range of customer services including consumer affairs, fulfilment processing, order-entry and field dispatch.

In addition, Internet services and call centre services are being combined whereby Internet users can click on an icon and either initiate a call or request the call centre to contact them at the number that they input on the screen.

Case study

LEAVING THE CUSTOMERS ALONE

Rejecting the anonymity that has characterised mass marketing for decades, corporations want to know everything about their customers so they can reward their most loyal buyers and devise new products for them. Following a trend set by airlines, companies in dozens of industries – including hotels, supermarkets and even car washes – have launched frequent-buyer clubs. Corporations flood their customers with special offerings, e-mails and news-letters in a bid to inspire brand fidelity. Consumers might be expected to feel flattered by such attention. Instead, they feel smothered by unwanted advances, says Susan Fournier, a professor at HBS. Ms Fournier has documented hundreds of cases of consumer alienation. Consumers, it turns out, may want nothing more than to be left alone. Many feel besieged by too many choices, too many sales pitches, and too many questions about their lives and buying habits. They develop defensive habits to cope with the barrage, such as screening telephone calls and tossing away all junk mail.

'A surprising number of corporations place themselves in an adversarial relationship with consumers,' says Ms Fournier. She says the problem with relationship marketing is that too many corporations want a relationship that gives them the upper hand. One woman complained that AT&T would make her special offers only if it initiated the call. When she phoned the company's customer relations office she was rebuffed. 'AT&T wanted to set the rules of the relationship on its own terms,' says Ms Fournier.

Companies that place themselves in the role of invisible servant may do better. The Internet bookseller Amazon.com, for instance, wins loyalty through maintaining a certain degree of reserve. It contacts customers only to confirm orders, and to make purchase suggestions only when a buyer logs on to the site. 'They are like the good butler who brings slippers and pipe at just the right moment and doesn't ask questions,' says Ms Fournier. Indeed, old-fashioned service providers are the model for many relationship marketing advocates. Companies would like to inspire the kind of loyalty normally reserved for hairdressers who know just how to trim their clients' hair, and butchers who set aside the best cuts for loyal customers. Fournier doubts that companies can amass such subtle information on vast numbers of customers. As one woman pointed out: 'If a hotel did "remember" what drink I ordered the last time I stayed there, who's to say I'd want it again? I don't always order a diet soft drink.' Relationship marketers, moreover, seem obsessed with winning the devotion of their buyers. They would do better to content themselves with a more casual acquaintance, says Ms Fournier. A Kentucky woman she studied purchased one of five brands of laundry detergent, depending on which was on sale, a habit the relationship marketing movement would scorn. 'But if she's only buying five brands, that still adds up to a lot of sales over the years. A company should be pleased with that.'

Many of the strongest relationships that consumers have with products, says Fournier, are based on old-fashioned brand building, rather than constant two-way communication. Fournier interviewed consumers who felt passionate about hundreds of products, from Progresso breadcrumbs to Diet Coke, although they had never had any personal contact with the company making the product.

Companies that fail to see the importance of these anonymous relationships may be led astray, says Ms Fournier. She interviewed a Range Rover owner who was furious over Land-Rover's launch of the cheaper Discovery model on the US market a few years ago. 'For him, owning a Range Rover had always been a status symbol,' Ms Fournier explains. 'Exclusivity was an unwritten rule of his relationship with the company. When they made the downmarket model, it was as if his wife had an affair. The company broke the implicit contract of the relationship.' Land-Rover's management may have simply failed to understand that they had a relationship to uphold. 'A relationship is not getting a newsletter, responding to a questionnaire or holding a frequent-buyer card,' says Ms Fournier. 'It has to do with product quality, consistency, image, and what is going on in people's personal lives. It's not about giving power to the companies, but placing it in the hands of consumers. That is what the relationship marketing movement has failed to recognise.' **FT**

Source: Financial Times (12 February 1998).[24]

Questions

1 'A surprising number of corporations place themselves in an adversarial relationship with consumers.' Discuss.

2 What do companies have to learn from old-fashioned service providers?

3 How should companies create a valuable relationship with these customers?

4 Analyse how three organisations that you are familiar with try to create a deeper relationship with their customers.

ASSIGNMENT QUESTIONS

1 Evaluate the differences between building a relationship and conducting transactions.

2 Discuss different approaches to building customer loyalty. Give examples of companies that, in your view, use IT effectively to build customer loyalty.

3 What is meant by 'delighting the customer'?

4 Visit the Broadvision site (www.broadvision.com) and discuss how their products can assist in relationship marketing.

References

[1] Berry, L. (1983). 'Relationship marketing', in *Emerging Perspectives on Services Marketing* by Berry et al. (eds), Chicago: American Marketing Association.

[2] Levitt, T. (1983). 'After the sale is over . . .', *Harvard Business Review*, September–October.

[3] Gordon, I. (1997). *Relationship Marketing*. Toronto: Wiley.

[4] Christopher, M., Payne, A. and Ballantyre, D. (1991). *Relationship Marketing*. Oxford: Butterworth-Heinemann.

[5] Grönroos, C. (1990). 'Relationship approach to marketing in service contexts: the marketing and organisational behaviour interface', *Journal of Business Research*, Vol. 20, No. 3.

[6] Shostack, G. (1985). 'Planning the service encounter', in Czepiel, J., Solomon, M. and Surprenant, C. (eds), *The Service Encounter*. Lexington Books.

[7] Bushanan, R.W.T. and Gillier, C.S. (1990). 'Value managed relationships: the key to customer retention and profitability', *European Management Journal*, Vol. 8, No. 4.

[8] Reichheld, F.F. and Sasser, W.E. (1990). 'Zero defections: quality comes to services', *Harvard Business Review*, September–October.

[9] Reichheld, F.F. (1996). *The Loyalty Effect: The Hidden Force Behind Growth, Profits, and Lasting Value.* Boston: Harvard Business School Press.

[10] O'Connor, J. (1992–5). Unpublished research based on analysis of customer profitability of two banks.

[11] Jones, T.O. and Sasser, W.E. (1995). 'Why satisfied customers defect', *Harvard Business Review*, November–December.

[12] Hart, S., Smith, A., Sparks, L. and Tzokas, N. (1999). 'Are loyalty schemes a manifestation of relationship marketing?', *Journal of Marketing Management*, Vol. 15.

[13] Sharp, B. and Sharp, A. (1997). 'Loyalty schemes and their impact on repeat-purchase loyalty patterns', *International Journal of Research in Marketing*, Vol. 14, No. 5.

[14] Miller, R. (1998). 'Locked in by loyalty', *Marketing*, 2 April.

[15] Beenstock, S. (1999). 'Supermarkets entice the "ultra" customers', *Marketing*, 15 April.

[16] Cook, R. (1998). 'Football clubs seize the chance to target their fans directly', *Campaign*, 31 July.

[17] Pearson, S. (1994). 'Relationship management: Generating business in the diverse markets of Europe', *European Business Journal*, Vol. 6, No. 4.

[18] The Economist (1998). 'Market makers', *The Economist*, 14 March.

[19] Pearson, S. (1994). 'Relationship management: Generating business in the diverse markets of Europe', *European Business Journal*, Vol. 6, No. 4.

[20] Quinn, F. (1990). *Crowning the Customer*. Dublin: The O'Brien Press.

[21] McKenna, R. (1995). 'Real-time marketing', *Harvard Business Review*, July–August.

[22] Bowen, D.E. and Lawler, E.E. (1992). 'The empowering of service workers: what, why, how and when?', *Sloan Management Review*. Vol. 33, No. 3.

[23] Peppers, D. and Rogers, M. (1996). *The One to One Future: Building Relationships One Customer at a Time.* New York: Currency Doubleday.

[24] Financial Times (1998). 'Knowing when to be of service', *Financial Times*, 12 February.

DEVELOPING THE CUSTOMER OFFERING

Part IV of this book deals with the impact of information technology on the marketing mix. It contains four chapters:

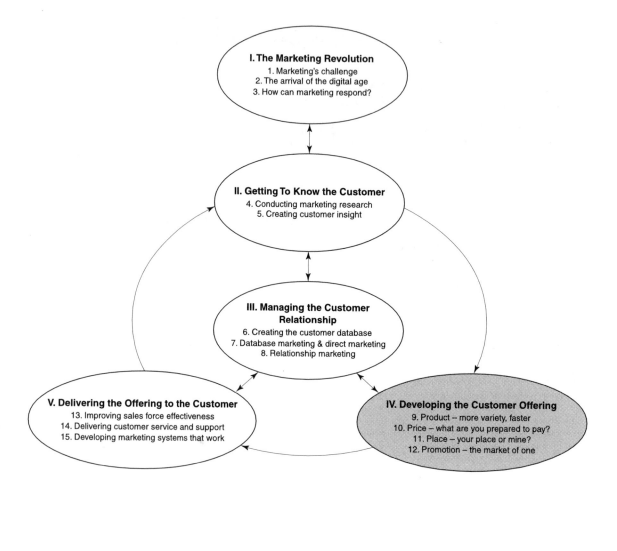

9

PRODUCT –
MORE VARIETY, FASTER

SUMMARY

The ability to develop and launch new products and services rapidly is a key competitive advantage in the digital age. Developing new products and services presents the marketing manager with a number of challenges:

☐ The failure rate for new product/service concepts is very high.

☐ New product/service introductions typically require large investments, particularly if the objective is to develop a global brand.

☐ The number of potential product/service configurations is often extremely high, making it difficult to decide on what options to pursue.

☐ Co-ordinating development across different parts of an organisation such as R&D, production and marketing, is difficult.

However, information technology can be used to improve the introduction of new products and services. Marketing managers need to understand that:

☐ IT can be used to improve the range of viable product/service offerings.

☐ IT can help in increasing speed to market.

☐ IT can help in almost all stages of the product development life cycle, right up to the commercialisation of the product.

☐ Advanced manufacturing techniques can be employed to speed up commercialisation and reduce investment costs.

USING IT TO IMPROVE THE RANGE OF VIABLE OFFERINGS

Incorporating IT into products

While new technologies such as high-definition TV (HDTV), mobile telephones and the Internet create large new markets, IT is also being incorporated into products and services in a more subtle fashion. For example, washing machines, toys and many household goods contain computer chips that give these products new functions. Even contraceptive products have entered the digital age (*see* Exhibit 9.1).

Exhibit 9.1

WHEN GREEN MEANS GO FOR IT

It has been heralded as the best development in contraception since the 1960s. After 15 years of research and development Unipath, the healthcare division of Unilever, has launched Persona, its computerised version of the rhythm method. The handheld device monitors hormone levels in urine and indicates on which days it is possible to have sex without fear of pregnancy. A green light means go and a red light means no. It went on sale in selected branches of Boots last week with little fanfare but the entire stock sold out twice.

Source: Financial Times (10 October 1996).[1]

Cars now employ IT to control many functions that were traditionally operated by mechanical means, including ignition control, central locking, braking systems and air conditioning. Automatic braking systems in cars employ a particular branch of technology known as fuzzy logic, which is used in the control systems of many products today. Consider Canon's handheld camera that uses only 13 rules to tune the autofocus on the lens. The fuzzy logic control system requires little memory and uses image sensors to measure picture clarity. The data from the image sensors, combined with these decision rules that drive the new lens settings, help the new system to focus twice as well as other controllers. Other products employing fuzzy logic include:

- *air conditioners*, where fuzzy logic is used to prevent temperature fluctuations and to reduce power consumption;
- *dishwashers*, to adjust cleaning cycle and rinse and wash strategies based on the number of dishes;
- *elevators*, to reduce waiting time based on passenger traffic;
- *toasters*, to set toasting time and heat levels for different thicknesses of bread;
- *transmission systems*, to select gear ratios based on engine load and other driving conditions;
- *video camcorders*, to cancel handheld shake and to adjust autofocus.

Another industry that has been transformed as a result of the digital age is the toy industry. Microchips and other computing devices have been incorporated into many of today's toys. One of the leaders in the electronic toy business is profiled in Exhibit 9.2.

Exhibit 9.2

VTECH – THE MICROSOFT OF TOYLAND

The toy industry is dominated by American giants such as Hasbro, Mattel and Fisher-Price – huge marketing machines that control most of the shelf-space at Toys 'Я' Us and other retailers. But VTech dominates the market for electronic learning toys on a global basis. Its market share in Britain and Germany is more than 80 per cent; in the US, just under 80. Allan Wong, VTech's founder, runs out of fingers as he counts the big toy firms that have entered his market in the past 15 years. But most soon leave: VTech's chief competitors

---

today are Team Concepts, another Hong Kong company, and Tiger, a Japanese firm bought earlier this year by Hasbro. From his offices in a dusty industrial complex near Hong Kong's border with China, Mr Wong seems genuinely bemused by VTech's dominance, if not its success. It did not invest in the market – indeed, Mr Wong got into electronic educational toys in the early 1980s when Sears asked the former NCR engineer to come up with something that could compete with Texas Instrument's *Speak and Spell*, the first toy to have a synthetic-speech chip.

Source: The Economist (21 November 1998).[2]

▦ Turning products into services

Because commodity products do not command a premium in the marketplace, marketing managers strive to augment the products, or even turn them into services, using information technology. In doing so they enhance their value and make them more difficult to replicate. Take, for example, remote monitoring services:

▦ *Industrial equipment.* Remote monitoring sensors are routinely incorporated into machine tools, chemical processing and other industrial equipment to monitor their operations. In the event of a problem, the machinery is either repaired remotely, or an engineer dispatched before a machine component fails and causes further damage. GE provides such services for its aircraft engines and medical systems.
▦ *White goods.* Remote monitoring is not just confined to industrial equipment. Exhibit 9.3 depicts how one company, Merloni, is launching a new service that will link domestic appliances in people's homes with remote 'diagnostic centres'.
▦ *Security services.* House alarms no longer simply let the neighbourhood know that an intruder is on the premises – many will automatically notify the police or security company as well.
▦ *Automobiles.* Many taxis are now equipped with global positioning system (GPS) technology that allows the taxi companies to schedule their movements more accurately.

Exhibit 9.3

TAKING THE WORRY OUT OF WASH DAY

Do you worry about your washing machine wearing out without you noticing? Do you fret about your freezer seizing up while you are on holiday? If so, your anxiety may be eased by a new service that links domestic appliances in people's homes with remote 'diagnostic centres' around Europe via the telecommunications network. The service, being offered by Merloni, the Italian white goods company, is intended to bring to the humble oven or dishwasher the type of 'on-line' monitoring that is routine for many large pieces of capital equipment such as machine tools or chemical processing systems.

Francesco Caio, Merloni's chief executive, says the new service is part of the company's effort to add value in a highly competitive market for kitchen goods. The diagnostics procedures will be available to people buying a variety of Merloni appliances from next

▶

year. For a fee of perhaps £30 a year, the consumer's appliance will be hooked up with Merloni's network of service centres around Europe. Instead of reacting to phone calls from people who spot a fault in one of their machines, the service centre will use computers to monitor the appliance around the clock. For instance, special software could spot when an electric motor is about to seize, or check whether a power cut might be stopping the electricity supply to a freezer – in the latter case alerting the owner by telephone.

Merloni, best known for its Ariston and Indesit brands, sells about 7 million kitchen appliances throughout Europe. Mr Caio said that he hopes that within a few years, up to 10 per cent of Merloni appliance owners might be taking advantage of remote monitoring.

Source: Financial Times (1 October 1998).[3]

Car manufacturers have also started to bundle value-added services into their products, through the use of advanced digital technologies. For example, if the driver of a General Motors car equipped with its On-Star system locks his key in the car by mistake, an emergency centre can transmit a digital signal via satellite to unlock the doors. On-Star also automatically calls for help if an accident triggers the airbags to open.

Toyota and General Motors are also among a growing list of car manufacturers to introduce in-car navigation systems as standard. In Europe, BMW and Mercedes-Benz recently introduced navigation hardware that not only plots the route but also alerts the driver to traffic jams along the way.[4]

■ Using IT to 'mass customise' products

Another option enabled by technologies such as the Internet is the facility that allows customers to design the product – an extension of 'mass customisation'. Here are four examples of how consumers are invited to design their own products:

- ■ *Dell Computers.* Dell is the world's leading direct seller of personal computers, and sells more than 50 per cent of its products over the Internet. Customers can visit Dell's Web site[5] and design and assemble a PC to their own specifications. Once the order is taken over the Internet the PC is assembled to order, and shipped within days.
- ■ *Andersen Windows.* In the USA, Andersen Windows uses multimedia applications in retail stores to integrate its customers into its supply chain and, effectively, to sell to a 'market of one'. It has built a system that allows customers to design a 3D representation of their home, pick the spot where the windows are to be located and experiment with different window frames.
- ■ *Rover Group.* Multimedia point-of-sale systems are also used by UK-based Rover Group to allow prospective customers to 'configure' their own model. The kiosks have been rolled out to Rover's dealers in the UK and elsewhere across Europe.
- ■ *General Electric.* At GE Power Systems customers can use technology to design their air conditioning systems. By answering a series of questions they are guided towards the most appropriate system to meet their needs.

USING IT TO INCREASE SPEED TO MARKET

▦ Introducing more products

Before marketing managers can define the role of IT they must set their overall objectives for new product/service development. For example, 3M has such a commitment to new products that more than 30 per cent of every division's annual sales must come from products invented in the previous four years. 3M employees are encouraged to spend up to 15 per cent of company time on 'skunkwork' projects that interest them and that do not require corporate approval. Another company that has turned product innovation into a competitive advantage is Casio, which brings out a regular stream of new competitive products. Rather than postpone profits until the later stages of the product life cycle, Casio aims to make its money on products with very short life cycles. It achieves this by integrating design and development with marketing so that those closest to the market are responsible for developing new products and meeting customers' needs.

▦ Accelerating time to market

Increasingly, speed to market is a key competitive advantage, and information technology is a driving force behind this (*see* Exhibit 9.4).

As in the case of Casio, payback and profitability is increased by extending the front end of the traditional product life cycle. The time to market from product conception to adoption is shortening and organisations are accelerating this trend using new processes facilitated by information technology.

Exhibit 9.4

DRUGS AND DATA

A senior executive of Eli Lilly, the US drugs company, described his company's business as '50 per cent information technology, 50 per cent pharmaceuticals'. His comment highlights the increasingly crucial role played by computer and telecommunications technologies in the fast-changing, high-pressure world of the global pharmaceutical manufacturers where a day's delay in bringing a product to market can cost $1 million in lost revenues.

Some companies believe they can cut the clinical trial process by half, from 30 months to 15 months, by managing the process better. Traditionally, a clinical trial depended on a lengthy and largely paper-based process which began with a general practitioner filling out a piece of paper after seeing a patient, sending this report back to the company conducting the trial which then had to input the data for analysis. More recently, doctors have been given computers to enter the data directly and clinical research assistants, who normally visit the GPs every six weeks, have been provided with mobile computers and digital telephones so that they can access the latest clinical trial information remotely.

Given the escalating costs and risks involved in new drugs, many pharmaceutical companies are also attempting to manage the spread of risk by forming research partnerships. In these cases, secure telephone links can help geographically remote teams

▶

exchange data and work more closely together. Similarly, companies such as SmithKline Beecham have begun to make extensive use of videoconferencing networks. The need to reach out and communicate with existing or potential customers has also encouraged drug companies to become early business adopters of the Internet as a marketing medium. Today, pharmaceutical companies' Web sites are among the best presented and most informative on the Internet.

Source: Financial Times (10 June 1996).[6]

In rapidly changing businesses such as telecommunications the difference in timing can be the difference between success and failure. Ericsson, a leader in telephone-switching equipment, has cut its development time dramatically by using 'concurrent engineering' rather than sequential development. Using this new system has allowed Ericsson to cut the time from order to delivery of a switching system from six months to ten days.[7] The speed of development in this industry is further illustrated by the fact that 30–40 per cent of sales come from products launched over the previous two years. Figure 9.1 provides a graphical representation of how these changes are changing the shape of the traditional product life cycle.

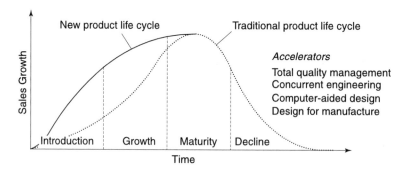

Fig 9.1 New product life cycle

USING IT TO SUPPORT THE PRODUCT DEVELOPMENT LIFE CYCLE

■ Six stages of product development

The success rate for new products is low and managing the new product development process is a complex task. Information technology can help marketers and new product development managers throughout the development process. In order to understand its full impact, we will now look at the role of information technology in the six different stages of the product development life cycle (*see* Figure 9.2):

■ *Stage 1: New idea/concept generation and screening.* A full 50 per cent of new product ideas are developed internally.[8] IT has a role to play in the sharing of ideas and obtaining feedback from remote locations. Executives from different offices or countries can be involved in the idea generation and screening process through the use of videoconferencing and e-mail. Products like Lotus's Domino groupware tool, and internal Web sites (intranets) allow team members to share ideas. Expert system software can also be used to evaluate each idea by asking a series of questions and attaching a predetermined weighting to each response.

▨ *Stage 2: Development and testing of new idea/concept.* Software tools such as computer-aided design (CAD) programs can be used to design the product and illustrate what it will look like. If the members of a design team are split up and located in different countries, they can stay in touch using videoconferencing and e-mail.

▨ *Stage 3: Business and marketing analysis.* In Chapter 4, we examined the use of IT in the six stages of marketing research. Basic software applications such as spreadsheets can also be used to perform the business analysis, sensitivity and 'what if' analyses.

▨ *Stage 4: Product development and testing.* IT applications such as virtual reality can be used to prototype the product design so that it meets the needs and requirements of customers better than if the design was created in two dimensions.[9] Car manufacturers such as Ford and Rover routinely build virtual models to check ergonomics and help develop a new model before it has been physically built. An Israeli company called eSim provides tools to build 3D models of products that can be used during the design stage.

▨ *Stage 5: Test marketing.* Geographic information systems and geo-demographic analysis tools have become commonplace in determining the most appropriate locations for test marketing particular products. Simulated test marketing (STM) is also used to speed up the test-marketing process.

▨ *Stage 6: Commercialisation.* A variety of advanced manufacturing techniques are available to speed up the commercialisation (see last section in this chapter).

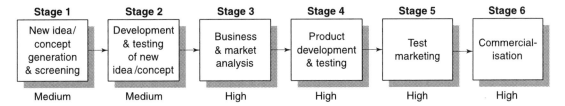

Fig 9.2 Applicability of IT in the six stages of product development

▨ Simulated test marketing

One of the most important developments in test marketing is the use of simulated test marketing, which improves the likelihood of new product success. Clancy and Shulman (1991)[10] believe that STM is the best way of reducing risk when launching a new product or repositioning an existing product. A typical STM will use information on each element of the marketing mix and assess the effect of changes to any part of the plan. The STM allows a marketing manager to test key components of his plan and do 'what if' analysis. Using an STM has a number of advantages over traditional methods of test marketing:

▨ *It reduces risk.* Typically eight out of ten new products fail. An STM costing $100,000 to $150,000 can provide feedback in three to six months, compared to several million dollars to test market and substantially more to launch nationwide.

▪ *It increases efficiency.* An STM can help prioritise different projects by providing feedback on which provides the greatest potential return (*see* Exhibit 9.5).

▪ *It maintains security.* Real test marketing alerts competitors to a company's intentions and allows them to react.

▪ *It can save company time.* As time has become a key competitive weapon, identifying and serving a customer's needs quickly is critical and an STM test can give results in three to six months as opposed to over a year for a real test.

Exhibit 9.5

IMPROVING THE EFFECTIVENESS OF POINT-OF-SALE DISPLAYS

Strange as it may seem, more than 70% of all purchase decisions are made at the point of sale. And yet the marketing effort, and marketing research, that goes into this much neglected area is puny.

Now, there's help at hand. One of the largest market researchers, Research International (RI), has developed a technique for assessing the impact of display stands before they hit the retail floor. Research International had already developed a well-established modelling system, the MicroTest, for pre-testing and analysis in other marketing areas. It has been around for some ten years and has been used extensively by such major manufacturers as Unilever, Kraft and Lyons-Tetley. The MicroTest, according to Maureen Johnson, managing director of RI's retail division, 'was developed to help clients go beyond standard diagnostic information collected in concept or product testing, and actually provides formal sales volume estimates based on the same type of interview. RI claims a margin of error of plus or minus 20% and says that out of the 150 or so validations it has run (out of a total of 1,750 MicroTests), 80% have fallen within this margin. While that may sound like a wide margin, it's an awful lot better than an uninformed guess.'

Here's how it works: MicroTest involves a series of intensive interviews with both consumers and shop-floor staff. Typically, there are 10 to 15 'accompanied shopping interviews' per category with each consumer. Each interview lasts about two hours and encompasses visits to three to five different retail outlets. The interviews are designed to allow modelling and analysis of sales volume estimates. The responses are processed and the model is used to fine-tune the stands before they go into action.

Source: Marketing (17 April 1997).[11]

USING ADVANCED MANUFACTURING TECHNIQUES IN PRODUCT COMMERCIALISATION

▪ Design for manufacture

Increasingly, organisations are using design for manufacture principles in their development efforts. Design for manufacture is an attempt to get away from the traditional product development process, where designs were passed from the design

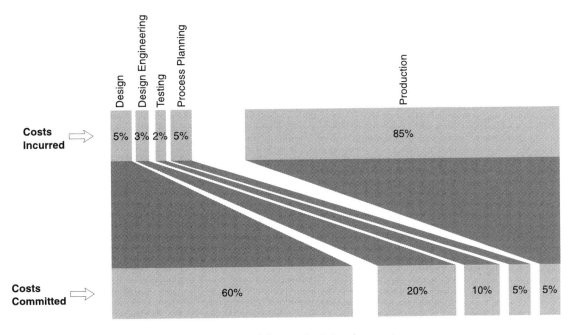

Fig 9.3   Costs committed at different stages of the product development process

Source: Business Week (30 April 1990).[12]

teams to the production unit that had the job of manufacturing them. Difficulties arose when the original design was found to be very expensive or difficult to produce.

There are several approaches to bridging these gaps between the marketing, engineering and manufacturing functions. Cross-functional teams can be used to integrate design and engineering with the manufacturing process and the customers' requirements. Indeed, leading-edge companies often closely involve their customers in the process. By focusing effort on the design process potential problems or break-throughs can be identified before significant costs are committed (*see* Figure 9.3).

Design for manufacture allows leading-edge manufacturing companies to simplify both product and process, leading to:

▩ *Fewer components in the product*. With fewer components, the product is not only easier and less costly to produce, it will probably have greater reliability.
▩ *Fewer steps in the process flow*. With the emphasis on the elimination of unnecessary steps, more value is added to the product. This applies to any process, whether factory operations or office procedures.
▩ *Fewer components in the fixtures and tooling used for machining*. The simplest fixtures and tools require the least time and cost to alter when a machine is changed from producing one item to another.

Implicit within design for manufacture is the design of the production process itself. As Exhibit 9.6 shows, the factory that manufactures major industrial products can be reduced to a digital map, allowing designers to create and build production facilities more quickly and with less capital expenditure than in the past.

Exhibit 9.6

THE BATTLE FOR THE DIGITAL FACTORY

Carmakers are under pressure to put out new models every two years instead of every four, yet redesigning a factory so frequently is very inefficient. Until recently, the IT revolution had failed to help companies to lower the costs of redesigning factories from the ground up when they develop a new product model. But IT manufacturing technology is now taking a big step towards the 'digital factory' model that could revolutionise production planning procedures, with big time and cost benefits to industry.

The virtual manufacturing battle is heating up between market leader Technomatix Technologies, the Israeli pioneer of the computer-aided production engineering (Cape) software market, and Deneb Robotics, the US-based competitor owned by Dassault Systemes. According to Daratech, a specialist market research company, the $200m Cape market is growing at around 30 per cent a year and is made up of three main products:

- robotic simulators account for about 45 per cent of the market;
- shop floor simulators – used to run product designs through virtual production lines – account for another 23 per cent;
- discrete event simulation tools – which allow manufacturers to optimise a sequence of manufacturing activities – account for the remaining 32 per cent.

Cape technologies have provided enormous efficiency gains. For example, Volvo speeded up the time it took to design, manufacture and install equipment on a single welding line by 20 per cent.

Source: Financial Times (2 June 1999).[13]

▪ Advanced manufacturing techniques

Computer-integrated manufacturing (CIM) is a concept describing how computers are used in advanced manufacturing. Some of the applications that can be part of a CIM program or used on their own include:

- *Computer-aided design (CAD).* CAD programs help design products using 3D perspectives of the product. Designers can view the design from any angle and obtain customer feedback on how it looks. CAD programs can be used to test different product designs based on the characteristics of the materials used without building the products.
- *Materials requirement planning (MRP) and manufacturing resource planning (MRPII).* MRP is used to plan the types of materials required in the production process with the aid of computers. MRPII helps integrate MRP with production scheduling and shop-floor control.
- *Computer-aided manufacturing (CAM).* CAM is used to manufacture products and can have a number of components including shop-floor control (monitoring and controlling the production process in a factory), process control (directly controlling a physical process), machine control (directly controlling machines) and robots (controlling a machine with human-like capabilities).

The benefits of computer-integrated manufacturing include:

▓ higher productivity through process simplification, better production scheduling, planning and workload balancing;
▓ increased utilisation of production facilities and better quality through continuous monitoring, feedback and control of factory operations, equipment and robots.

▓ Building to order

The biggest revolution in manufacturing in recent years has been the principle of 'building to order'. Using this system, manufacturers only begin building or assembling the product when they receive a firm customer order. This contrasts with a 'build-to-stock' system whereby products are built to a forecast of demand and stored as inventory. Dell Computers is one of the greatest proponents of this system, and one of its biggest success stories. The benefits of building to order include:

▓ lower investment in inventories and work in progress through just-in-time policies, better planning and control of production and finished goods requirements;
▓ higher customer service by reducing out-of-stock situations and producing high-quality products that better meet customer requirements.

Case study

GENERAL ELECTRIC

It took seven years for General Electric (GE), the US industrial group, to bring to market its F-class gas turbine, which is now being installed in power stations throughout the world. Its successor, the H-class gas turbine, will come to market in half the time, even though it incorporates more new technology, including a revolutionary way of using steam to cool the fast-spinning rotor blades. The speed at which GE is developing the new turbine is a reflection of the rapid advance of research and development tools, notably computer modelling, and of an overhaul of GE's research efforts ordered five years ago by Jack Welch, the group's chairman and chief executive officer. Welch, who took over in 1981, has included R&D in his wider-ranging efforts to extract bigger profits from the company's acknowledged technological and industrial prowess. Even the group's legendary research and development centre, home of two Nobel prize winners, has not been spared from the demands of change.

'It was a culture shock for some of us,' says Gene Kimura, manager of the mechanical systems laboratory, one of 13 units at the R&D centre. 'But it was absolutely necessary that the company got value for money.' The centre, built in wooded hills in New York state, is GE's equivalent to AT&T's Bell Laboratories. Until the 1950s, 75 per cent of its funds came from group headquarters and most of the rest from US government programmes. Many of its researchers became remote from commercial realities. For some the site seemed more like a university campus than a factory – except that the salaries were higher.

In the early 1990s Welch decided that this had to change. The group cut its contribution to the central laboratories' budget to 25 per cent, leaving GE's 13 operating divisions to make up the difference – and demanded commercially relevant research in return. Now the operating divisions pay 40 per cent of the costs. The remaining 35 per cent is split between the government and Lockheed, the aerospace company that acquired the former GE aerospace business in 1994 in a takeover of Martin Marietta, the defence contractor.

GE also laid down rules for how these funds should be spent – 15 per cent on improving current products, 35 per cent on developing successors, 35 per cent next generation products, and 15 per cent on blue-sky ideas. The central laboratories have an annual budget of just under $400m (£250m) a year, about 20 per cent of GE's total R&D spending. They produce about a quarter of the group's patents and about half its scientific papers. The new financing arrangements have given priority to the needs of operating divisions. The change was reinforced by a management restructuring at the central laboratories in 1993, which saw the appointment of 13 business managers – one for each division – to monitor R&D work done for their divisions. They have tried to ensure that the traditional strong links between technical staff at the laboratories and at the divisions have been matched by an equally tough commercial tie. At the same time, GE threw out a hierarchical system in which laboratory managers reported to branch managers who in turn were answerable to more senior executives. In its place, GE introduced a four-man technical council, headed by Lonnie Edelheit, the senior vice-president in charge of corporate R&D. Kimura says that as well as cutting office bureaucracy, the new system created more flexible ways for ideas to be passed between laboratories and discussed among different teams of researchers. 'At the top, things are mushy, which is great for communication.'

Teamwork, says Kimura, is important in commercial research. 'It's a culture we have to create. This isn't a university. We can't have people who stay in their labs and come out and give a paper once a year.' For example, developing aero engines required expertise in high temperature materials, fluid dynamics, emissions, manufacturing techniques and information technology. Hand-in-hand with organisational change at the laboratories has come a rapid advance in research technology, particularly in computer modelling. Sophisticated hardware and software enable researchers to produce ever more accurate computer simulations of products. The techniques help virtually all products, but are particularly useful for large items such as power turbines that are very expensive to construct in physical prototype. Kimura says: 'IT management is critical to our future.'

Yet even the overhaul of R&D management and the introduction of the latest R&D tools have not been enough to save GE last year from an embarrassing and expensive technical problem. The group's F-class turbines developed faults that only became apparent after the first machines went into service with customers. Some turbine sections had to be flown back for repairs while others were put right by roving teams of GE engineers. The problems cost the group at least $100m. Ironically, the faults were not caused by any high-technology features but by the rotors rubbing against the turbine casing at high temperatures. Kimura says valuable lessons have been learnt: 'We have learnt how to improve the management of launching new products. We put a lot of emphasis on using the latest design tools. We should have paid more attention to traditional fatigue tests.'

Source: Adapted from S. Wagstyl, 'Blade runner', *Financial Times*, 23 July 1996.

FT

Questions

1 'In the early 1990s Welch decided that this had to change.' What were the main driving forces for changing the way in which R&D was carried out at GE's research centre?

2 How did IT play a part in improving the R&D and product development effort at GE?

3 Describe how you think researchers work, collaborate and share ideas in the R&D centre now, paying specific attention to the types of information technology they would employ to assist them in their day-to-day work.

4 How can GE's new R&D capability be used in the marketplace?

5 Discuss the comment from Gene Kimura that 'IT . . . is critical to our future'.

ASSIGNMENT QUESTIONS

1 Describe how technology is driving the development of new products and services.

2 Access the Dell site on www.dell.com and describe the advantages for a) Dell and b) the consumer.

3 Briefly describe the product development life cycle.

4 Discuss the role of IT in manufacturing.

References

[1] Jones, H. (1996). 'When green means go for it', *Financial Times*, 10 October.

[2] The Economist (1998). 'The Microsoft of Toyland', *The Economist*, 21 November.

[3] Marsh, P. (1998) 'On-line machines that take the worry out of wash day', *Financial Times*, 1 October.

[4] The Economist (1998). 'Sorry, officer, I was just surfing', *The Economist*, 17 January.

[5] www.dell.com

[6] Taylor, P. (1996). 'Increasingly crucial role', *Financial Times*, 10 June.

[7] Nilson, T.H. (1995). *Chaos Marketing: How to Win in a Turbulent World*. Maidenhead: McGraw-Hill.

[8] Kotler, P., Armstrong, G., Saunders, J. and Wong, V. (1996). *Principles of Marketing, European Edition*. London: Prentice-Hall.

[9] Bradbury, D. (1996). 'Out of this world', *Computer Weekly*, 18 July.

[10] Clancy, K.J. and Shulman, R.S. (1991). *The Marketing Revolution*. New York: HarperBusiness.

[11] Dwek, R. (1997). 'Predictions of success', *Marketing*, 17 April.

[12] *Business Week* (1990). 30 April.

[13] Machlis, A. (1999). 'The virtual world of robotic production', *Financial Times*, 2 June.

10

PRICE –

WHAT ARE YOU PREPARED TO PAY?

SUMMARY

Price is a crucial element in the marketing mix for a number of reasons. Prices can usually be changed very quickly, marketing and sales managers often have a high degree of discretion on the prices they set and, perhaps most important of all, price has a direct impact on the total revenue a company generates and an even greater impact on its profitability.

In developing an appropriate pricing strategy, the marketing manager faces a number of challenges. These include:

☐ Setting prices requires accurate data on costs that may be difficult to gather.

☐ Different customers or customer groups have different sensitivities to price changes.

☐ Competitors may be rapidly changing their prices.

☐ New Internet-based technologies such as shopping agents can commoditise products, where customers have greater access to information.

☐ International companies increasingly have to develop a pricing strategy across different countries.

Given these challenges, the marketing manager can use IT in a number of ways to improve the effectiveness of pricing decisions. To use IT effectively the marketing manager needs to understand:

☐ how e-business is rewriting the pricing rules

☐ how IT can be used to identify costs accurately

☐ how to make well-informed and rapid pricing decisions.

E-BUSINESS IS REWRITING THE PRICING RULES

The impact of the Internet

The Internet is changing the rules of pricing[1] by transferring the balance of power from the manufacturer to the consumer. The impact of the Internet is at least threefold:

▪ *It is easier to find and compare sellers' prices.* Customers can easily compare the price of products ranging from hotel rooms to CDs.

▨ *It is cheaper and easier to change prices*. Electronic price tags in supermarkets can be altered at minimum cost and the Internet allows global price changes to be implemented immediately.

▨ *Prices are harmonising across the globe*. Buyers from all parts of the world pay the same price for books from Amazon.com.

There are exceptions. Prices are likely to change less frequently when the quality of the product is hard to assess, when consumers dislike frequent changes to prices, and when the market is dominated by a small number of firms.

In the case of Amazon, the Internet bookseller, different prices are quoted from different sites. The latest John Grisham thriller is priced in US dollars on Amazon.com, in pounds sterling on Amazon.co.uk, and in Australian dollars on Amazon.au, allowing slightly different pricing strategies to be adopted from each site. However, the overall effect is to make it more difficult to maintain major price differentials in different countries.

Many marketing managers fear that the popularity of the Internet will lead to significant price reductions and margin erosion as more and more companies flood the market with low-price offers in an attempt to win market share. Certainly, building market share through discount pricing has been a feature of many successful Internet companies to date. Amazon offers books at up to 40 per cent below recommended retail prices. Banks such as Citibank are also offering attractively priced loans in order to build up their on-line customer bases (*see* Exhibit 10.1).

Exhibit 10.1

CITIBANK OFFERS CHEAP LOANS

Citibank is offering the cheapest personal loans available in the UK in 20 years in a move that will increase pressure on banks and building societies to reduce their unsecured lending rates. The rates offered by Citibank, which has only three branches in the UK and operates mainly as a telephone bank, start at 13.9 per cent for loans of £3,000 but its cheapest rate is for large loans of £15,000 or more where the rate is 7.9 per cent. According to data provider MoneyFacts, the next cheapest lenders are Tesco, Royal Bank of Scotland Direct and First Direct – all non-traditional players in the banking industry. Citibank, which is based in the US, has 100,000 current account customers in the UK but aims, with the introduction of cheap loans, to widen its appeal beyond wealthy international professionals. About 20 per cent of new Citibank customers are opening accounts via the Internet.

Source: Financial Times (17 July 1999).[2]

▨ Internet shopping agents

Internet shopping agents have significant implications for customers and marketers. These agents are software programs capable of accessing a large number of Internet sites to identify the lowest price for an item that the customer has specified. In some cases retailers have felt so threatened by these pricing agents they have created software

Table 10.1   Selected Internet shopping agents (1999)

Shopping agent	Internet address	Description
Bargain Dog	www.bargaindog.com	On-line price alert service
Bottom Dollar	www.bottomdollar.com	Comprehensive shopping search service
DealTime	www.dealtime.com	Searches retailers, auctions and classifieds for the best price
Excite Shopping's Product Finder	www.jango.com	Searches the Internet for the best price
MySimon	www.mysimon.com	Searches the Internet for the best price
PriceScan	www.pricescan.com	Takes the hassle out of finding the best price on thousands of computer hardware and software products
RoboShopper	www.roboshopper.com	Searches the Internet for the best price
Sales Channel	www.thesaleschannel.com	Free news service that sends e-mail updates when department stores are having a sale
SALEseeker	www.saleseeker.com	Free on-line service that helps you find sales and specialists at local, department, specialty stores and catalogues
Top10guide.com	www.top10guide.com	
Valulinks	www.valulinks.com	Membership club providing discount shopping tips for brand name merchandise and wholesale products

Source: Yahoo.com (July 1999). [3]

to block the intelligent agents from accessing price information on their sites. Some of the more well-known shopping agents are shown in Table 10.1.

These Internet shopping agents will undoubtedly put pressure on retailers to remain cost competitive and put power firmly in the hands of the customer (*see* Exhibit 10.2 for the results of some of our own searches). There is also the possibility that some of the more successful agents will become well-known retail brands just like the major retailers.

Exhibit 10.2

HAVE A CIGAR (OR A BEANIE BABY, OR SOME EROTICA?)

Cigars are less easy to find on the Internet than Beanie Babies. At least, that's the opinion of Jango, the Internet shopping agent from Excite Shopping. On 5 August 1999 we searched for the best-value Arturo Fuente Brevas Royale cigars on the Web. Jango could only find two on-line retailers that sold them: Cigar Express and The Cigar Box. Beanie Babies were a different matter altogether. Although we specifically told Jango that he had to find the cheapest *Scoop the Pelican* beanie baby, it was no problem to our digital shopping assistant. Within seconds Jango returned 353 results from a variety of Internet classified advertising sites and on-line auctions. For $7.00 we could purchase Scoop from one of Yahoo's classified advertisements. Alternatively we could choose from a variety of auctions, including 19 different Yahoo! auctions, all of which were due to start within eight hours. Guide prices ranged from $3.00 up to $9.00, the highest prices being reserved for Scoops with free heart-shaped tag protectors or similar value-added paraphernalia. If we were in a hurry, the on-line auction house eBay had an auction starting within six minutes and, yes, there was a *Scoop the Pelican* going for $9.99.

To go with the cigar and the beanie baby, some soothing music, perhaps? This time, we asked mySimon if he could find Madonna's Erotica CD (there's no accounting for taste). MySimon was almost as efficient as Jango, returning quickly with 73 results from 42 different merchants, including Amazon.com, Compact Disc Connection, Border.com, BestPrices.com, and even Wal-Mart. BestPrices.com even offered a choice between the clean version and the stickered version of the CD. Unfortunately, it was out of our price range at over $14.99. Eventually we settled for Amazon's offer of shipping within 24 hours for a mere $12.99.

All in all, a good evening's shopping. Now, where's that cigar?

Source: O'Connor & Galvin (5 August 1999).

▦ Internet auctions

One other factor to consider in cross-border price management – the Internet. General Electric purchases more than $1 billion of goods a year over the Internet, receiving tenders from companies all over the world in the process.[4] Electronic sales of CDs and books are also a global business, typically priced in US dollars. In Europe many companies will be forced to adopt a 'one price fits all' policy for goods and services, regardless of national boundaries, as the Euro currency comes into force and as Internet sales become commonplace. One specific aspect of Internet selling that deserves a special mention is the Internet auction. These electronic auctions are ideal for selling off 'perishable' services as their 'best by' date approaches. Examples of perishable services include flights and holidays – as the departure date approaches the value of unsold seats and hotel rooms plummets to zero.

Most major airlines have begun to auction unsold seats, following the lead of American Airlines and Hong Kong-based Cathay Pacific in 1996. For airlines and travel agents the economics of Internet auctions is inescapable – selling off unsold capacity by auctioning them at a discount one or two days before their 'best by' date can improve profitability dramatically. Achieving 100 per cent passenger loadings on planes can quadruple net profits, even if the airlines discount prices of unsold seats by 25 per cent.[5]

More recently specialist Internet auction houses like Priceline have set up auctions on the Internet that have become hugely successful (*see* Exhibit 10.3).

Exhibit 10.3

REVERSE AUCTIONS

In the off-line world, this would be a strange market indeed. Buyers attach money to a board, along with a note stating what they want to buy for the sum. Later, sellers come along and have a look. If they like an offer, they take the money and deliver the goods. This

▶

> sort of reverse auction has made Priceline.com (www.priceline.com), which went online with much fanfare in April 1998, one of the more interesting airline-ticket bidding services on the Internet.
>
> *Source: The Economist* (15 August 1998).[6]

Priceline.com is not the only auction on the Internet. By mid-1997, the year before Priceline opened its doors on the Internet, there were more than 150 on-line auction sites, selling everything from industrial machinery to rare stamps.[7] Today there are thousands, as both traditional and Internet-based companies move into the on-line auction business.[8] For example, in March 1999 many Amazon.com customers received this e-mail from Jeff Bezos, the founder and CEO of the Internet bookstore:

> *Dear Amazon.com Customer,*
>
> *I'm excited to tell you that we've opened Amazon.com Auctions. Auctions is something truly different for Amazon.com. In the past, when you bought something at our store, you were always buying directly from us. Now, with Auctions, our community of almost 8 million customers (including you – thank you) can sell anything they want to on the Amazon.com Web site. Letting millions of sellers participate at Amazon.com is another way for us to give you the broadest selection possible. You'll find rare books and signed first editions, rare music, vintage toys, antiques, sports memorabilia, collectibles of all kinds, etc., etc.*

The Internet's chief advantage for auctioneers is the size of its audience. Its global reach brings a critical mass of buyers and sellers to the most popular auction sites, avoiding the problem of insufficient trading that bedevils many of their cousins in the physical world. Indeed quick, easy, virtual auctions carry a hint of the sort of hyper-efficient capitalism that Internet fans have long been promised.

More importantly, Internet auctions are not just confined to North America. Most western countries can boast a growing number of on-line auctions today. The case study at the end of this chapter examines QXL, a UK-based Internet auction company that is expanding across Europe. Australia can boast a wide range of on-line auctions, including:

- Aus auctions
- Austweb Auctions
- Chalon Stamps
- EZY Systems
- Melbourne Flower Auction
- ShopZone Bidder Network.

ESTABLISHING ACCURATE COSTS

■ The importance of understanding product costs

Even if the pricing rules are being rewritten in the digital age as power is concentrated in the hands of the buyer, the starting point for many pricing decisions will still be the cost of production. As we have seen above, this does not mean that pricing is simply a matter of adding a given margin to the cost of production, although many companies still take this approach. However, production costs must be understood. Otherwise companies will cross-subsidise one product with another and can easily end up in a situation where they are generating large sales (and losses) on the subsidised products, while losing out to the competition on the profitable products.

Using activity-based costing (ABC) systems

One solution to the problems facing traditional management accounting systems is activity-based costing. ABC allocates overhead costs to the activities that generate the cost. The costs in these 'activity pools' are then further allocated or traced to individual products based on the level of activity associated with the product. Because ABC is more concerned with identifying activities that cause cost it is able to deal more easily with non-volume-related overheads. Using ABC information marketing managers are better positioned to consider options such as dropping unprofitable products or raising the prices of existing products.

Searching an organisation for all the information about the direct and indirect costs of a product or service can be a major undertaking. Creating an IT system to track cost-contributing activities and presenting the information to management is equally challenging. In many cases the old accounting system is replaced and new measurement and incentive systems are tied to the new ABC figures. When an ABC system is implemented managers can use it to answer many questions, including the following:

▓ What does a given product or process cost?
▓ What are the non-value-adding activities that contribute to its current cost?
▓ If a given distribution channel or market is unprofitable, where can the company reduce costs to make it profitable?
▓ If the company eliminates an unprofitable product or customer, how much will it save in costs?
▓ If the company lowers the price of a product to increase sales volume, what will be the impact on the cost per unit?
▓ What can the company do during the design and engineering stages of a product to avoid unnecessary costs in the first place?

Many companies have used ABC in one-time profitability studies to help them decide which products or customers to keep. But ABC can be much more than an accounting technique that shows how much profit individual products are really making or losing. When ABC is woven into critical management systems it can serve as a powerful tool for continuously rethinking and improving not only products and services but also processes and marketing strategies.

MAKING WELL-INFORMED AND RAPID PRICING DECISIONS

Basing pricing strategies on accurate information

In a survey of US companies Clancy and Shulman (1991)[9] found that many made pricing decisions without any serious formal research. They found that only about 8 per

	Serious Strategy	Little or No Strategy
Serious Research	Sophisticated players (8%)	Radical empiricists (4%)
Little or No Research	Gamblers (47%)	Losers (41%)

Fig 10.1 Strategy/research pricing matrix

Source: Clancy & Shulman (1991).

cent of companies were sophisticated players with a serious pricing strategy based on primary research (*see* Figure 10.1). Forty-one per cent fell into the losers' category, with neither strategy nor research capabilities.

▪ Using IT to support the six key pricing actions

Clancy and Shulman identified six actions that companies need to take in order to be successful in their pricing strategies:

▪ Examine the environment.
▪ Tie pricing to the target market, competitive positioning and product.
▪ Examine many alternative pricing strategies.
▪ Study manufacturing and distribution costs and their relationship to product demand.
▪ Undertake serious pricing research to develop a price elasticity curve that shows how sales change as price goes up or down.
▪ Select the optimal price based on the best strategy, costs and price elasticity curve.

Information technology can assist in all six of these actions. For example, a major car rental company in the USA has developed a decision-support system that allows its marketing staff to analyse changes in competitor prices quickly. The system scans price data from the company's five main competitors for more than 160 locations across the USA and Canada, across six car classes, 12 regional market segments and five potential rental segments. Data is collected on a daily basis and significant changes or exceptional movements reported to the marketing department. The reports allow pricing analysts to view the information by competitor or by geographic area. The primary benefit of the system is that it allows the pricing analysts to spend more time making pricing decisions and less time being submerged in a sea of data.

▪ Pricing for different segments of the demand curve

A key responsibility of marketing managers is to determine demand for a product. They use market research and forecasting to establish the relationship between a product's price and demand. For most products there is an inverse relationship between the price and the quantity demanded; as the price goes up the quantity demanded goes down and vice versa. Drawing an accurate demand curve for a product requires information on historical purchasing patterns. The availability of large amounts of scanning data, such as price and quantity sold from many different retail stores, can be used to calculate and graph the demand curve for products.

Once identified, this price information can be used very effectively to define new pricing strategies. Tesco uses data from till receipts and social profiling to develop nationwide 'direct pricing'. This approach means that price-sensitive customers pay less for everyday items than busy professionals. A key factor for Tesco is not just being able to use IT systems to identify new pricing strategies but to quickly implement price changes. Being able to dramatically change prices across a large number of stores requires well-developed systems.

Employing yield management techniques

One of the most powerful applications of the demand curve is the concept of maximising revenue across all customers. It is moving away from the 'one price for all' concept to true demand-based pricing. This trend is being driven by IT that allows companies to develop and market product offerings at different prices. Marketing managers are now faced with a much more complex task of identifying a range of product or service options targeted at different customers and charging different prices.

Probably the most sophisticated use of this technique is in the airline industry where 'yield management' is supported by complex computer software. The system works by calculating different prices depending on the length of the stay, the time of week the person wishes to travel and the flight times. The airline's objective is to identify and target the business traveller who is less price sensitive than the tourist traveller. Early-morning flights are more expensive, as are tickets purchased at short notice. Tickets that include a weekend stopover are usually cheaper, as business people like to return home at the weekend. All of these conditions help the airline identify the business traveller, whom they can charge a premium for effectively the same service. Efficient yield management has increased the revenues of US airlines by 5–10 per cent.[10]

Changing prices rapidly

One of the main impacts of IT is the increased speed with which pricing decisions can be implemented. A good example is the retail trade, where traditionally changing prices took a long time to implement. Head office marketing managers would decide on a price change that would then be sent to the individual stores in the form of a paper-based price list. If products had been individually labelled the price stickers would have to be removed and replaced with the new prices. IT enables the process to be carried out in a shorter time and with less manual effort. Once the marketing manager has decided on a price change the new price is keyed into the central computer system and is usually downloaded that night to the stores. The next morning the store manager receives a report that indicates all the prices that have been changed and the new price stickers are also printed. It is important to synchronise the price changes on the shelf and at the checkout. As Exhibit 10.4 shows, this does not always happen. However, if done correctly, the time required to change prices is significantly reduced and this provides an important advantage in the highly competitive retail industry.

Exhibit 10.4

BAR-CODE BOO-BOOS

Six thousand complaints about discrepancies between bar-code prices and shelf prices were made to the Institute of Trading Standards (ITSA) in the last 12 months. Martin Fisher, pricing specialist for the Institute of Trading Standards, said: 'Such discrepancies crop up quite often. Sometimes, head office decides on a price change, changes the prices on the computer and does not inform stores in time for them to change the shelf price.' The price held on the computer is the one recorded by the till when a bar-code on a product is scanned at the supermarket checkout.

New developments are underway that should make the whole process even faster and more accurate. Electronic displays on each shelf showing the name and price of each product would remove the need for any manual intervention once the new price has been set. Once the price has been changed at head office it could be updated simultaneously on both the electronic shelf display and the computer that stores the prices for the checkouts. Many new retailing systems also allow different prices to be set for different stores. Based on demographic analysis and an understanding of the demand curves in different store locations, higher prices can be set in more affluent areas.

Case study

QXL

Economists have long recognised the virtues of auctions. In 1880 Leon Walras, a French economist, described the entire price mechanism as an auctioneer, attaching a body to Adam Smith's 'invisible hand'. The 'Walrasian auctioneer' would call out a price, see how many buyers and sellers there were, and if these did not balance, adjust the price until demand equalled supply. The Internet, thanks to its cheap interconnection of millions of people, makes well-functioning auctions far easier. So far, the leading on-line auctions are fairly simple, but highly popular, affairs. Already the US-based eBay boasts 2.4m sale items in 1,627 categories. One reason for its success (its market valuation is $25bn) and for that of auctions more recently offered by uBid, Amazon, Yahoo! and others, is that they are entertaining. On eBay, auctions are transparent: all bids and bidders are published. This generates valuable information for buyers and sellers, though it increases the risk of collusion.

The battle for on-line auction business is heating up. FairMarket is hosting auctions for many e-retailing sites, including Lycos, ZD Net, CompUSA and Cyberian Outpost. And then there is Priceline, a quasi-auction, that sells airline tickets (and hotel rooms, mortgages and cars, with more to come) by inviting customers to submit bids for travel on a particular day.

And now the circus is coming to Europe. Enter QXL, an Internet-based auction house with some straightforward objectives:

■ Aim to help informed buyers find excellent value products – and buy them quickly, conveniently, and at exactly the price they're willing to pay.
■ Aim to provide world-class service and support, and to make the process of buying a product easy, secure and exciting.

Like its US counterparts, QXL doesn't tell the customer what to pay. The customer makes a bid depending on what he or she thinks the product is worth. Auctions are opened every day, offering a variety of computer and electronic goods, jewellery, gifts, household and travel products. Because the auctions only run for a limited time customers can (potentially) get a great deal. Customers can bid over the Web from any computer, at any time of the day.

QXL has revenues of perhaps £20m and is preparing to float in September 1999 with a price tag of up to £500m in what would be the second largest public offering by a UK-based Internet company. If the valuation is achieved it will underline the rapid development of the UK Internet sector. QXL, founded by Tim Jackson, a freelance journalist who is now a non-executive director, was valued at only £28m in February 1999 when Apax Partners, the venture capitalists, bought a 25 per cent stake. Since then the group has consolidated its position as market leader in the UK and launched sites in France, Germany and Italy. It has also launched a service to allow individuals to auction second-hand goods, in addition to its service for manufacturers wishing to sell products to the highest bidder.

All good stuff. A California gold rush in Internet stocks is one thing. But this is Europe, after all. What about the fundamentals? Surely, if the market puts such a value on a start-up company, it is being so long term as to be positively reckless? Peter Englander of Apax Partners says: 'The valuations of QXL and other Internet stocks are very high on traditional measures, but on the other hand, the Internet is not a traditional phenomenon.'

QXL could face a rocky road. US auction house eBay plans to move abroad, and with a market value of over $16bn it has the firepower to blow QXL out of the water. Priceline.com could do the same. Can QXL establish enough of a foothold to see off the US competition? Or is this a global market where QXL is simply another nimble follower trying desperately to catch up? One thing is for certain. It's all good news for the consumers – with a wider variety of low-cost auctions a mouse-click away.

Based on: 'QXL: On-line auction house set for £500m flotation', by Thorond Barker, *Financial Times* (5 July 1999); 'Investment: the long and the short of it', *Financial Times* (10 July 1999); 'Is the Internet bubble going to burst?', by James Mackintosh, *Financial Times* (17 July 1999); 'The heyday at the auction', *The Economist* (24 July 1999); and the QXL Web site (www.qxl.com).

Questions

1 As an on-line auction, how does QXL compare to eBay or Priceline?

2 How can off-line retailers compete against the on-line auctioneers?

3 Compare a consumer-based auction such as www.qxl.com to a business-to-business auction site such as www.ventro.com.

4 How can on-line auctions continue to generate traffic to their sites?

ASSIGNMENT QUESTIONS

1 How is the Internet rewriting the rules of pricing?

2 Why have on-line auctions grown so rapidly? Which is your favourite on-line auction?

3 Evaluate the effectiveness of different pricing agents.

4 What are the implications of the Internet for international pricing? Give examples.

5 Choose a well-known retail chain. Examine the prices for a selection of products, in different stores (e.g. city centre vs suburban). Are the prices the same?

References

[1] The Economist (1999). 'Is this the end of sticky prices?', *The Economist*, 16 May.

[2] London, S. (1999). 'Citibank offers cheap loans', *Financial Times*, 17 July.

[3] www.yahoo.com

[4] www.ge.com

[5] Financial Times (1996). 'Passengers take a seat at the Internet auction', *Financial Times*, 17 June.

[6] The Economist (1998). 'It was my idea', *The Economist*, 15 August.

[7] The Economist (1997). 'Going, going...', *The Economist*, 31 May.

[8] www.internetauctionlist.com

[9] Clancy, K.J. and Shulman, R.S. (1991). *The Marketing Revolution*. New York: Harper Perennial.

[10] Cross, R. and Schemerhorn, R. (1989). 'Managing uncertainty', *Airline Business*, November.

11

PLACE –
YOUR PLACE OR MINE?

SUMMARY

The 'place' element of the marketing mix deals with how products get to consumers, and choices about whether companies should market directly to the customer or go through intermediaries. Channel management decisions affect pricing, product management, brand image and promotion decisions. The choice of channel affects all the other elements of the marketing mix. One of the traditional features of channel decisions was that they took a very long time to develop. This is changing rapidly with e-business. Many organisations are following the lead of companies like Dell and selling their products direct to the end consumer. For companies that have already chosen direct distribution, the Internet offers the opportunity to target a wider audience. There are a number of key changes happening in distribution:

☐ the increasing importance of direct channels

☐ the changes that are taking place in indirect channels

☐ the management of multiple distribution channels.

THE INCREASING IMPORTANCE OF DIRECT CHANNELS

The rise of direct channels

Traditionally, the firm with well-entrenched distribution channels dominated the market and created very high barriers to entry for newcomers. For example, one of the biggest barriers to entry in petrol retailing is the presence of large networks of petrol forecourts, most of which are tied to one of the major oil companies. Over the last 10 to 15 years the oil companies have moved from using independent garages to directly owning garages. This has allowed them to standardise forecourt layouts and service quality, and develop very important forecourt retail businesses. It also gives them control of the distribution channel and makes it very difficult for other oil companies to enter the market.

More significantly, the application of information technology has created turmoil in the area of distribution. Direct marketing and telemarketing have allowed organisations like the Virgin Group to bypass traditional channels and build relationships directly with their customers in a much shorter period of time than it took the petrol retailers to gain control over their distribution channels (*see* Exhibit 11.1).

Exhibit 11.1

PUTTING A ROCKET UP THE PENSIONS INDUSTRY

Almost a quarter of working adults in the UK – 7m people – make no pension arrangements whatsoever, relying on the state for support during old age, a survey reveals. Pension funding is woefully inadequate, and Britain is on the very edge of a pensions crisis, the survey suggests. Of those that do save for retirement, almost half make personal contributions of just £50 or less a month. The survey, commissioned by Barclays, is believed to be one of the most comprehensive investigations into pension planning and makes alarming reading. The figures reveal a growing 'misery gap' – the difference between actual monthly pension contributions and the recommended monthly contributions for a comfortable retirement. 'People are simply deluding themselves,' said Nigel Waite, marketing director of Barclays Life. People spend about 20 years in retirement,' said Waite. 'Proper pension planning determines the quality of life in old age and should not be treated as a low priority.'

Virgin Direct, the financial services arm of the £1.6 billion Virgin Group, has launched a personal pension which it claims will 'put a rocket up the pensions industry'. Rowan Gormley, managing director of Virgin Direct, said: 'The pension rules are fine, the tax breaks are spectacular – the problem is the industry. It has hijacked the personal pension for its own gain.' Virgin staff will offer advice over the phone on the Virgin Personal Pension, which is one of the cheapest on the market. New customers pay a 1% annual management fee and a £2 charge per payment. There are no policy fees, no front-end-loaded charges and no bid-offer spread. Policy holders can also change or stop payments at no extra cost.

Source: Sunday Times (20 October 1996).[1]

In the UK companies like Virgin have blazed a trail with new ways of developing propositions and taking them to the customer. Many others have followed. The primary means of bypassing the intermediary in the mid-1990s was the telephone. Today it is increasingly the Internet, often in conjunction with the telephone, while other mechanisms such as automated teller machines (ATMs) are being reinvented as multimedia channels.

■ The telephone as a distribution channel

Telemarketing is a direct sales channel that uses the telephone and associated technologies for marketing purposes. The advantages are its flexibility, its interactive nature, its immediacy and the opportunity to make a high-impact personal contact. It has suffered somewhat in the past from misuse and 'cold calling' and some of its disadvantages include a high cost per call, its association with pressure selling and its lack of a visual presentation. However, as consumers become more accustomed to telesales and telemarketing, as telecoms markets are deregulated and prices are driven down, the telephone will continue to gain acceptance as a mainstream distribution channel.

Telemarketing can be described as either inbound or outbound. If a customer hears an advertisement on the radio for car insurance for lady drivers and phones the (freephone) telephone number mentioned at the end of the ad, her call will be received by an *inbound* telemarketing group in the insurance company. Twelve months later, if the insurance company phones the same customer to remind her that her insurance is due for renewal, the insurance company is employing *outbound* telemarketing.

Companies are increasingly outsourcing their telemarketing to external organisations that have both the sales skills and the capacity to handle very high response rates. Exhibit 11.2 shows how this trend to outsource telemarketing operations has led to the creation of four major telemarketing firms in Japan.

Exhibit 11.2

DISTRIBUTION BY PHONE IN JAPAN

Even as corporate Japan slides deeper into the mire, telemarketing is finding its feet. Everywhere there are signs of distress: companies are cutting operations, deregulation is opening markets and foreign competitors are appearing. Telemarketing thrives on all three. Since the mid-1990s Japan's top 20 telemarketing agencies have seen their total sales increase by, on average, 30% a year. The biggest agency, Bell Systems 24, is part of CSK Corporation, which is Japan's largest information-services company and also owns such firms as Sega, a video-game maker. Behind CSK comes NTT, a telecoms giant; Mitsui, Japan's top trading company; and Benesse, Japan's largest supplier of correspondence courses. Altogether, these four agencies account for roughly 70% of sales. They have thrived on the very changes that have hurt other businesses in Japan. Foreign companies coming to sell things such as insurance and investment trusts need distribution. Some have gained access to existing outlets by finding domestic partners. Those loath to spend in advance have taken the cheaper course of employing a telemarketing agency on their behalf. And costs of distributing by telephone are coming down. Deregulation has cut the price of long-distance calls in Japan by 75% over the past decade.

Source: The Economist (3 October 1998).[2]

The management of telephone call centres and the technology used to handle large volumes of calls is a major topic in its own right and greater coverage of the subject is provided in Chapter 14.

▨ The Internet as a distribution channel

Today a shopping trip involves travelling to a store, selecting items, taking them to the checkout, queuing, paying, and then taking them home. It can be a lot of work and many consumers consider shopping an unpleasant experience. In comparison, shopping over the Internet is rapidly gaining in popularity. In today's retail world up to 20 per cent of the price of a product goes to covering the costs of running retail stores, which represents a very significant opportunity for Internet retailing. The implications for retailers are enormous as location no longer becomes a barrier to entry. Two major PC manufacturers that have been fighting a battle to distribute over the Internet are depicted in Exhibit 11.3. As the Exhibit shows, the valuations of both companies have been determined to a great extent by their ability to win this battle.

Thanks to the convergence of telecommunications and computer technology, and the rapid take-off of the Internet, many consumer industries have moved quickly to embrace

Exhibit 11.3

DELL VERSUS COMPAQ

Thanks to the convergence of telecommunications and computer technology, and the rapid take-off of the Internet, many consumer industries have moved quickly to embrace direct delivery channels. Or, at the very least, to increase the number and variety of delivery channels to give consumers greater buying choice. The personal computer (PC) industry is a case in point. Despite its strong growth and success, Compaq, the industry leader with annual sales of more than $30 billion, realised that survival in an increasingly cut-throat industry meant adapting its existing distribution model. Compaq had always depended upon its reseller network to provide service and support to its customers, and to expand the company's breadth and depth in the market. However, it now faced intense competitive pressure from rivals Dell Computer and Gateway 2000, both of which have been building market share by selling directly to their customers. Dell, in particular, had turned itself into one of the top five personal computer companies in the world by concentrating on sales over the Internet and by telephone. By early 1999, less than two years after it began taking electronic orders from its Web site, it was generating sales of more than $6m a day. Compaq's share price suffered dramatically in the face of the onslaught from Dell and other direct sales competitors. During the first half of 1999, as Compaq's share price dropped from a high of more than $50 to around $20, it removed its chief executive and embarked on the difficult task of implementing a direct sales model that would complement, not cannibalise, its channel of resellers.

The scale of the change is impressive. For example, part of Compaq's new direct model outside of North America centred around the creation of a pan-European call centre based in Dublin. With 450 agents speaking 15 different languages, the centre provides technical support for queries from Compaq's channel partners, key corporate accounts and end-consumers across Europe, the Middle East and Africa. In the Asia/Pacific region, Compaq created a one-stop-shop Internet site, called 'Compaq Club', to serve the needs of distribution partners and customers in the region. In addition, it has revamped its global account management programme, which provides a single point of contact for its major corporate accounts across the globe.

Source: O'Connor and Galvin (1998)[3].

direct delivery channels. The Internet is a disruptive technology that has created a new breed of retailer, sometimes referred to as an 'e-tailer'. E-tailing has been adopted more quickly in some industries than others. For example, the travel industry has seen the arrival of a number of non-traditional players like Microsoft's Expedia and Sabre Holding's Travelocity (*see* Exhibit 11.4).

Exhibit 11.4

ONLINE TRAVEL

More than 1 million households in the US have already booked travel online and by the end of 1998, 27 per cent of all households who had shopped on the Internet – 1.3 million in total – had purchased airline tickets online, thus beating all other consumer categories except software, books and computers. This growth threatens to reshape the highly fragmented travel industry and lead to the emergence of a new tier of online agencies. The online leisure travel business, which has increased in value from less than $300m in 1997 to over $3 billion in 1998, has been pioneered in the US by the airlines and online travel agencies like Preview Travel, Sabre Holding's Travelocity and MSN Expedia. Now these Internet-based agencies are broadening their horizons and targeting the expected surge in electronic commerce in Europe. For example, MSN Expedia has launched local sites in the UK and Australia while Travelocity, which has been doing business in Britain since 1997, established a UK site five months ago. Since then it has become the biggest online travel site in the UK with an estimated 40 per cent of the online market.

Source: Financial Times (5 May 1999).[4]

Although the newer, on-line companies have quickly won market share, some research companies believe that air and hotel suppliers will leverage the power of their brands and frequent travel programmes to increase their share of on-line direct bookings. Jupiter Communications believes that the traditional players can increase their share from 48 per cent in 1997 to 61 per cent in 2002.

■ Automated teller machines and multimedia kiosks

The ATM is ubiquitous. There are nearly 150,000 machines already installed across Europe – one for every 3,000 people. On average, more than 3,000 withdrawals are made from each machine every month.[5] However, ATMs are more than simply a means of withdrawing cash or making routine transactions. Many banks have added new marketing functions to their ATM networks. In the USA, for example, 4 per cent of ATMs already offered full motion video by the end of 1995.[6] Today the figures are significantly higher. More interestingly, many of them are now becoming Web enabled as well, providing the promise of bringing eCommerce directly to your local cash machine (*see* Exhibit 11.5).

Exhibit 11.5

THE FUTURE OF THE ATM

ATMs are losing their fixation with cash and beginning to offer other services. The latest ATMs, located away from banks, enable customers to withdraw cash, buy cinema tickets, which the machine prints itself, and make hotel reservations. The technology company Moneybox announced it would install 1,000 ATMs in convenience stores and petrol stations in the UK, later spreading to nightclubs and betting shops. As well as dispensing cash, they will sell cards for prepaid mobile phones and run promotional advertising. At present, Moneybox's ATMs will not be linked to the Internet. But later, says Moneybox's managing director Paul Stanley, they will be – enabling customers to purchase goods and bring eCommerce to the cash machine.

In another development, full-motion advertisements are now running on the screens of ATMs at some 7-Eleven stores in New York, Chicago, San Diego and, of course, Los Angeles. Trailers are a natural choice for showing off the video capabilities of new, sophisticated ATMs, says Cassie Metzger, a marketing manager at Diebold, a big ATM maker. And since people often stop to pick up cash before going to see a flick, she says, a 15–30 second trailer, with sound, could influence what they see. The ads don't lengthen the transaction time – they play while the ATM is already processing. It's an advertiser's dream – customers can't change channel and they can't walk away, at least not without leaving their cash.

Sources: *Financial Times* (21 July 1999)[7] and *Business Week* (26 April 1999).[8]

Multimedia kiosks are unmanned outlets designed to provide product information, customer service and sales functions through the use of multimedia. Although the outlet itself may be unmanned, the kiosk can provide a teleconference or videoconference link to a call centre where human operators can answer more complex questions than the kiosk is designed to handle. Applications of kiosk technology include the provision of tickets and information in the travel industry.[9] Kiosks can be used for providing train and airline tickets to customers either as a means of improving customer service, or as part of a premium service where, for example, airline frequent fliers can use a magnetic stripe or smart card to provide kiosk access.

INDIRECT CHANNEL CHANGES

■ Electronic point of sale systems

Indirect sales channels include retail stores such as supermarkets as well as dealers, value-added resellers (VARs) and wholesalers. The retail industry, and supermarkets in particular, have invested heavily in IT over the past number of years. One of the biggest changes has been the implementation of electronic point of sale (EPoS) bar-code scanning systems that have the capability of providing retailers with much higher levels of sales information. Where credit cards are used and payments are made electronically, the process is referred to as EFTPoS (electronic funds transfer at point of sale). EPoS and EFTPoS applications are not just confined to supermarkets. Mobile EFTPoS can be found in taxis. Scandinavian and Australian taxis have accepted credit cards for several years.[10]

■ Efficient consumer response and supply chain management

When manufacturers distribute through wholesalers and retailers, information about products, product sales and deliveries must be shared across the entire distribution chain. This has become increasingly important as manufacturers and retailers alike are striving to achieve efficient consumer response (ECR), a term coined to describe the efficient management of supplying goods and services from the manufacturer to the consumer. ECR traces its origins to a growing awareness in the early 1990s that the traditional adversarial relationships between manufacturers and retailers in the grocery industry were not delivering best value to customers. ECR involves manufacturers and retailers sharing information about buying trends and co-operating to manage the supply chain. Inventory can be reduced without loss of product availability, allowing prices to be reduced or margins to be increased. Full-scale ECR is not easy to achieve because, like other forms of partnering, it requires companies to make available information previously regarded as confidential. But the benefits of sharing such information are clear. For example, Procter & Gamble, the consumer products group, was able to reduce product costs by more than $2 a case between 1990 and 1997 through the implementation of ECR. Total savings over the period were $2.5 billion.[11]

The sharing of information across the supply chain and the implementation of ECR have put enormous pressure on manufacturers to manage the supply chain effectively. Most European manufacturers do not have the skills or resources to manage everything themselves and the industry trend is to outsource some or all of the supply chain activities to specialist third party logistics operators like Exel Logistics, Royal Nedlloyd, TNT and McGregor Cory (*see* Exhibit 11.6). Netherlands-based logistics companies, for good geographical reasons, tend to dominate this business as more and more European manufacturers start treating Europe as a single strategic unit, rather than as a series of national markets.[12]

Exhibit 11.6

RECKITT & COLMAN

Even a UK manufacturer as large as Reckitt & Colman, with global sales of more than £2bn – one-third in continental Europe – is rarely in a position of delivering a full truckload of products to a retailer. As the supermarkets have put the squeeze on the stocks they are prepared to hold in-store, their suppliers have been forced to make increasingly frequent delivery of smaller amounts of products. The company which is only delivering a pallet or two to each store or to a distribution centre will find its trucks relegated to inconvenient times. 'Coca-Cola may be able to deliver a truck full every day to a distribution centre but we don't have full loads,' says John Doran, logistics director Europe for Reckitt. 'Supermarkets want daily deliveries but they don't want a lot of lorries turning up.'

The answer increasingly has been to go to a third party logistics company (3PL) that can combine one company's products with those of several others to deliver a full truckload to the supermarket. It is the changing patterns of retail supply which have persuaded Reckitt to sign up McGregor Cory, the logistics service company, to handle its distribution in the UK and Spain. In June, the two companies reached agreement on a five-year deal, worth up to £5.5m a year to McGregor, for McGregor to handle all of Reckitt's UK deliveries from its distribution centre at Bawtry, near Doncaster, South Yorkshire. McGregor also handles Reckitt exports to the Middle East, Israel, Cyprus, the Caribbean and North Africa. The Bawtry centre handles 400 Reckitt product lines involving an annual volume of 160,000 pallets.

But harmonising IT systems required the greatest effort. The contract negotiations coincided with an upgrading of Reckitt's IT systems to provide a business-wide enterprise resource planning (ERP) capability. 'We will be able to provide Reckitt with information from our links with retailers,' says John Winston, managing director of McGregor's logistics division. 'They will get a greater understanding of their product flows.' McGregor will also install a bar-coding scanning system to allow the progress of products through the system to be monitored more closely.

Source: Financial Times (1 December 1998).[13]

MANAGING MULTIPLE DISTRIBUTION CHANNELS

■ Managing distribution conflicts

Choosing a distribution channel is a strategic decision with major investment implications. Similarly, entering another country by setting up an agency or distributor agreement will usually involve a multi-year contract that can be both expensive and difficult to break. In some businesses, such as the airline industry, it is more profitable if customers order directly from the airline rather than going through travel agents. There are major drawbacks, however. If the same airline promotes its direct channel heavily, travel agents may recommend other airlines in retaliation. The prospect of 'channel conflict' has deterred many manufacturers from going direct to their end-customer. The case of Body Shop in Exhibit 11.7 provides another good example of these drawbacks.

Exhibit 11.7

BODY SHOPPING

Early in 1996, 30 Body Shop franchisees trooped into the Army & Navy Club in Piccadilly in London. It was an unruly group of clashing personalities and opinions, but all had one thing at stake – their livelihood. Amongst other grievances about inaccurate and misleading profit projections, the franchisees are concerned about plans by Body Shop to introduce Body Shop Direct, a home shopping arm it has been piloting since 1993. Faced with saturation in the number of British stores, Body Shop is planning to boost sales by setting up networks of agents who will operate rather like the people who run Tupperware parties. They will sell Body Shop beauty products directly in people's homes. The franchisees are concerned the plan will bite into their sales, and this is a big concern, with Body Shop's latest figures showing that profits are stagnant in Britain. The group said in a recent letter to Body Shop: 'There are four key principles enshrined in the existing agreement – exclusivity, renewability, mutuality and transferability. We need to establish that these principles will be honoured in any new agreement.' The letter speaks of Body Shop's moral obligation to respect the contracts under which the franchisees bought into the business. But Body Shop wants the group to sign new agreements to pave the way for Body Shop Direct, agreements the group members have so far refused to sign. For the Body Shop the contract wrangling comes at a time when it desperately needs to build its business.

Source: Sunday Times (29 September 1996).[14]

■ Hybrid marketing

Increasingly there is a trend towards using a number of different channels simultaneously to target different market segments. Many banks are now using telephone call centres and on-line banking in parallel with normal branch operations and ATMs. Each of these channels has its own set of advantages and disadvantages. Moriarty and Moran (1990)[15] coined the term 'hybrid marketing' to describe this situation, where companies use a number of different channels to go to market. They cite the example of IBM, which started to expand in the late 1970s from just using a direct sales force to new channels such as dealers, value-added resellers, catalogue operations, direct mail and telemarketing. In less than ten years it doubled its sales force and added 18 new channels to communicate with customers. The advantages of employing a hybrid marketing system include increased coverage, lower costs, and customised approaches. In adding a new channel companies must have a clear understanding of how it will affect their overall marketing strategy. As Moriarty and Moran describe it, the co-ordination of multiple distribution channels can be a complex business, which relies upon IT for its successful management:

> '*Once a hybrid system is up and running, its smooth functioning depends not only on management of conflict but also on coordination across the channels and across each selling task within the channels. Each unit involved in bridging the gap between the company and the customer must "hand off" all relevant information concerning the customer and the progress of the sale to the next appropriate units.*'

Case study

ON-LINE STOCKBROKING
(MERRILL LYNCH, CHARLES SCHWAB, E*TRADE AND CONSORS)

Another electronic trading milestone was passed in December when the $255bn market capitalisation of Charles Schwab, the biggest on-line broker, passed that of Merrill Lynch, the traditional US retail brokerage firm that vies with Morgan Stanley Dean Witter for the title of the world's largest securities group. The event signalled the astonishing success of Schwab and other leading on-line brokerage firms like E*Trade, the most popular Internet-only brokerage. Their low-cost, Internet-based, execution-only share-dealing services have helped them grab up to 50 per cent of retail share trading in the USA within the last four years. In 1998, Schwab opened 1.4 million new accounts, bringing its total customer base to 5.6 million. Schwab operates a direct model, using telephone and Internet. Two million of its customers have on-line accounts. It also has an office network, opening 55 new offices in the past two years, taking its total to 289. Schwab believes that the continued emphasis on traditional services is helping to boost the acceptance of on-line trading among investors.

Even though Charles Schwab is opening more offices, the Internet service is saving it money while introducing the brokerage to potential clients outside the USA where it is not well known. 'We sometimes get 20 million hits a day from across the world, and we have worked out that to handle that number of interactions in the traditional way, we would need 15 more call centres whereas we currently have four,' says director Greg Gable. Even so, Charles Schwab still had to announce plans to open a new customer service centre at Milton Keynes to handle the rapid growth of Internet share trading in the UK. The move will position Schwab for an explosion of competition in the UK Internet market. At present, it faces a handful of rivals such as Barclays and Stocktrade, but in the next few months E*Trade, DLJ Direct, NatWest, Freeserve and Killik are due to enter the market. The call centre will start with 450 staff and is expected to grow to 1,200 in five years. Its initial investment is £30m, rising eventually to £50m. Customer service staff will advise the 500–1,000 new Internet customers it is signing up every week. It hopes that by getting a head start it will have built up a loyal customer base. It said: 'We aim to be seen as the premier execution-only stockbroker.'

And the on-line trading phenomenon has caught on in Europe as well. In Sweden, where the long nights have boosted Internet take-up and there is a culture of owning equities, the big traditional brokers moved on to the Internet two years ago and there are now 14 operating through that medium. Germany is also producing its own on-line brokers. Chief among these is ConSors, a discount broker whose shares have soared since it was floated on the Neuer Markt in April, turning it into Germany's fifth-largest bank by market value. Quite a feat for a company that was founded five years ago as part of a family-owned private bank, with an initial investment of a mere DM2m ($1.2m). It is now adding 1,500–2,000 new accounts a week to the 140,000 it already has. Its customers are active traders: ConSors handles a quarter of all Internet trading accounts in Germany, but a third of all trades. Having shaken up Germany, ConSors' go-getting 30-year-old boss Karl Matthaus Schmidt is looking elsewhere. In January he signed a deal with Web Street Securities, a US stockbroker, to give his customers cheap access to US shares. More recently ConSors snapped up a French broker and Schmidt is now looking for targets in Italy and Spain.

And what of Merrill Lynch? In what many viewed as a humiliation, Merrill changed its Internet strategy in July 1999 by launching a flat fee Internet-trading service. The launch took place after some internal wrangling that apparently involved both Herb Allison, the anointed heir to the throne at Merrill, and brokerage chief Launy Steffens. Days later, Herb Allison resigned amid much speculation. Allison's departure 'is a sign that there are still a lot of rival constituencies to worry about at Merrill', said one senior executive at a rival firm. While Launy Steffens, who could have faced difficulties over the Internet issue, commanded fierce loyalty from Merrill's vast network of brokers, Allison does not appear to have had a strong support base. How the infighting between the well-paid traditional brokers and their new Internet-based broking colleagues at Merrill will end is anybody's guess.

Based on: 'Investors click a path to new online markets', by Paul Taylor, *Financial Times* (3 February 1999); 'Long-term future looks bright', by James Mackintosh, *Financial Times* (3 February 1999); 'Web site attracts up to 20m hits a day', by John Kavanagh, *Financial Times* (3 February 1999); 'Merrill loses shine in a year of stumbles', by Tracy Corrigan, *Financial Times* (20 July 1999); 'Charles Schwab plans to boost UK Internet trading', by Brian Groom, *Financial Times* (14 July 1999); and 'Prost', *The Economist* (31 July 1999).

Questions

1 What are the advantages of on-line banking from a customer perspective?

2 How should Merrill Lynch manage the tensions between its existing distribution channel (the well-paid traditional brokers) and the newer channel (those supporting execution-only Internet trading)?

3 Which is the most likely to win out in the retail stockbroking market: traditional firms such as Merrill Lynch that are only now moving into on-line stockbroking; telephone and Internet-based stockbrokers such as Charles Schwab; or Internet-only stockbrokers such as E*Trade?

4 Can ConSors become a pan-European on-line stockbroker?

ASSIGNMENT QUESTIONS

1 Comment on the role of distribution channels in the marketing mix.

2 What is the impact of e-business and the Internet on distribution?

3 Why should a manufacturer consider using an intermediary?

4 What do you understand by the term 'hybrid marketing'?

5 Why are EPoS systems important to the retail marketing manager?

References

1. Caine, N. (1996). 'Millions face pensions "misery gap"', *Sunday Times*, 20 October.
2. The Economist (1998). 'Japan's Bell curve', *The Economist*, 3 October.
3. O'Connor, J. and Galvin, E. (1998). *Creating Value Through eCommerce*, London: Financial Times Pitman Publishing.
4. Taylor, P. (1999). 'Strength of sales indicates radical change to industry', *Financial Times*, 5 May.
5. Electronic Payments International (1996). 'Sweden heads ATM league table', *Electronic Payments International*, April.
6. Whybrow, M. (1996). 'Nipped in the bud', *Banking Technology*, July–August.
7. Buxton, J. (1999). 'Cashing in on the hole-in-the-wall', *Financial Times*, 21 July.
8. Business Week (1999). 'Grab some cash, check out a flick', *Business Week*, 26 April.
9. Guptill, B. and Thomson, W. (1995). 'Full-service applications for travel ticket kiosks', *Gartner Group*, 30 June.
10. Electronic Payments International (1995). 'Taxis to try mobile EFTPoS', *Electronic Payments International*, March.
11. Batchelor, C. (1998). 'Buzzword – or the way of the future?', *Financial Times*, 1 December.
12. Terry, M. (1998). 'Taking a continent-wide view', *Financial Times*, 1 December.
13. Batchelor, C. (1998). 'Working with mixed pallets', *Financial Times*, 1 December.
14. Bernoth, A. (1996). 'Body shopping', *Sunday Times*, 29 September.
15. Moriarty, R.T. and Moran, U. (1990). 'Managing hybrid marketing systems', *Harvard Business Review*, November–December.

12

PROMOTION –
THE MARKET OF ONE

SUMMARY

The promotional mix contains advertising, personal selling, sales promotions and public relations. The digital age has already made significant changes to each of the elements of the promotions mix. In the coming years the changes are likely to be far more significant as the Internet, digital television, customer databases and other information-rich promotional methods become more sophisticated. We will focus on five key trends that marketing managers need to understand:

☐ fragmentation of television advertising

☐ trends in other advertising media

☐ the increasingly targeted nature of sales promotions

☐ the growth of the Internet as an advertising medium

☐ the potential of digital television and radio

☐ growth of public relations on the Internet.

FRAGMENTATION OF TELEVISION ADVERTISING

Historic growth of television advertising

In most western countries total expenditure on mass media advertising amounts to between 0.5 and 1 per cent of gross domestic product (GDP), typically through one of the following primary media:

- newspapers and magazines
- television
- radio
- cinema
- outdoor/transport.

Newspapers and magazines account for the majority of advertising expenditure but the medium of choice depends on the nature of the product or services being advertised, as well as the country or region in question. Food, drink and consumer goods tend to carry a much greater proportion of their expenditure on television than other media, while

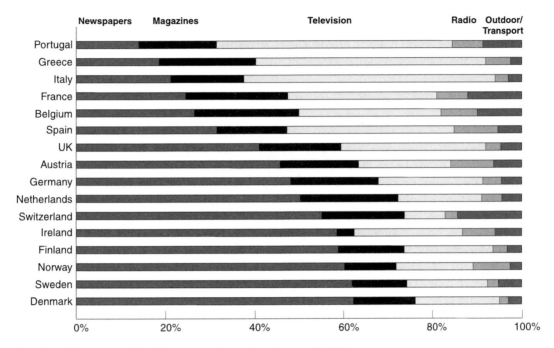

Fig 12.1   European advertising expenditure by category (1996)

advertising of property and items such as clothing and computers is dominated by newspapers and magazines. For example, in the UK, where one-third of all advertising expenditure is spent on television, Kellogg's and Procter & Gamble spend nearly 95 per cent of their advertising budget on this medium.[1]

There are significant differences across Europe as well. In the UK and southern Europe a far greater proportion of advertising expenditure is directed to television, while northern European, and Nordic countries in particular, are more likely to spend their advertising budgets on newspaper and magazine advertising (*see* Figure 12.1). The historic trend has been for television to capture an increasing proportion of advertising expenditure.

■ Fragmentation of television audiences

Most western economies have seen a dramatic increase in the number of television channels as television is deregulated and opened up to greater competition. In the UK, the BBC was the only broadcasting company until 1995, when Independent Television (ITV) was launched. This was followed by BBC2 in 1967 and, more recently, by Channel 4 and Channel 5. However, the range of television services has really only increased dramatically in the last decade with the launch of the multi-channel satellite systems. The arrival of BSkyB's satellite channels has altered fundamentally the balance of power between the traditional broadcasters and the newer upstarts.

With greater choice, audiences have become smaller. Today's top television programmes in the USA command smaller audiences than those of 20 years ago. In the 1970s the ratings of *Seinfeld* would have got it only to the bottom of the top 20.[2] However, the good news is that it allows advertisers to be more focused on targeting specific audiences by regional, ethnic or social differences.

Direct response television

If the marketing message is sent directly to the customer other than through the post, the process is known as direct response advertising. The message can be delivered via television, radio, newspapers or magazines and customers are asked to respond directly to a specified telephone number or address. Direct response advertising has increased in popularity as a marketing tool in the 1990s. In 1994, approximately 20 per cent of commercials on television carried a telephone response number, a substantial increase on the previous year.[3] The *Sunday Times* dated 15 September 1996 contained 63 half-page or full-page advertisements for companies or products, of which 50 included a telephone number to call; 22 of these were freephone numbers to encourage the reader to make the telephone call.

However, the subsequent handling of the telephone calls can leave a lot to be desired. Over one-third of telephone calls generated by direct response advertising on television are not picked up by the company that advertised, or by a call handling company acting on its behalf. In the case of call centres, the major problem appears to be the lack of advance warning that they receive on the exact timing of the advertising campaign, and their inability to staff up for the ensuing deluge of phone calls. Some television channels such as Channel 4 in the UK are now allowing call handling centres direct access to their advertising schedules so that they can make the appropriate arrangements for staffing.

A good example of how direct response television advertising has been used to build up a database of customer information comes from the drinks company Britvic (*see* Exhibit 12.1).

Exhibit 12.1

PUTTING THE FIZZ INTO THE DATABASE

Four years ago, Tango was just another boring fizzy drink. Now it's one of the most famous brands in the UK, thanks to a brilliant marketing strategy. Steve Kay is the real life Mr Tango who has built the once-ailing soft drink brand into one of the marketing successes of the 1990s. Since Kay took the reigns as marketing director of Britvic Soft Drinks, Tango has become the star performer of its sector – not through its taste but through a marketing approach that can be regarded as ground-breaking or deviant, depending on your point of view. Kay attributes the success of Tango to his ability to keep a finger on the pulse of the 16 to 24-year olds who buy the brand. More than two and a half million people have responded to the phone number flashed at the end of Tango commercials. On a more prosaic level, these have given Britvic a massive database of its customers to target with further promotions.

■ Teletext

Teletext is an information service in which pages of text are transmitted together with normal analogue television broadcasts for display on a domestic television set. In the UK, the BBC offers Ceefax and ITV transmits Teletext UK. Teletext works very well in complementing other advertising media. While a TV advertisement usually only lasts a minute or less and does not convey much detailed information, the teletext service can provide additional detail. For example, when the Midland Bank in the UK underwent a massive rebranding exercise in 1999 as it changed its name to HSBC, it took out television advertisements that referred viewers to page 396 on Teletext UK for more information.

One of the biggest growth areas is in providing travel information and the service is very effective in listing plane, shipping and rail schedules. Another major growth sector has been the advertising of last-minute travel bargains. While teletext is very effective when the customer knows what they are looking for, the initial prompt to look for additional information must be provided by traditional TV and print advertising. Its advantages over the Internet are the penetration of TVs and speed. The advantage of the Internet is that it is a two-way communication and it is likely that many companies who provided information on teletext will eventually migrate to Internet Web sites. Ultimately the two technologies will converge as digital television and digital teletext become pervasive.

■ Future decline of television advertising

A 1997 survey[4] of marketing and senior executives in over 200 UK companies by KPMG found a decline in the traditional means of promoting products and services such as sales force and advertising, while newer means were predicted to rise. Respondents were asked to name the top three activities currently used and to predict what these might be in five years' time. The only activities that respondents thought would increase were telemarketing, direct mail and database marketing, and Internet or new media. The traditional sales force was predicted to decline while traditional advertising was predicted to decline by a slightly smaller margin.

Already major FMCG companies such as Procter & Gamble have started to move some of their traditional advertising expenditure out of television into the newer media (*see* Exhibit 12.2). This is a trend that is set to continue.

Exhibit 12.2

MARKETING BREAKTHROUGH 2000

The American consumer giant, Procter & Gamble (P&G), is cutting back its spending on advertising to pay for a new wave of lower prices on some of its best-known brands. The company plans on reducing the level of marketing support from a quarter of net sales to a fifth or less by the end of the decade. P&G spends $8.3 billion (£5.4 billion) worldwide on marketing, and the cuts could deprive the advertising world of more than $1.6 billion a year in revenue. In Britain this will translate into an average 10% cut in TV advertising budgets this year. The internal memo, called Marketing Breakthrough 2000, confirms the

▶

company's drive to reduce prices. 'In many markets our major competitor is own label,' the memo says. 'We're reducing our selling prices so that our premium versus private label is less of a barrier to the growth of our brands.' The memo to regional managers around the world also instructs them to 'become true experts in non-TV media'. P&G, along with fellow consumer goods manufacturers such as Unilever and Colgate-Palmolive, spends the vast majority of its advertising budget on TV. The impact of P&G's new marketing style will therefore be a double blow for the TV industry – more media outlets to share a smaller amount of advertising money. The effects are already being felt across Europe. P&G recently cancelled all its brand advertising on London's weekday channel, Carlton – usually it spends an estimated £1.5m a month.

Source: Sunday Times (18 February 1996).[5]

TRENDS IN OTHER ADVERTISING MEDIA

■ Commercial radio services

Although radio started in the UK when the BBC began transmitting in 1922 some industry commentators believe that commercial radio really only took off in the early 1990s.[6] In 1989 the UK Radio Authority began to license more local stations, stipulating that they must also diversify output. New radio stations such as Jazz FM, Kiss FM and Melody Radio sprang up. Radio stations were allowed to go national following the 1990 Broadcasting Act, led by Classic FM in 1992 and followed by Virgin Radio and Talk Radio.[7]

It was only in the 1990s that commercial radio had sufficient listenership to pull in the advertising revenues and shake off the so-called '2 per cent tag', which refers to the proportion of advertising revenues taken by this medium.[8] In 1998 there were more than 200 commercial radio stations in the UK, reaching more than half of the UK population and generating more than £390m in advertising revenue – approximately 5 per cent of total advertising revenues and a far cry from the first radio advertisement for Bird's Eye fish fingers in 1973. Indeed, the popularity of commercial radio was supported by the fact that the average person in the UK spent more time listening to radio in 1998 (15 hours a week) than watching television (14 hours).[9]

■ Newspapers and magazines

Improvements in printing and binding technology are making it easier and more cost effective to customise magazines for selected target audiences. Advertisers can use these customised editions to more selectively target advertising messages. This allows magazines to produce several different editions, each addressing the needs of different constituencies. Magazines are facing competition from on-line computer services. In the future consumers may be able to select articles of interest to them and create their own personal magazine on a computer terminal. This trend is part of a wider technology movement sometimes referred to as 'the electronic newspaper'. In the USA over 100 newspapers offer daily information ranging from traffic reports to soap opera updates. The reports are given to customers using a telephone service and freephone numbers.

The *New York Times* and the *Los Angeles Times* fax several page summaries of the day's top stories to companies in Japan and Russia. Most newspapers and magazines, from the *Financial Times*[10] to *Playboy*,[11] are now posting summary articles on the Internet, a trend that will eliminate the need for the fax machine.

■ Place-based media

Technology developments will allow advertising to be targeted to individual stores on large and small screens. Such advertising can be very effective. For example, an advertisement for baked beans at a store entrance will have a higher impact on the purchase decision than one seen the previous night on television. Research in the 1980s indicated that the average American was exposed to 150 advertisements a day from television, radio, newspapers and magazines. Non-traditional media will significantly increase consumers' exposure to advertising messages. Exhibit 12.3 shows how outdoor advertising is becoming more sophisticated and more targeted.

Exhibit 12.3

BUS SHELTERS AND ADVERTISING

The More Group and TDI account for 90% of the Irish outdoor advertising industry. More's subsidiary Adshel, a bus-shelter and advertising company, uses geographic information systems (GIS) to manage its poster sites and allows advertisers to tailor campaigns based on demographic and retail proximity criteria. Kristi O'Sullivan, executive director of Adshel said that, 'We see GIS as a vital tool in the provision of a quality service to our clients. For example, food companies can target families with children while a car manufacturer can target their dealer outlets. The new GIS system allows us the extra targeting dimension and improves the service we can provide to our clients.'
Source: Sunday Business Post, Computers in Business supplement (September 1998).[12]

Outdoor electronic displays are also becoming more sophisticated. For example, Lighthouse Technologies a leading European supplier of electronic display technology uses modern LED (light emitting diode) technology to construct massive television screens that are used for outdoor advertising. Recent developments have enabled LED screens to produce a true red, green and blue, which means that they can reproduce colour as faithfully as television and cinema. As one commentator has put it: 'Unlike television, when you book an advertisement on a giant LED screen, you can be guaranteed that viewers are not watching the other channel when your advert is playing'[13] (see Exhibit 12.4).

Exhibit 12.4

DISPLAYING EMOTION TO KAI TEK AIRPORT

10,000 spectators shared an unforgettable evening at Kai Tek and bid farewell to the airport with popular Hong Kong artistes and celebrities live and on display on the world's brightest superscreen at the Farewell Concert at Kai Tek Airport on Saturday 27 July 1998.

▶

> The Lighthouse SuperScreen LVP50, the first ever true colour LED big screen for outdoor displays, is the brightest and most impressive video system on the market. During the Farewell Concert, the SuperScreen LVP50 lit up the stage and allowed every spectator to enjoy the concert in as much detail as if they were standing in the front row. The screen measured 6.4 metres by 4.8 metres and featured a definition of 50 lines per metre, the highest performance screen available today. In contrast, the LVP100 series is an indoor LED screen with a very thin 10-centimetre profile, which offers instant set-up and low cost and is perfect for trade shows, conference arenas and shopping malls.
>
> *Source:* Lighthouse Technologies Web site (1999).[14]

■ Growth of direct mail

Direct mail's share of promotional expenditure has increased steadily over the years. For example, the average person in the Netherlands received 82 pieces of direct mail in 1996, almost double the figure of five years earlier. In the UK the 1996 figure was 54 pieces, up 35 per cent from 1991. Again there are significant differences across Europe. Germany and Austria are among the greatest proponents of direct marketing in the world while the markets in Portugal and Greece are almost non-existent (*see* Figure 12.2).

Direct mail's share of advertising expenditure in the UK has steadily increased over the years. Between 1988 and 1992 its share rose from 7 per cent to 11 per cent, mainly at the expense of press advertising, which dropped from 60 per cent to 55 per cent over the same period. The average household in the UK now receives between six and seven pieces of direct mail every month.[15] The more highly targeted groups, typically ABs and those over 35, will clearly receive significantly more. There is evidence to suggest that particular segments of the market are already being overtargeted. For example, 84 per cent of the 'grey' market (those over 55) consider the level of targeting to be excessive.[16] Other findings from such surveys give a similar and somewhat predictable picture:

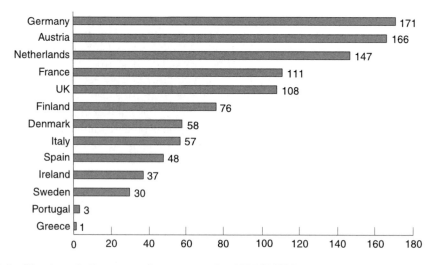

Fig 12.2   Direct marketing expenditure per capita 1995 (ECUs)

Sources: FEDMA; Eurostat; IFS.

- 95 per cent consider telemarketing to be unethical
- 76 per cent consider direct mail to be unethical
- 71 per cent consider the sale of lists between companies to be unethical behaviour
- 67 per cent of respondents do not consider that direct communications provide information
- 47 per cent consider direct marketing to be an invasion of their privacy.

As the amount of material dropping through the letterbox increases, the chances of it being read decreases. There is some evidence that people react well to material that is of interest or directly relevant to them and that the key to successful direct mail advertising is very close analysis of the target audience. The ability to target customers closely is dependent on building an accurate database with sufficient information to identify key customer groups. As Evans et al. (1995) describe it:

> 'The sooner marketers move to using direct mail in response to customers' requests, rather than "cold" prospecting, the better it will be for all concerned. Marketers will be able to target more accurately and more effectively, and consumers will see a phenomenal reduction in unsolicited direct mail. This will lead to more true "relationships" between marketer and consumer and will probably significantly alleviate privacy concerns among consumers and legislators, and will clearly be beneficial for the industry.'

Direct mail should not simply be seen as a stand-alone means of communicating with a customer. All forms of communication with a customer offer the opportunity to include a marketing message. Companies that have regular correspondence with customers, by way of monthly statements for example, can tailor marketing messages for inclusion with the correspondence. Although direct mail has received bad publicity through the proliferation of unsolicited 'junk mail', it does have a number of advantages:

- It is more targeted than traditional media advertising (*see* Figure 12.3).
- In many cases, it is also cheaper than traditional advertising.
- Its effectiveness can be measured.

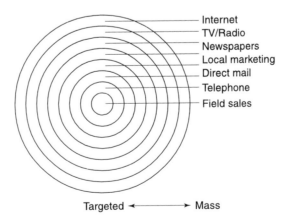

Fig 12.3   Degree of targeting of advertising messages

THE INCREASINGLY TARGETED NATURE OF SALES PROMOTIONS

■ Trends in sales promotions

Over the last 10 to 20 years sales promotions have become an increasingly important element of the marketing mix. In the USA in 1977 the ratio between advertising and promotion was 60:40. By 1987 the ratio had been reversed. Not all of these promotions have been successful, as the case of Hoover in Exhibit 12.5 illustrates. In the past promotions served to jump start sales and rarely involved the use of IT. Many campaigns were aimed at a broad audience with little differentiation made on the basis of a customer's past activity or behaviour. Customer databases were rarely used as they tended to be out of date or inaccurate. Using information technology, marketers can now address customer behaviour. Detailed transaction databases using information on previous purchase histories can be used to generate offers aimed at changing customer behaviour. They can be used to either retain existing customers or acquire new ones. Using the concept of customer life cycle profitability, companies can use promotions that lose money in the short term but generate profitable relationships over the longer term. The modern promotions are more effective because they relate directly to the customer's likes and lifestyle. Opportunities exist in marketing to the customer when they are about to make a purchase and are most susceptible to a marketing message. This can be called 'just-in-time marketing' and examples include point of purchase coupons tailored to the buying preferences of the customer.

Exhibit 12.5

HOOVERING UP THE FREE FLIGHTS

One of the most spectacular corporate mistakes in recent years was the UK Hoover promotion in the autumn and winter of 1992–93. The net result of the promotion was a cost to the company of over £20 million plus an effect on reputation which is difficult to evaluate. In contrast, the effect on the executives responsible was very measurable as most of them lost their jobs. The Hoover promotion ran in two stages. Stage one, during the early autumn of 1992, offered customers two free return air tickets to continental Europe if they purchased any Hoover product worth more than £100. Stage two, which began on 1 November, was an offer of two free flights to the United States if the customers purchased a Hoover product worth more than £250. Stage one of the promotion started off fairly well with satisfied customers and little general attention. It was only months after the promotion had ended that adverse comments started to appear.

Stage two was almost instantly a news story. The Hoover promotion was not the first of its kind; several companies had run free flight promotions previously but without the attention and side-effects Hoover was soon to experience. The Hoover promotion caught the imagination of people, especially when alert journalists realised that the company had not made any commitments as to how they would send the participants in the promotion over the Atlantic. Then, they started to fuel doubts as to how the details of the promotion were designed. The promotion was created so that prospective participants would be discouraged to go through the whole process. One such aspect was that there were six steps to be taken, five by post, within eight weeks to obtain the free tickets. The customers were expected to tire of the process and not bother to complete the offer. In the case of Hoover that did not happen. In addition, the company also misjudged the way the customers would respond to the offer. Normally one would expect a 5–10 per cent redemption rate; the Hoover promotion went significantly over that.

The end result was that a large number of appliances were sold but the costs to the company proved to be enormous. The attention to detail that is necessary in a turbulent world was missed and safeguards to allow for the unpredictability of the consumers were not installed – actually the reverse, as apparently no tickets at all were purchased prior to the promotion.

Source: Nilson (1995).[17]

■ Loyalty programmes

Another aspect of sales promotions is the use of loyalty programmes to build stronger relationships with existing customers (*see* Chapter 8 for a wider discussion of relationship marketing and customer loyalty). Having recognised the importance of a core customer group that remains loyal to a brand, many organisations are implementing loyalty programmes to identify and reward these customers. Customer loyalty programmes are not new. For years savers could collect Green Shield Stamps and motorists have been able to collect Tiger Tokens every time they filled up their car with Esso petrol. A multitude of retailers have offered stamp-based schemes to entice consumers away from the competition and to turn them into loyal customers of their own. Information technology had a very small role in these early programmes but is increasingly becoming a vital component in developing customer loyalty.

In the UK supermarket industry Tesco is a leader in the area of loyalty programmes. It launched its Clubcard scheme in February 1995 and, in less than 18 months, built up a customer base of 8.5 million cardholders.[18, 19] Its 1996 variation of the scheme, Clubcard Plus, went even further by offering customers 5 per cent interest on credit balances on the card while charging 9 per cent on debits. This initiative was regarded in the industry as an extremely innovative means of winning customer loyalty. Most of the other large retailers in the UK have followed Tesco's lead by introducing loyalty schemes of their own. J. Sainsbury's ABC loyalty card has 3.8 million customers but it is revamping it at an estimated cost of up to £20 million.[20, 21] The new card, known as the Sainsbury Reward Card, is expected to gain 6 to 7 million users within six months of launch.[22, 23] Asda, with the help of GE Capital, the US finance company, is following the example of Sainsbury and Tesco.

The reason for the investments is the belief that it will make the customers much more loyal to the store, and reduce the need for multimillion pound advertising and discount battles to gain or retain market share. Will it work? It seems to have for Tesco. In 1996, for the first time ever, it moved ahead of Sainsbury with nearly 23 per cent of the £2.8 billion packaged grocery market in the UK, compared to Sainsbury's 19 per cent.[24] Will it continue to work? Inevitably the competition will retaliate, but if it gives Tesco a lead for a couple of years until the next major marketing battle, Tesco will regard it as worth the investment.

Companies need to understand that the loyalty scheme itself is no substitute for a good product or a good brand.[25] They must also understand that a successful loyalty programme will not happen overnight. In addition, investments in analysing the data to develop marketing campaigns must be made to capitalise on information gathered from customers. Other initiatives such as self-scanning in supermarkets can be linked into loyalty schemes.[26, 27]

THE GROWTH OF THE INTERNET AS AN ADVERTISING MEDIUM

■ Web sites and 'brochureware'

The Internet is increasingly seen by companies, and FMCG organisations in particular, as an important medium through which advertising messages can be directed towards consumers. Today the debate that is referred to in Exhibit 12.6 is being repeated among marketing executives in many organisations across the world.

Exhibit 12.6

MARKETING BREAKTHROUGH 2000 – PART II

You're Procter & Gamble, the consumer products group; you're the world's biggest advertiser; and a nagging worry has worked its way to the forefront of your mind. Where are you going to be advertising your soaps, detergents and toothpastes in five years' time? In the 1940s, Procter & Gamble spent more than half its advertising dollars on the radio. Then came television; and in only five years, from 1950 to 1955, the new medium's share of P&G's advertising budget shot up from nearly nothing to 80 per cent. With the advent of the Internet, another media revolution is under way. That poses at least two important questions for P&G. Should the company be prepared to switch 80 per cent of its advertising budget to this new medium in the next five years? And if so, just how is it supposed to advertise its mundane household products on the Internet?

In August 1998, P&G hosted an extraordinary two-day summit to discuss these issues – extraordinary in that it included representatives of arch-rivals such as Colgate-Palmolive as well as scores of people from the advertising and interactive media industries. The conference turned out to be better at questions than answers. But it forced some serious thinking about the problems confronting consumer goods companies such as P&G as they enter the Internet age.

Source: Financial Times (28 August 1998).[28]

By the end of 1999 most large organisations had established some sort of presence on the Internet. The most common form of Internet advertising is still the creation of 'brochureware' – using the corporate Web site to advertise the company's range of products and services. However, without the rich 'content' to attract visitors to a company Web site, it is difficult to see how such brochureware can, on its own, be an effective form of advertising.

Many companies try to combine the Internet with traditional forms of advertising. There is an increasing propensity for companies to include their Internet addresses alongside other forms of advertising – on posters, magazine advertisements, and even on television advertising. Some companies have taken the concept one step further: companies like EasyJet,[29] the low-cost airline carrier, and Joe Boxer,[30] a manufacturer of men's underwear, have emblazoned their Web addresses clearly and visibly across their respective products – airlines and boxer shorts.

■ Internet banners

A more effective form of Internet advertising recognises that Internet traffic is concentrated around a relatively small number of 'high-content' sites, or through portals, the access gateways that Internet users have as their starting point to surf the 'net. These sites are particularly attractive to advertisers, who are increasingly anxious to market their products on them. The Internet ratings company Nielsen NetRatings[31] predicts that spending on Internet advertising will reach $4.2 billion in 2000, $5.8 billion in 2001 and $7.8 billion in 2002. Web advertising is managed by a new breed of company such as DoubleClick,[32] the US-based marketing organisation that delivers approximately 10 billion advertisements per month, across 7,500 Web sites, to 100 million Internet customers.[33] The mechanism for carrying these advertisements is the banner, the rectangular advertising space on the Web site that is often animated and that attracts consumers to 'click through' to the relevant page on the advertiser's own Web site. For example, when British Airways used DoubleClick's animated banner advertisements to attract customers to a screen where flights could be booked, it achieved click-through rates of between 13 and 18 per cent, a very high achievement in the Internet advertising industry.[34]

But not everybody is happy with the banner advertisements that form a major proportion of this Internet advertising expenditure (*see* Exhibit 12.7) and not surprisingly, there is some scepticism about the effectiveness of this form of advertising. Falling click-through rates are even causing some companies to rethink the migration of advertising expenditure to the Internet. Despite this scepticism, the Internet will undoubtedly account for a growing proportion of advertising revenues for the foreseeable future as research shows that even if 99 per cent of the people who see a banner do not click on it, the banner can still build up brand awareness and perception.[35]

Exhibit 12.7

WEBWASHERS AND CYBERSITTERS

Anyone who uses the Internet knows about banner ads. These omnipresent rectangles account for 80 to 90 per cent of Web site advertising revenues (pop-ups account for the bulk of the rest). Running banner ads is sort of like tossing water balloons at passing cars: Every so often a target will stop and take notice. But unlike television commercials that take up the whole screen and will eventually go away on their own, or print ads that can be skipped over, banner ads stubbornly conceal what you are trying to see until you physically banish them with mouse clicks. And since they tend to be overloaded with graphics and animation, they can slow transmission to a maddening creep. The majority of US users pay a flat rate for unlimited Internet access, but most users outside the USA must pay for content by the minute – thus downloading Web pages with graphic-intensive banner ads proves extremely costly.

▶

To avenge consumers, a number of companies have made ad-blocking software available at little or no cost. The software recognises ad content and filters it out, a move that can result in download speeds as much as 500 times faster. A broken image icon loaded by your browser is the only visible trace of the ad you were spared. Siemens' WebWasher (www.siemens.de/servers/wwash.de.htm) is available free from the company's home page (and is reportedly gaining ground in Germany, where Internet-access charges are notoriously high). The 1.2 million parents who have coughed up $40 for the popular smut 'n' spam strainer, CyberSitter, can activate a feature that keeps on-line ads from reaching their surfing progeny. A host of other blockers such as Internet Junkbuster Proxy, AtGuard and InterMute round out the field.

These blockers, occasionally referred to as Roach Motels for Internet ads (ads check in ... but they don't check out) are, not surprisingly, frowned upon by advertisers, Web-based businesses that rely on advertising income, and related organisations.

THE POTENTIAL OF DIGITAL TELEVISION AND RADIO

■ The interactive power of digital media

Analogue television and radio services made significant progress in the 1990s but they suffer from one drawback — they are media that do not allow any form of interactivity between the broadcaster and the viewer (or listener). Even teletext is not interactive — the broadcaster decides what information to send to the television, not the viewer. Interactivity requires greater bandwidth and different technology, both of which can only be provided by digital media.

As Figure 12.4 shows, digital media do not automatically mean interactivity, only the *potential* for interactive services.

We have already discussed the growth of the Internet as a marketing medium. Now let us briefly examine the potential of the other interactive digital media services.

■ Digital television

Digital television (DTV) is an improved way of transmitting television pictures — improved because it can compress the digital signal and fit five digital channels into the

	Broadcast	Interactive
Digital Media	Digital television Digital radio Digital teletext	Digital television Videotex Digital radio Digital teletext Internet
Analogue Media	Television Teletext Radio	N/A

Fig 12.4 Interactive services

frequency bandwidth currently used by a single conventional station. Digital television is delivered in one of three generic ways:

- *Satellite*. Satellite television requires a satellite dish and a set-top box but is generally available to anybody who is willing to purchase the requisite equipment and pay for the service.
- *Cable*. Cable requires no new hardware for existing cable television subscribers but requires non-cable subscribers to have cable installed.
- *Terrestrial*. Somewhat confusingly entitled, digital terrestrial television (DTT) refers to television that is received via an ordinary aerial. It requires no new wiring but does require a set-top box and is more limited in bandwidth than satellite or cable.

Satellite is the delivery channel used for all the pioneering digital services. The UK's first digital satellite service was SkyDigital, which went on the air in late 1998 (*see* Exhibit 12.8).

Although the launch of SkyDigital marked a major point in the history of television in the UK, it was not the first digital service. Digital services have been set up in many western countries including the USA, France, Germany and Spain. By early 1999, there were already 4.3 million digital television subscribers across Europe (*see* Table 12.1).

From a marketing perspective, some of the more interesting developments in digital television are the interactive services that are being promised to consumers. Although not yet widely available, they will eventually provide home shopping, home banking and a variety of other services through the television screen.

Exhibit 12.8

HEAVENS ABOVE!

In 1945, the science fiction writer Arthur C. Clarke wrote an article outlining the possibilities for establishing a global communications system using three satellites placed in geo-synchronous orbit equidistant from each other. In 1962, the first satellite transmission was made from France to the US via the Telstar 1. Thirty years after Arthur C. Clarke's article, Home Box Office (HBO) began its satellite service with the 'Thrilla from Manila' heavy-weight boxing match. But all these were analogue transmissions. Now the world has gone digital – PrimeStar rolled out its digital broadcast by satellite (DBS) service in 1994, closely followed by the DirecTV/USSB digital service.

In the UK, the launch of digital television on 1 October 1998 was essentially the launch of SkyDigital, and with all its multi-channel experience Sky is undeniably the leader in the field, with up to 200 channels dedicated to films, sport, news, music, general entertainment, documentaries, lifestyle and children's programmes. All these will be available to subscribers in various combinations along with the so-called free-to-air channels – BBC1, BBC2, Channel 4, Channel 5 (ITV has yet to join) – as well as BBC Choice, BBC News 24, and 10 audio music channels. And in Spring 1999, British Interactive Broadcasting (BIB), a venture between BSkyB and BT (British Telecom) will introduce home shopping, home banking and the facility to book tickets for events and holidays through digital television sets. The joint interactive television service, called 'Open', has signed up the first four companies to offer shopping and banking over TV: Great Universal Stores, Iceland Group, Kingfisher's Woolworth stores and HSBC (Midland Bank).

Source: www.skyreport.com, *Sunday Times* Digital Television supplement (4 October 1998).[36, 37]

Table 12.1 Digital television services in selected countries

Country	Service	Delivery medium	Subscribers ('000s)	Launch date
France	Canal Satellite Numerique	Satellite	1100	1996
	TPS	Satellite	615	1996
	AB1	Satellite	150	1996
Germany	DF1	Satellite	230	1996
	Premiere	Satellite/cable	200	1997
Japan	PerfecTV!	Satellite	500	1996
	DirecTV	Satellite		1997
	JSkyB	Satellite		1998
Scandinavia	Canal Digital (pan-Scandinavia)	Terrestrial	50	1998
	Tele Danmark	Cable	36	1998
	Telia (Sweden)	Cable	20	1997
Spain	Canal Plus España	Satellite	575	1997
	Via Digital	Satellite	350	1997
UK	SkyDigital	Satellite	200	1998
	ONdigital	Terrestrial	20	1998
US	PrimeStar	Satellite		1994
	DirecTV/USSB	Satellite		1994
	DISH (EchoStar)	Satellite		1996

Source: Based on Department of Trade and Industry (April 1998) [38] and *Financial Times* (3 March 1999). [39]

■ Videotex

Videotex, or *viewdata,* is the term used to describe any two-way system for transmitting text or graphics across a telephone network, for display on a television screen or PC. Typically, these videotex services are provided by the post, telegraph and telephone (PTT) companies. Examples of videotex services include Prestel in the UK and Teletel in France. Prestel was the world's first public videotex service when it was launched in the UK in 1979. [40] It was initially a very popular service, with more than 1 million customers in the 1980s. Teletel began service in France in 1984 and built up a customer base of 3 million by 1988.

In general, videotex has been less than commercially successful as a vehicle for marketing promotion. Videotex promised to provide the business user with a wide variety of electronic services available from a single terminal. In practice it worked out quite differently:

- Videotex was beset by technical problems related to the speed at which information could be accessed and transactions could be carried out.
- Despite the initial rush of subscribers, the end-consumers did not feel that they received sufficient value to continue paying for the service.
- Customers also did not want to pay for separate terminals when they already had expensive personal computers on their desks.
- Other technologies such as CD-ROM (and, more recently, the Internet) were beginning to provide a faster, more reliable service than videotex.

By 1989 there were less than 100,000 terminals attached to Prestel, less than one-tenth of the peak customer numbers. In 1994 the service was relaunched as New Prestel with 30,000 customers. In France, the fact that France Telecom had provided the 'Minitel' terminals free of charge to their customers helped to sustain the market. Even now, the installed base of Minitel is formidable. For example, France's largest mail order company, La Redoute, gets 20 per cent of its orders via Minitel.[41]

▦ Digital radio

Digital radio brings listeners CD-quality sound, more channels and interactivity via small screen displays. However, it does not have the same obvious benefits associated with digital television. Most commentators believe that it will take 10 to 15 years before digital radio overtakes analogue (*see* Exhibit 12.9).

Exhibit 12.9

MAROONED IN AN ANALOGUE WORLD?

The industry is divided about how radio will evolve. One of the issues that confronts the industry is digital radio. Only one consortium, Digital One, has bid for the national licence. The group is made up of media company NTL, Talk Radio, and GWR, which owns Classic FM, the country's largest commercial radio station. GWR's chief executive Ralph Bernard says: 'Digital is happening in TV, music recording and all types of media. It is not likely that radio will be the only medium to stay marooned in an analogue world.' However, the managing director of another major commercial radio station is more blunt. He says: 'Digital TV has sports and movies that will drive the product. But what is the consumer benefit of digital radio? People aren't thinking about that. We are asking people to pay about £400 for clearer sound and that is obviously too much.'

National Economic Research Associates (NERA) economist Mark Shurmer comments: 'We are reasonably pessimistic about digital radio. Price is a key barrier.' NERA predicts that by 2007 penetration will hit between 5 per cent and 11 per cent – a lot depends on whether car manufacturers take up the product for in-car radio.

Source: Marketing (8 October 1998).[42]

▦ Digital teletext

In the future digital teletext will offer a faster, more comprehensive service than its conventional analogue rival. In time the graphics and 'look and feel' of digital teletext will also change, and may eventually look similar in format to the Internet. The advantages of digital teletext claimed by Teletext Limited, the operator of the UK teletext service on ITV and Channel 4 are:[43]

■ *Greater interactivity.* Viewers will be able to interact with the service rather than being limited to the narrow range of information broadcast to them by ordinary teletext. More information will be available on sport, weather, travel, education, entertainment, polls, games, listings, community news, leisure and activities.

■ *Greater viewer control.* Digital teletext will have easier-to-use navigation that is more intuitive to use than the existing analogue service.

■ *Enhanced graphics and animation.* This includes photographs, video clips and much higher resolution, which cannot be supported by traditional teletext.

Exhibit 12.10

RUMOURS, GOSSIP AND LIBEL

What digital interactive television will not be – and should not be confused with – is the Internet. For all that is said about the global computer link-up as the universal medium of the future, it remains essentially uncontrollable. There is literally no way anyone can prevent something from being 'published' or 'broadcast' on the Internet. Whether or not it comes into your home is your decision; in most cases you have to go and look for it.

And what is out there, despite what agents Mulder and Scully might believe, is not always the truth. Quite apart from the notorious pornography, the Internet is a minefield of unconfirmed rumours, gossip and libel. Television is altogether different. As an established medium, it already has a watchdog body: the Independent Television Commission, which will scrupulously monitor the quality of what is broadcast by television companies.

Source: Sunday Times Digital Television supplement (4 October 1998).[44]

GROWTH OF PUBLIC RELATIONS ON THE INTERNET

■ PR activities on the Internet

The Internet is being used more and more for a variety of marketing and corporate public relations activities. Typical public relations activities that are conducted using the Internet include:

■ *Investor relations.* Many companies will place the annual, half-yearly or quarterly accounts or financial statements on the Internet for investors to view or download. Almost all major investors will use corporate Web sites as a key source of information and intelligence about target companies.

■ *Product and service information.* The Internet has become a key distribution channel for marketing PR material. Most corporate Web sites will devote most of their Web pages to descriptions of their products or services. The general 'look and feel' of a corporate Web site can significantly enhance (or detract from) the organisation's overall public image.

■ *Press releases.* Most companies who distribute press releases on the Web will archive these releases so users can access them again easily. Most corporate Web sites will have one or more pages devoted to recent press releases. Marketing departments will now e-mail statements to newspapers for immediate release, as opposed to using fax, courier or mail.

■ *Recruitment.* A company's Web site can be an invaluable source of reference material for prospective employees. Many companies solicit and receive job applications over the Internet nowadays.

ONDIGITAL VERSUS SKY DIGITAL

If you are wondering whether to spend a couple of hundred pounds switching to digital television, spare a thought for the gamble big business is taking. Billions of pounds are being invested by a handful of players who are betting digital television will become a huge success. Most analysts agree the bonanza will come. The big question is: when, and which companies will reap the rewards?

The most common prediction is of a digital war, in which the operators of the three different systems will attempt to overthrow each other. But not everyone is convinced the war will materialise. 'I think there is room for all of them,' says Neil Blackley, media analyst at Merrill Lynch. The three systems each have distinctive qualities. BSkyB, which is 40 per cent owned by News Corporation, launched Sky Digital on 1 October 1998[45] and broadcasts using its satellite dish and a set-top box. It has promised up to 200 channels, including the closest the industry has come to video on demand. ONdigital will be a terrestrial operator, a 'plug and play' service needing neither a satellite dish nor a cable link.[46] But customers will have to buy a set-top box or, eventually, a new digital television and a card that will give them access to the pay-TV services. One potential disadvantage of the ONdigital package is that it promises only about 30 channels, including all the BBC free digital services plus ITV's digital innovation ITV2. Less is more. And on that oxymoron rides ONdigital's hope of success. Third come the cable companies that have promised to pick up the cost of turning digital themselves rather than handing on part of the bill to customers. The cable companies will deliver the digital service through their existing cable networks, which means that all the digital paraphernalia will stay out of the customers' living rooms.

Cable, say some, is best placed to deal with the next step in digital television – interactive programmes. 'Cable is the most future proof,' says Blackley. 'As you get interactive services, the most efficient way of doing that is via a broadband mechanism like cable.' So who is likely to win the battle? Matthew Horsman, media analyst at Henderson Crossthwaite, says it is more a question of timing than absolute success or failure. His company has recommended that investors sell Carlton (ONdigital is a 50:50 joint venture between Carlton and Granada, the ITV companies that hold the commercial franchise for digital terrestrial television) but he believes ONdigital will eventually become a success. Carlton and Granada's own optimism for ONdigital is based on the fact that upwards of 17 million British homes – about three-quarters of the total – do not have cable or satellite. ONdigital's chances of success? Well, the proposition is this:

▨ Set-top boxes at £199 – from Philips, Pace at launch and from Nokia and Toshiba by Christmas 1998.
▨ Free help to any subscribers with DTT reception problems, promising an engineer within 24 hours of a call.
▨ Free-to-air channels including four BBC channels, two ITV, Channel 4 and Channel 5 (for the first time in many parts of the country).
▨ A basic subscription of £7.99 per month, for which customers get total flexibility in the form of six channels from the 12 or so available; or £9.99 for all of them.
▨ Some premium channels will only be available for an extra fee. (SkyDigital's premium channels range from £11 per month for one up to £18 per month for three; Film Four is £6 per month; Manchester United TV is £5 per month.)

The cost to companies of developing and marketing the three delivery platforms will be high, particularly as they will have to subsidise equipment to encourage customers to sign up. BSkyB is investing more than £1 billion in digital. ONdigital has put a £300 million price on its investment, although analysts believe the real figure is likely to top £400 million. According to analysts, the cost to cable companies of shouldering the burden of going digital themselves could easily reach £1 billion. The rewards are also measurable. Horsman calculates that ONdigital should start breaking even with 1.7 million subscribers, and producing profits on 3 million subscribers.

Adapted from: 'Playing for high stakes' by Kirstie Hamilton, 'How to surf a digital wave' and 'Aerial automatic' by Breda Maddox, *Sunday Times* Digital Television supplement (4 October 1998) and ONdigital's Web site.

Questions

1 'Less is more.' What are ONdigital's chances of success?

2 Browse the Web sites of both Sky Digital (www.sky.co.uk/digital/) and ONdigital (www.ondigital.co.uk) and compare the services they offer.

3 How successful has ONdigital been to date, and what is its likely future?

4 What lessons can be learned from the way digital television and digital services have developed in the USA?

ASSIGNMENT QUESTIONS

1 What are the main trends in television advertising?

2 What advertising media would be most appropriate for a small local retailer?

3 What is the likely future of videotex and teletext?

4 Choose a company and examine how effectively it uses the Internet for public relations.

References

[1] (1997). *European Marketing Pocket Book, 1998 Edition*, Henley-on-Thames: NTC Publications Ltd.

[2] The Economist (1998). 'Infinite variety', *The Economist*, 21 November.

[3] Croft, M. (1996). 'Right to reply', *Marketing Week*, 12 July.

[4] Baker, P. and Stone, D. (1998). 'A research report into data warehousing', London: KPMG Management Consultants.

[5] Mellor, P. (1996). 'P&G slashes advertising to cut price', *Sunday Times*, 18 February.

[6] Baird, R. (1998). 'Next 25 years for commercial radio', *Marketing Week*, 8 October.

[7] Littlewood, F. (1998). '25 years of commercial radio', *Marketing*, 8 October.

[8] Hewitt, M. (1988). 'Tuning in to radio's success', *Marketing*, 8 October.

[9] Douglas, T. (1998). 'Digital TV has radio to thank for the multichannel revolution', *Marketing Week*, 8 October.

[10] www.ft.com

[11] www.playboy.com

[12] Dunne, J. (1998). 'Targeting the best locations', *Sunday Business Post*, Computers in Business supplement, September.

[13] Roche, A. (1998). 'Ways to catch attention', *Sunday Business Post*, 20 September.

[14] www.lighthouse-tech.com

[15] DMIS (1994). *Direct Mail Information Services (DMIS) Report*. London.

[16] Evans, M., O'Malley, L. and Patterson, M. (1994). 'Direct marketing: rise and rise or rise and fall?', *Marketing Intelligence and Planning*, Vol. 3, No. 6, August.

[17] Nilson, H.T. (1995). *Chaos Marketing: How to Win in a Turbulent World*. Berkshire: McGraw-Hill.

[18] Brown-Humes, C. (1996). 'Tesco plans services to challenge banks', *Financial Times*, 4 June.

[19] Teather, D. (1996). 'Asda joins queue to offer supermarket credit cards', *Sunday Business ComputerAge* 5 May.

[20] Burton, G. (1996). 'Sainsbury's shops around for cheap loyalty card technology', *Sunday Business ComputerAge*, 23 June.

[21] Ham, P. (1996). 'Store wars: now Sainsbury launches loyalty card', *Sunday Times*, 16 June.

[22] Brown-Humes, C. (1996). 'Sainsbury card for customers offers BA link', *Financial Times*, 18 June.

[23] Randall, J. (1996). 'Sainsbury plays its loyalty card', *Sunday Times*, 23 June.

[24] Moore, L. (1996). 'City loses its taste for Sainsbury's', *Sunday Business*, 5 May.

[25] Stead, J. (1996). 'Loyalty is back in fashion – at any price', *Sunday Business*, 7 July.

[26] McNevin, A. (1995). 'Loyalty pays', *Computing*, 30 November.

[27] Computing (1996). 'Supermarket chain adopts self-scanning', *Computing*, 2 May.

[28] Tomkins, R. (1998). 'Net ads fail the soap test', *Financial Times*, 28 August.

[29] www.easyjet.com

[30] www.joeboxer.com

[31] www.nielsen-netratings.com

[32] www.doubleclick.com

[33] Poynder, R. (1999). 'Stakes are raised by net advertising', *Financial Times*, 4 August.

[34] Wheelwright, G. (1999). 'Counting the clicks for their profit potential', *Financial Times*, 5 May.

[35] Newing, R. (1999). 'Flying corporate banners for the Internet audience', *Financial Times*, 3 March.

[36] Payne, S. (1998). 'Sky high', *Sunday Times* Digital Television supplement, 4 October.

[37] Miller, J. (1998). 'Here it comes', *Sunday Times* Digital Television supplement, 4 October.

[38] www.dti.gov.uk – 'Moving into the information age: international benchmarking survey 1998'.

[39] Price, C. (1999). 'Sending the right signals to attract a wider following', *Financial Times*, 3 March.

[40] Zorkoczy, P. and Heap, N. (1995). *Information Technology, an Introduction, 4th edition*. London: Pitman Publishing.

[41] Salz-Trautman, P. (1996). 'French prove resistant to change', *Digital Media*, Issue 1.

[42] Littlewood, F. (1998). '25 years of commercial radio', *Marketing*, 8 October.

[43] www.digital-teletext.co.uk

[44] Miller, P. (1998). 'Your gateway to the world', *Sunday Times* Digital Television supplement, 4 October.

[45] www.sky.co.uk/digital

[46] www.ondigital.co.uk

DELIVERING THE OFFERING TO THE CUSTOMER

In Part V, we examine how information technology can be used to deliver a product or service offering to the customer. We begin by looking at how technology allows sales forces to sell more effectively. We then examine how call centres and the Internet have transformed customer service and we finish with a brief tour of the 'dos' and 'don'ts' of developing effective marketing systems.

Part V contains three chapters:

13 Improving sales force effectiveness

14 Delivering customer service and support

15 Developing marketing systems that work.

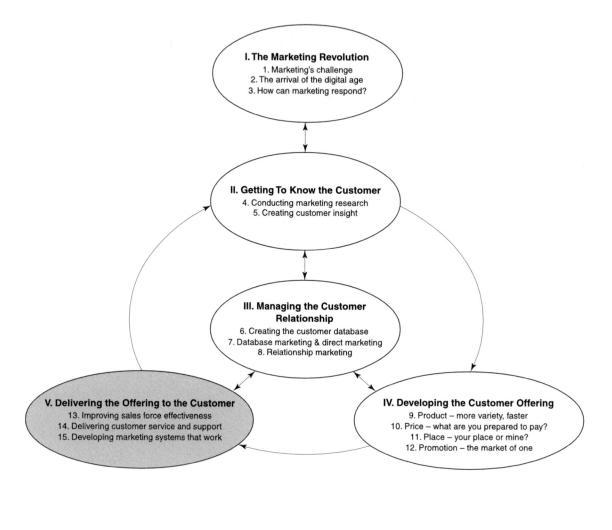

13

IMPROVING SALES FORCE EFFECTIVENESS

SUMMARY

ECommerce and information technology are transforming the role of the traditional sales force. Where previously the sales force performed a range of tasks from lead generation through to order taking and after-sales service, many of these tasks are now either automated, migrated to the Internet or performed in call centres. Even where face-to-face interaction is still required (and in industrial sales or business-to-business situations this is still predominantly the case) the role of the salesperson has changed radically.

Today's marketing managers need to understand that:

☐ the digital age has changed the traditional sales function considerably, with the demise of the traditional sales force and the rise of the mobile sales force;

☐ we are now into the third generation of sales force automation tools;

☐ there are several critical success factors that marketing managers need to understand if they are to achieve the greatest effectiveness from today's sales function.

THE IMPACT OF THE DIGITAL AGE ON THE SALES FUNCTION

The changing role of the sales function

While FMCG companies rely heavily on promotions and advertising to market their products, industrial goods such as raw materials, major equipment, component parts and industrial services are marketed in a different fashion. Personal selling, using a direct sales force, is more effective in business-to-business situations than advertising and receives a correspondingly higher share of the overall marketing budget (*see* Figure 13.1).

Personal selling is becoming more sophisticated, with sales people requiring consulting and advisory skills in addition to their traditional sales skills. One of the greatest changes in the sales function has been the move from a product focus to a customer or account focus, with the resulting dramatic changes in the mindset of the sales manager and sales people. There is now a much greater focus on understanding the likely buying patterns of individual accounts at a local level and aggregating them into an overall sales plan. With a focus on individual accounts or customers, many companies are now spending more time trying to increase the profitability of specific accounts. This has only become feasible with the use of IT to enable sales departments to track sales and profitability at an individual customer or account level.

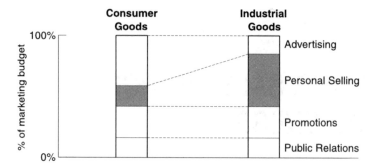

Fig 13.1   Importance of personal selling in industrial marketing

Sales people have always relied on relationships with their customers but companies are now moving more towards a team approach to selling where the depth and breadth of that relationship is increased and the chances of follow-on or repeat sales are enhanced. Team selling requires greater co-ordination and relies heavily on good quality information to be shared between different members of the sales team. Figure 13.2 provides a summary of the major changes that have taken place in the sales function in the past decade.

From: Product Focus (1990s)	To: Customer or Account Focus (2000s)
▨ product focus	▨ customer focus
▨ product marketing	▨ regional brand marketing
▨ national promotional plan	▨ local account strategy
▨ volume focus	▨ profitability focus
▨ 'sell to' philosophy (push)	▨ 'sell through' philosophy (pull)
▨ relationship selling	▨ relationship and information-based selling
▨ single-brand focus	▨ category focus
▨ uniform sales force	▨ team selling:
	– account
	– category market specialists
	– merchandising

Fig 13.2   The changing focus of the sales function

▨ The demise of the traditional sales force

In many industrial organisations sales force costs are the largest single marketing cost. A typical field representative will have a car, mobile phone, expense account and bonus scheme but there are limits to the number of customers who can be met in any particular day. By the mid-1990s many organisations had begun to question the effectiveness of the traditional sales force, feeling that:[1]

▨ sales force effectiveness was difficult to measure
▨ business leads were being lost
▨ vital customer information was kept on scraps of paper or in the salesperson's head
▨ if a salesperson left the company, important customer information also left
▨ salespeople were always busy but sales results were often mediocre.

As sales migrated to the Internet and other direct channels throughout the late 1990s the impact on the traditional sales force was dramatic. According to one US survey, the average US sales force was 26 per cent smaller at the end of 1998 than it was two years previously.[2]

The drive for improved sales force effectiveness

As pressure on the traditional sales force increased throughout the 1990s, many organisations invested in automating and modernising in order to improve productivity. The benefits of sales force automation can be significant. For example, Canterbury Clothing International, a leading supplier of football jerseys in Australia and New Zealand, has equipped its sales force with laptops. Sales staff use the laptops to download up-to-date sales and stock information, as well as to send and receive e-mails.[3] Many other companies have followed a similar route, often at significant cost. In the USA, the Prudential Insurance Corporation has invested $100 million in sales force automation (*see* Exhibit 13.1).[4]

Exhibit 13.1

FUTURE-PROOFING THE SALES FORCE

In the age of the Internet and the inexorable rise of electronic commerce, one big insurance group is relying on that most traditional of all sales methods – agents in the field. But the Prudential Corporation of America has given its nationwide sales network a new digital twist. Faced with the prospect of a growing online market in financial services, as in numerous other sectors, it decided not to cut down on its 12,000-strong sales force but to equip it with the latest mobile computer systems.

At a cost of some $100m – part of the group's overall information technology budget of $1bn a year – it has provided its agents with notebook computers and access to a variety of financial solutions over a network. 'We've got to make the sales force more productive and effective,' says Barbara Koster, Prudential's chief information officer. 'Technology is the only way to do that. Otherwise, you price yourself out of the market. Technology is critical to our future.'

Despite some reservations from the less IT-minded sales agents, she says the new programme has been accepted positively. 'Agents want to know how to use technology to make better sales presentations. Prudential began with a six-month pilot programme, involving nearly 500 agents and managers. Together with other streamlined new business processes, the technology enabled agents to more than double the number of life products sold, with commissions rising by 153 per cent.

Source: Financial Times (7 April 1999).

Optimising sales territories

In many instances, sales reps spend considerable time 'on the road'. The allocation of territories to particular salespeople can be automated using statistical techniques to optimise the ratio of time spent with clients to time spent on the road. Geographical information systems (GIS) that are commonly used by retailers to locate stores (*see* Exhibit 13.2) are now being used to allocate territories to sales force reps.

Exhibit 13.2

USING TECHNOLOGY TO LOCATE YOUR STORES

In an age of tough planning restrictions and cut-throat competition, location is a critical factor in the success of a supermarket. Now, a growing number of retailers are turning to powerful Geographic Information Systems (GIS) to help find the best sites for their new stores. Retailers have woken up to the potential of these new systems to create 'intelligent' maps to help them rapidly analyse the many factors that influence the location of a new store, such as journey times, catchment areas and distance from competitors. 'Location is of pre-eminent importance in food retailing,' says a spokesman for Tesco, one of the UK's leading food retailers. 'The time needed for potential customers to drive to a new store is crucial and we have built a wealth of data and trading models over the past 15 years to help us make better decisions and forecast turnover.'

But where does the information come from to make these GIS systems work? The Ordnance Survey, the principal source of commercial maps in the UK, provides the retailer Tesco with digital versions of its large-scale maps. The maps give Tesco planners a detailed picture of population centres and roads, but offer little insight into where Tesco's best customers are likely to live or how long it will take them to drive to the new store. Tesco enriches the map by adding data that allows it to precisely calculate the time taken for potential shoppers to drive to the new store using the most likely routes. The Department of Transport supplies information on the speed limits and the number of lanes on each road. But this is still insufficient and so Tesco adds its own proprietary data on the location and direction of one-way streets and whether junctions are controlled by traffic lights, roundabouts or give way signs. Fifteen minutes is the longest time that people will take to drive to a new store, according to Tesco. The results of the drive-time analysis are then superimposed on the on-screen map to identify those population centres that fall within the 15-minute drive time.

Source: Financial Times (3 September 1997).

▨ Improving sales forecasting

The effect of accurate sales forecasts can be profound. Raw materials and component parts can be purchased much more cost effectively when last-minute, spot market purchases can be avoided. Such expenses can be eliminated by accurately forecasting demand. Perhaps most important of all, accurate forecasting can have a profound impact on a company's inventory levels. In many firms inventory exists to provide a buffer for inaccurate forecasts. Thus, the more accurate the forecasts, the less inventory that needs to be carried.[5] And sales forecasts are rarely near the mark. In a 1997 survey by the magazine *Purchasing* nearly 60 per cent of the purchasing outfits surveyed said the sales forecast information they received was only somewhat accurate. Another quarter said the information was not accurate.[6]

So how can sales forecasting be improved? Technology alone is not the answer. Another survey of 478 US companies revealed that most companies used only personal computers and had very little access to mainframe systems where the really useful information to support accurate sales forecasting is often held.[7] The answer is to create an integrated forecasting function, allowing both your customers and your suppliers into the process. The technology comes in through:

- electronic data interchange (EDI) and extranet links between manufacturers and retailers to allow everybody to see where the inventory is in the supply chain;
- electronic point of sale systems (EPoS) to provide instant feedback on how well different products and product lines are selling.

The ultimate effects of sales forecasting excellence can be dramatic. Mentzer and Schroeter (1993) describe how Brake Parts, Inc., a manufacturer of automotive after-market parts, improved its bottom line by $6 million per month after launching a company-wide effort to improve sales forecasting effectiveness.

THE THREE GENERATIONS OF SALES FORCE AUTOMATION

▩ The benefits of automating the sales force

Traditionally sales reps operated with limited additional IT support, but in recent times technology has been employed with considerable success to improve productivity. Applications of IT to improve the productivity of the sales force are sometimes referred to as sales force automation (SFA) applications.

Technology can increase the overall professionalism of salespeople as they work through the sales cycle with potential customers. Some of the benefits provided by the type of laptop software applications used by Prudential and Canterbury Clothing include:

- freeing salespeople from routine office administrative tasks, enabling them to spend more time with customers;
- providing better customer service because the salesperson has immediate access to information such as stock levels or quotations;
- capturing information that allows management to measure and monitor sales performance;
- helping to create sales opportunities and manage them so that a greater proportion are converted into sales.

The Yankee Group,[8] a consultancy, thinks that the current technology is actually the third generation of sales force automation software to be released on to the market.[9]

▩ Generation 1: Personal information and contact management

The first generation involved equipping the sales force with laptops and other types of computing and data storage devices. At first these machines contained the typical office productivity applications such as spreadsheets and word processors. Before long salespeople clearly saw the value of personal information managers (PIMs) and, over time, these applications became tied into the other personal productivity applications on the PC. Products such as ACT!, GoldMine and Maximizer were designed to help a salesperson manage contacts and time, and increase their selling effectiveness. Such powerful time and contact management tools had not existed previously, and were accepted quickly and enthusiastically.

▩ Generation 2: The networked sales force

As management realised that this technology was helpful to their field sales representatives, they began to wonder how they might also harness this information for corporate purposes. The second generation of SFA tools were essentially networked versions of the first, connecting the contact tracking database and personal productivity tools of the sales force to the corporate network, contact, and prospect database. This was usually accomplished via data replication, by plugging the PC into a phone line, typically at night.

While sales representatives retained their interest in time and contact management, these tools offered them little if any additional advantage over the first generation, although some were much smaller, portable and lighter than their predecessors (*see* Exhibit 13.3).

Exhibit 13.3

A SALE IN THE HAND   **FT**

While sales of contact management software have soared in recent years – with titles such as ACT!, GoldMine and Maximizer making an impact in North America and Europe – several trends have started to change the nature of contact management applications. The first of these is the move towards handheld computers by salespeople. The release of Windows CE 2.0, the handheld computer operating software produced by Microsoft in 1997, is encouraging many of the leading lights in the contact management software arena to create 'handheld' versions of their products. The other big issue facing contact management software developers is how to make best use of the Internet, e-mail and desktop applications that have become popular. It was these trends that prompted Maximizer Technologies to launch its Maximizer 97is (the 'is' stands for 'Internet-savvy') earlier this year.
Source: Financial Times (5 November 1997).[10]

▩ Generation 3: Technology-enabled selling

Technology-enabled selling is the name given by the Yankee Group to the latest generation of SFA tools. Technology-enabled sales systems incorporate a much richer variety of functions to help salespeople acquire and close more business, including some combination of the following:

▪ *Lead management.* The ability for sales to receive leads from marketing and other departments. This is important given that an estimated 75–90 per cent of sales leads that companies receive from advertising are not followed up.[11]
▪ *Opportunity management.* The ability to convert leads into sales. This organises all information around the opportunity to give a complete view of sales cycles, co-ordinate schedules and resources, and bring the sales process to closure.
▪ *Account management.* The ability to track successfully closed opportunities. Also, tracks business entities through companies, subsidiaries, branch offices, departments etc. with multiple addresses and contacts. Provides the ability to roll up to company level and master accounts, and to maintain existing business relationships, leverage repeat business, and review order and delivery status.

■ *Proposal management.* The ability of the sales force to produce on-the-spot, customised, accurate product configurations and proposals. It is critically important for complex product and service sales opportunities (*see* Exhibit 13.4).

■ *Win/loss reporting.* The ability to objectively evaluate wins, losses, and return on investment. It allows people and companies to learn and improve their sales and customer support processes.

Exhibit 13.4

CITIPOWER GOES ON THE CAMPAIGN TRAIL

Deregulation of Australia's energy market was the driving force behind the creation of CitiPower in the mid-1990s, serving a customer base of 230,000 in Melbourne's Central Business District and its surrounding suburbs. The first to benefit from deregulation were those with annual consumption of about 4,400 gigawatts, like manufacturing organisations. In 1996, a second block of customers became contestable – the mid-range consumer, the very segment that comprised a substantial proportion of CitiPower's customer base. Customers from hospitals and large hotels to casinos were now able to choose their energy provider from a larger pool of suppliers. More than 15,000 customers began to look critically at energy providers. CitiPower had a small window of opportunity in which to impress prospective customers with the kind of service they could offer; a small window, and a lot of competition.

'Competition was new to these customers,' said Samantha Bartlett, CitiPower's manager of marketing and business sales. 'Their whole view of an energy provider would be based on the sales process, and the speed with which their sales queries could be answered.' CitiPower looked at Customer Relationship Management (CRM) solutions that could link its sales, marketing and customer care operations with its back office systems. It conducted a lengthy evaluation of the marketplace and eventually selected TeamPOINT, a third generation CRM solution from POINT Information Systems. 'With TeamPOINT, we forced competitors to stay busy defending their turf, rather than attacking ours,' said John Walker, project manager at CitiPower. 'TeamPOINT's speed and flexibility enabled the company to flood the market, and then turn around offers and counter-offers in less than a day. CitiPower can fax responses back to prospects within 20 minutes. In contrast, some of the competition took three or four weeks to respond,' said Walker. The system created an efficient, easy-to-use system for outbound campaigns, maximising the effectiveness of CitiPower's legacy systems.

'When the market opened up, we had a 10% market share,' says Samantha Bartlett. 'We have been able to maintain that share throughout the development of competition, and we will not use the system to grow our market share in 1999.'

Source: POINT Information Systems Web site (1999).[12]

SUCCESSFUL TECHNOLOGY-ENABLED SELLING

■ Key success factors

The sales and marketing world is littered with examples of failed implementations of sales force automation projects. In general, salespeople are reluctant to waste time on anything that is unlikely to have a relatively quick pay-back period. Rasmussen (1999) has five steps for the successful implementation of technology-enabled selling:[13]

- *Know what you want to accomplish.* One way of establishing this is to ask the sales force questions such as: What part of the sales process can be improved? What information is not available now? What administrative tasks are the most time-consuming? What ideas are our competitors using? What are we overlooking?
- *Involve the sales force in vendor selection.* Software must be easy to use and have the minimum amount of administrative overhead if salespeople are to spend the maximum amount of time with customers. The performance and ease-of-use of the system must be such that salespeople will want to use it rather than being forced to use it. The best way to achieve this is to get them involved in designing the system.
- *Get executive buy-in.* Given the high rate of failure of SFA initiatives, it is important that they have the strongest sponsorship from within the organisation. These initiatives must be seen by all employees as critical to the organisation's future success.
- *Take time to implement.* Rushing a sales force automation is often a good way to ensure poor user compliance and ultimate failure. Software should be tested on a small 'pilot' group initially before the entire sales force is converted to the new system. The pilot group should consist of people with a positive attitude towards the new system and who will act as 'product champions' during its roll-out.
- *Train and support like crazy.* Not all salespeople are computer literate and some will be apprehensive about IT-based selling. After all, these people have carried out their duties for years (often decades) without any support other than pen and paper and, more recently, a mobile phone. A training programme must be designed that will cater for those salespeople who are already familiar with PCs, as well as those who are computer illiterate.

Even if these steps are followed, success is not guaranteed. The Gartner Group estimates that more than 55 per cent of technology-enabled selling projects fail. Other commentators quote higher figures. Invariably, when a SFA programme is launched, there are initial teething problems. The provision of a telephone-based helpdesk can provide a quick response during this initial period.

While richness of functionality is important, the introduction of technology-enabled sales systems is often part of a much wider transformation of the sales function. The two additional features that they have are:

- They are often accompanied by a radical re-engineering of processes, from pre-sales through to delivery.
- They are also accompanied by the introduction of customer relationship management (CRM) initiatives.

▥ Re-engineering of processes

The business case for automating the sales force does not have to stop with the sales representative. Other processes can, and usually must, be automated as well. Campbell Soup, the US food company, invested $30 million in sales force automation in order to

	Before	After
Product/customer administration	▨ paper-based process with data often rekeyed	⇒ integrated customer service system results in data being keyed in only once
	▨ customer contract not captured in system	⇒ customer contract generated electronically and captured in system
	▨ redundant information with greater chance of error	⇒ elimination of non-value-added tasks across multiple departments
Order control	▨ orders not thoroughly checked	⇒ orders checked up front to eliminate downstream problems
	▨ special handling required for urgent orders needed within 48 hours	⇒ all orders immediately processed
	▨ customer order status information very labour intensive	⇒ order information available to distribution centre immediately
	▨ 18 hours from receipt of order to confirm order	⇒ customer enquiries answered immediately using on-line system
Settlement	▨ inaccurate invoices lead to penalties	⇒ accurate invoices significantly reduce penalties
	▨ finance department lacks information to settle disputes	⇒ finance department can investigate every discrepancy with facts
	▨ salespeople spend 40% of time on administrative work	⇒ salespeople spend very little time on administration
Accounting	▨ transactions feed into a number of different computer systems	⇒ transactions feed directly into customer service system
	▨ various system updates lead to inconsistent data and confusion	⇒ systems are integrated
	▨ considerable manual work required to produce MIS reports	⇒ timely accurate reporting delivered with minimal work

Fig 13.3 How automation improved sales at Campbell Soup

Source: Datamation (1 May 1995) © EarthWeb Inc. www.Earthweb.com.

achieve annual cost reductions of $18 million through shorter order cycle times, more accurate invoicing and better control of funds used for product promotions (*see* Figure 13.3).

▨ Incorporation of customer relationship management principles

We examined the principles of customer relationship management (CRM) in Chapter 8. Many of the major sales force automation vendors such as Siebel,[14] Clarify[15] and POINT market the CRM capabilities of their products (*see* Exhibit 13.5). Others combine the CRM messages with a more clearly commercial message about improving sales force productivity. For example, Vantive,[16] a sales force automation company, claims that:

'Vantive supports the entire sales and marketing process, giving you tools that not only make your sales reps more efficient but actually help them sell more effectively. Vantive's

unique approach delivers full functionality in all areas that are critical to your sales organisation:

- ■ *makes your sales reps more effective with tools to improve win rates, increase deal sizes, shorten sales cycles, and increase margins;*
- ■ *gives your sales reps more time to sell with tools for reducing administrative tasks, decreasing preparation time, using down-time effectively, and condensing training;*
- ■ *increases sales management precision with tools for accurate forecasting, territory and rep reporting, cost control and planning.'*

The software alone will not achieve this. Implicit in Vantive's claims is the need to restructure sales and marketing organisations to gain full benefits of the software tools. More important is the need to carry out such restructuring using customer relationship management principles so that the customer is guaranteed the same experience and quality of response, regardless of the channel through which contact with the company is made.

Exhibit 13.5

LUCKY STRIKE IN BELGIUM

British American Tobacco (BAT) has deep pockets to invest in large-scale change. It has spent £10m on a CRM operation pulling together data for staff in its wholesale distribution business. For Hans Niedermann, head of BAT's global trade marketing and distribution division, the real issue is what he calls micro-marketing. 'We want to look at particular customers in detail so that we can improve market share by a measurable amount.'

In Belgium, BAT has targeted specific stores and restaurants for increased sales of Lucky Strike cigarettes. While Mr Niedermann's staff do not sell direct to these locations, they will follow up the wholesale distributor by visiting retail outlets and promoting BAT brands – and in Belgium, Lucky Strike is a strategic brand for BAT. Software from US-based Siebel, which claims a dominant position among CRM product providers, pulls together historical data on BAT customers and gives Mr Niedermann's 'people at the sharp end' – the field sales force – the same information that BAT's marketing and distribution divisions possess. 'The customer information was traditionally held in functional silos. Now, we've integrated it all.'

Source: Financial Times (3 February 1999).[17]

Case study

DIAMOND HOME SERVICES

It is 21 June 1999 and Diamond Home Services declares lower-than-average sales for the first quarter of the year. Diamond, a leading US contractor of home improvement products, announced revenues in its home improvements sector that were 30 per cent lower than the same period in 1998, and claimed that the results were attributable to the restructuring of the home improvements segment. 'We are entirely confident that our operating processes and organisational restructuring are fundamentally sound for managing future sustained growth in the installed home improvements industry,' stated Geoffrey Foreman, the company's president and chief operating officer. 'While we were disappointed – though not discouraged – that all sales markets and newly consolidated district operations centres are up to speed, we remain encouraged with the potential benefits of our changes.'

Diamond Home Services is a leading marketer and contractor of installed home improvement products, including roofing systems, gutters, doors and fencing. Through its subsidiary, Reeves Southeastern Corporation, it is one of the largest manufacturers and distributors of fencing and perimeter security products to the industrial and residential markets in the USA. Reeves Southeastern operates 32 distribution centres primarily in the eastern half of the USA. Through its subsidiary Diamond Exteriors, the company markets installed home improvement products and services directly to consumers, primarily under the 'Sears' name. Diamond Home Services Inc. has approximately 1,300 employees across the country and achieved revenues of over $240 million in 1998. It has home consultants located in all major cities, providing the company with a presence in markets covering approximately 80 per cent of the owner-occupied households in the USA. The company also offers customers financing through its subsidiary, Marquise Financial Services.

Currently, Diamond Home Services Inc has 60-plus sales offices located in 44 states. The company maintains its headquarters in Woodstock, Illinois and operates a nationwide call centre in Lawrence, Kansas. The number of people managing the phones at the call centre varies from month to month based on the seasonal demands of home improvement services. However, during peak periods, as many as 80–100 people take service calls and enquiries. The large majority of Diamond's calls come as a result of Sears preprints, Yellow Pages and newspaper advertisements.

In late 1997 Diamond's management evaluated the systems used at the company's headquarters, call centre and sales offices. Given their existing infrastructure, the volume of calls they handled was making it difficult to respond quickly to business opportunities. Diamond Home Services knew they needed to make systematic improvements and increase their automation capabilities.

Stuart Davidson, vice-president of information systems, led the task force on an initiative to improve sales efficiency. 'We had been using a system that captured leads, batched them twice a day, and forwarded them to the corporate office, where they were subsequently sent via e-mail to the appropriate sales office,' said Davidson. 'To reach the information, we relied on a number of different software packages, including one we developed internally. However, we had an integration problem. The information was distributed to regional offices and then to the sales offices via e-mail or by fax. The number of hand-offs and volume of paperwork made it difficult to maintain accuracy and respond fast enough to leads. We had a built-in time lag of 48 hours with the transferring of data between the various systems.' Davidson claimed that a two or three-day lag time between the enquiry and the sales call could hinder Diamond's chances of winning the bid. 'Statistics show that the first person who reaches the potential customer is most likely to get the job,' said Davidson. The new sales system, supplied by Vantive, should help Diamond reach the customer faster. 'It's the best way to justify the investment we made. Now we can take a lead and follow up on that lead in sales offices the same day or at least within 24 hours. Our close ratio has increased this year over last year.'

Based on: information from Vantive's Web site (www.vantive.com), Diamond Home Services' Web site (www.dhms.com) and industry reports such as www.marketguide.com in August 1999.

Questions

1 Visit Diamond Home Services' Web site, and use the Internet to research whether the new sales system enables 'Diamond to reach the customer faster'.

2 What other choices did Stuart Davidson have to improve sales efficiency?

3 What other companies, that you know of, exhibit the characteristics of effective sales force management?

ASSIGNMENT QUESTIONS

1 What have been the major changes in the focus of the sales function over the last decade?

2 What is the difference between sales force automation (SFA) and customer relationship management (CRM)?

3 Visit the Web sites of sales force software vendors such as Siebel and Vantive. Are their claims to support CRM valid?

References

1 Marketing (1994). 'Marketing guide: computers in marketing', *Marketing*, 17 March.

2 Ligos, M. (1998). 'The incredible shrinking sales force', *Sales & Marketing Management*. December.

3 Asian Business (1999). 'Taking e-business on the road', *Asian Business*. January.

4 Fisher, A. (1999). 'How a 12,000-strong sales force builds better links with clients', *Financial Times*, 7 April.

5 Moon, M.A., Mentzer, J.T., Smith, C.D. and Garver, M.S. (1998). 'Seven keys to better forecasting', *Business Horizons*, September–October.

6 Genna, G. (1997). 'What's wrong with sales forecasts', *Purchasing*, 5 June.

7 Kahn, K.B. and Mentzer, J.T. (1997). 'State of sales forecasting systems in corporate America', *Journal of Business Forecasting*, Spring.

8 www.yankeegroup.com

9 Yankee Group (1997). 'Power to the field: technology-enabled selling', *Yankee Watch Enterprise Applications*, Vol. 2, Issue 12.

10 Wheelwright, G. (1997). 'Keeping track of customers', *Financial Times*, 5 November.

11 Donath, B. (1994). 'Roadkill in the back room', *Marketing*, 21 July.

12 www.pointinfo.com

13 Rasmussen, E. (1999). 'The 5 steps to successful sales force automation', *Sales & Marketing Management*, March.

14 www.siebel.com

15 www.clarify.com

16 www.vantive.com

17 Dempsey, M. (1999). 'Why so many companies are embracing the CRM trend', *Financial Times*, 3 February.

14

DELIVERING CUSTOMER SERVICE AND SUPPORT

SUMMARY

Customer service has moved into the age of the telephone. Large, specialist telephone call centres for customer service have become commonplace, often with the operations outsourced to third party organisations with the skills and the resources to handle thousands of customer calls every day.

The full potential of telephone-based customer service is only just being realised and companies using it are stealing a march on their competitors.

In this chapter, marketing managers will learn about:

☐ the growth in telephone-based customer service

☐ the various technologies employed in call centres

☐ the principles of good call centre management.

GROWTH IN TELEPHONE-BASED CUSTOMER SERVICE

▓ The increasing use of the telephone for customer service

Historically, large companies have been faster to use IT and call centre technology in customer service than small to medium size enterprises (SMEs). Nowadays, the call centre has become a key component of most companies. According to a recent survey, the most common functions supported by call centres are the provision of customer services and the handling of customer complaints.[1] However, successfully resolving a customer's query presupposes the availability of accurate information to deal with the query. It also assumes that the caller can get through to the right person in the organisation with the minimum inconvenience. Quite often the experience from the customer's perspective can be as follows (or similar to Adrian in Exhibit 14.1):

▓ 'The phone rings 20 times before somebody answers.'
▓ 'They keep passing me around.'
▓ 'I keep having to repeat information.'
▓ 'They never return my calls.'

ADRIAN'S GOT A HEADACHE

At 9.00 am, Adrian wrote a list of companies that he needed to telephone. He spent the rest of the morning trying to get through. Most lines were constantly engaged. Other times he got through, was put on hold and then forgotten about. One company had a touch-tone answering system that confused him with endless lists of names and coded numbers. Finally, Adrian got through to a company that had installed a Vocalis virtual operator. The phone was answered automatically after two rings and he was able to speak normally and to get the information he required in no time at all. In fact, the Vocalis system gave Adrian everything he needed. Except an aspirin.

Source: Vocalis advertisement (1996).

▓ Growth in call centres

Call centres are big business as customer service moves into the telephone era. Call centre services are either set up in-house or, increasingly, being offered as a third party service by specialist providers. Many organisations realise that they do not have the skills or the resources to manage a telephone-based customer service operation and an increasing number of companies are now making the decision to outsource their call centre operations to third parties with the required scale and expertise. The USA traditionally led the world in call centre implementation with more than half a million customer service representatives (CSRs), or agents, employed in 25,000 call centres. However, Europe has been catching up fast with 685,000 call centre seats in 1999, according to latest research estimates.[2]

▓ Multinational and multilingual call centres

Multinational and multilingual call centres are becoming increasingly important. In Europe, countries like Ireland and the Netherlands have attracted multinational organisations to establish pan-European call centres. With more than 100 Irish-based call centres,[3] Ireland has claimed more than its share of the major international call centre market (*see* Exhibit 14.2 and Table 14.1).

Ireland's success at attracting call centre investment is based on a combination of factors including tax incentives and a lower wage environment, although the cost advantages had eroded significantly by the late 1990s.

CALL CENTRES COMING OUT OF DUBLIN'S EARS

Dublin has call centres coming out of its ears. In Ireland as a whole, and the capital in particular, the sector has enjoyed rapid growth in recent years. The centres perfectly reflect the country's dual strengths of a highly trained workforce and a modern infrastructure. Although other countries such as Scotland are able to boast a greater number of call centres, Ireland has the distinction that the majority of its call centres are providing multilingual, pan-European services rather than national services. In addition to US multinationals like PC manufacturers Dell Computers and Gateway 2000 which support their European operations from Ireland, and software company Oracle which does direct marketing across Europe from its Dublin centre, a number of specialist call centre companies have chosen Ireland as their base for their third party operations. One is the Merchants Group which opened its call centre in Cork City in March 1998. The Merchants Group provides third party services for IT, financial services, pharmaceutical, healthcare and utility companies. It investigated sites in Scotland, England and Wales before choosing Cork. Scotland has an attractive grants regime, like Ireland, and the largest concentration of call centres in Europe but Andrew Whiteman, a director of the Merchants Group, says 'we decided not to go there because of the competition for staff. We train people to a very high standard and we don't want them going down the road for seven and sixpence more.' The Cork centre, which opened with 60 staff, will eventually employ 600, and represents an investment of several million pounds. The customers are in 40 different countries, requiring staff with skills in 16 different languages.

Source: Financial Times (22 September 1998).[5]

Table 14.1   Major international call centres in Ireland (1999)

Call centre	Year established	Number of agents
Gateway 2000	1994	850
IBM	1996	800
Dell	1993	720
AOL/Bertelsmann	1995	650
Hertz	1996	500
Citibank	1997	450
UPS	1995	300
Xerox	1998	300
Lufthansa	1998	270
Oracle	1996	250
Compaq	1996	200
Merchants Group	1998	145

Source: Industrial Development Authority of Ireland Web site (1999). [4]

The Netherlands and the other Benelux countries are good locations for multilingual call centres because citizens typically have more than one language. Some companies are also setting up call centres in Finland to serve the Russian market because they prefer the investment climate there.[6]

CALL CENTRE TECHNOLOGY

▓ Three main technology components

Modern telephone call centres are constructed using a variety of telephone and computer technologies from a range of suppliers. The three main technology components in a call centre are:[7]

■ *Automatic call distribution (ACD) systems.* The key technology component in the call centre is the ACD. These are the modern version of the older telephone exchanges and have a far greater range of features. They are designed to receive large volumes of incoming calls, answer the calls automatically, place them in a waiting queue and connect them to the next agent who becomes available. As well as managing call routeing, ACDs provide status information, such as average wait time, so that managers can make decisions about call handling. Information from the ACD is also very useful for tracking promotions, providing information on where calls are originating from, and other marketing purposes.

■ *Voice response systems.* Voice response systems are referred to as *interactive voice response (IVR)* and *voice response unit (VRU)* and, although both terms are used interchangeably, there is a subtle distinction between the two. VRUs provide a simple recorded message such as the reply that customers typically get when they dial a speaking clock or the local rail timetable. IVRs are interactive, using prerecorded messages and then accepting responses from touch-tone phones to answer queries from callers.

■ *Computer telephony integration (CTI).* The convergence of telephone and computer technology is known as computer telephony integration. CTI provides the ability to retrieve customer data and deliver it to the agent together with the incoming phone call. Automatic retrieval of customer data, based on information given to the IVR, reduces both the amount of time an agent has to spend before addressing the customer's needs and the amount of information the customer has to repeat. Using CTI, the caller's files can be accessed on screen in a matter of seconds and the caller's query answered. If the agent cannot deal with the call it can be diverted to a supervisor. When the call is transferred the supervisor's screen is automatically filled with that customer's details through the use of CTI. This 'screen-popping' reduces the frustration of the customer because the agent's questions need not be repeated.

■ Issues with computer telephony integration

CTI can be complex and expensive to implement, as it requires the call centre equipment to be linked to a variety of customer and other databases. Indeed, one of the biggest obstacles that call centres face is the lack of integration with other company systems.[8] However, as the example in Exhibit 14.3 shows, if integration can be achieved, the benefits can be significant.

Although CTI was first introduced in 1982 in the UK,[11] it only matured as a technology in the 1990s. Already a mature technology in the USA, it is now being employed in European and other call centres. In 1996 there were already over 170 different software and CTI solutions available for automating call centres.[12] By 2002 the CTI market will be worth an estimated $14 billion per annum.[13]

Exhibit 14.3

I'D LIKE TO TALK TO THE PERSON WHO MADE MY LAPTOP, PLEASE

With the recent announcement of 3,000 new jobs, in addition to the 1,400 already employed at its manufacturing plant in Limerick, and Dell Direct Call Centre in Bray, County Dublin, Dell Computers will soon be one of the largest private sector employers in Ireland.

Every Dell PC shipped in Europe, the Middle East and Africa, is custom-built in Limerick and sent directly to the customer. It takes four working days from order to delivery. Dell maintains a database of every machine it ships, giving full details of the configuration and service history. This provides customer support staff with a very precise history of the PC, which they can access as soon as they receive a call. It also allows support staff to talk directly to the person who made the machine, if necessary. All this happens because Dell uses CTI technology to link its call centre staff to the database.

The Japanese company Shimano, a manufacturer of bicycle components and fishing gear, also uses CTI technology to improve customer service. Shimano wanted a CTI system that could help it manage a wide variety of customer calls and enable it to capture customer information from those customers that could be fed back to its headquarters to help in product development and improving products. The CTI system, from Siemens Rolm, had to be integrated with the computer system that manages its customer database records. The Shimano account manager now receives the following information automatically from the CTI system:

- who is calling
- customer data from the customer database
- a history of previous calls made by the customer
- past queries and requirements of the customer
- how these queries were handled
- products bought by the customer, and
- the degree of customer satisfaction.

Source: Financial Times (3 June 1998)[9] and Financial Times (3 February 1999).[10]

■ Other call centre components

Other applications of information technology in the call centre include:

- *Predictive dialling.* Predictive dialling is an outbound IT application whereby customers or prospective customers are automatically dialled using a list of telephone numbers from a customer database. Predictive dialling also employs statistical techniques in the form of a 'pacing algorithm' to reduce the risk that there will be no free agents available to deal with a successfully connected call. The pacing algorithm monitors and controls a number of key variables in the call centre, such as the connect rate, average call length and customer wait time, and can predict when the next outbound call should be made.[14]
- *Tracking software.* Tracking packages normally serve two purposes. The first is to record and track customer interaction with the company, so every employee has the necessary information to deal with the customer. The second is to track customer problems from initiation to resolution, so if the problem happens again it can be resolved more quickly.
- *Imaging software.* Imaging software allows agents to view documents such as product catalogues, diagrams and customer correspondence. Viewing the actual documents online allows the agent to provide an accurate and up-to-date service.
- *Fax-on-demand.* Fax-on-demand allows information to be faxed automatically to the customer without any human intervention.

▨ Web-enabled call centres

By 1999 there was much speculation that the call centre was becoming an outdated concept. As companies moved into the digital age, would customer service functions not simply migrate to the Web? There is clear evidence that some companies are trying to persuade their customers to use the Internet for customer service (*see* Exhibit 3.1 in Chapter 3, for example). However, the call centre will still play a significant role in the delivery of customer service and support in the future. One clear trend, as evidenced by the case study at the end of this chapter, is the integration of call centres with the Internet. If properly implemented, Web-enabled call centres will improve the levels of service and support that can be provided to customers.

PRINCIPLES OF GOOD CALL CENTRE MANAGEMENT

▨ Characteristics of well-managed call centres

Cleveland and Mayben (1997)[15] describe a number of characteristics of well-managed call centres. Several relate to the interplay between people management and advanced technology:

- ▨ *They view the incoming call centre as a total process.* The days of the call centre as an island unto itself are fast fading. The reality is that the call centre is an important part of a much bigger process, and has to be integrated into the manufacturing, sales, delivery, fulfilment and after-sales support processes. It also has to be managed as an integral part of several delivery channels, including the Internet.
- ▨ *They have an effective mix of people and technology.* In the emerging call centre environment, personal contact with callers will need to be rationed. There is simply too much demand to have people handling routine calls that technologies such as IVR and the Internet can readily handle. But it is detrimental to force callers to use machines when a person is available or when they prefer a live answer.
- ▨ *They have a practical balance between specialisation and pooling.* Although pooling of resources is at the heart of incoming call management, a balance must be struck that both avoids unnecessary complexity in agent group structures and expands the responsibilities of call centre representatives.
- ▨ *They leverage the key statistics.* Good call centres ensure that the right statistics (see below) are generated accurately and used in an unbiased manner. Gathering the statistics is not enough. They must be acted upon as well.
- ▨ *They effectively hurdle distance, time and politics.* While new technologies have provided enormous new capabilities, they have not eliminated the natural barriers that exist between people who work in distributed environments. The best call centres work hard at getting results from people that work in different locations, have different reporting lines or who work at different times.

▨ Monitoring call centre performance

Regardless of whether an operation is outsourced or in-house, organisations using the telephone as a key customer service tool need to answer the following questions if they are to monitor the level of service they provide:

▨ How many calls do not get through?
▨ How long do customers have to wait?
▨ How many calls did not get through to the right person?
▨ How many queries were answered correctly first time, and how many required one or more follow-up calls to resolve the issue?

Other metrics should also be carefully monitored. Call centre revenues and costs must be measured accurately. Key ratios include:

▨ average call revenue (for revenue-producing call centres)
▨ forecasted call load versus actual load
▨ scheduled staff to actual staff
▨ average call time.

Most of these figures and ratios can be gathered through the combination of computer and telephone technology.

Case study

CALL CENTRES AT COMPAQ AND HEWLETT-PACKARD

Compaq, the world's largest maker of personal computers, manages to keep a healthy distance from one current technology vogue. Interactive Voice Response, or IVR, is the term for automated customer service lines that require callers to continue pressing buttons as they are transferred through different service options. Iain Murray, information management manager at Compaq's new £25m UK call centre in Glasgow, shares the popular distaste for IVR systems that demand too much time from the caller before a real human voice is found. 'As a company, we have a policy of minimum use of IVR systems. Some people hang up straightaway when they get an IVR system at the end of the line.'

The Compaq call centre does employ some IVR technology, but Murray stresses it is a limited use, primarily for late-hour calls. 'The whole point of having a call centre is that it allows you to *talk* to the customer.' One new method of getting in contact with those customers is a cheap and practical piece of software from a small UK company called PhoneMe. The service that PhoneMe offers to call centres consists of an Internet-related freephone number that callers access by clicking a button on the screen of the company Web site. So a customer making an enquiry about Compaq hits the PhoneMe button and is directed to type in his phone number, which is then linked via the PhoneMe switch to the Glasgow call centre. The PhoneMe switch reconciles the two numbers, automatically routeing a call from a Compaq call centre agent through to the prospective customer. Damon Oldcorn, founder and managing director of PhoneMe, explains that simplicity and speed of service are key to his product. 'For customers such as Compaq, the important objective is to capture the interest of someone who has come across the Web site while browsing on the Internet before that person wanders off to another site.' The temptation to click on the freephone button is considerable, and as the phone rings almost instantly, there is none of the frustration of working through the disembodied voice and numerous prompts of an IVR system.

But members of the public are slow to exploit the simple Internet-response option. According to the latest figures from Compaq, only 17 per cent of the visitors to its Web site who decide to speak to the company use the PhoneMe option, while the remaining 83 per cent pick up their phone and dial the number manually.

Not every transaction suits conventional phone contact. Trevor Crooks, UK senior manager for call centre solutions at Nortel, the Canadian telecoms giant, notes that some potential customers for credit card purchases prefer to enter their credit card details in a box on a Web site rather than divulge them to an anonymous telephone operator. Nortel's switching equipment sits at the heart of many call centres and company phone exchanges. For example, Hewlett-Packard has installed a Nortel ACD and associated call centre software at its computer products support centre in the Netherlands. According to Mr Crooks, the 450 agents there handle 18,000 calls a day from across Europe, the Middle East and Africa. 'HP has identified 650 types of call that might arrive there. So they have to be able to distinguish between types of call and route them to the right agent.' The Nortel ACD contains software that picks up the point of origin of each call, routeing it to an agent with the appropriate language. This is what Nortel calls 'granularity', the ability to filter each call through the structure of a massive call centre to the right human voice.

Call Centre Selection is a niche recruitment agency that helps select and train call centre staff. It places 500 staff in call centres every year. Managing director Malcolm Harris has watched the customer support line's love affair with IVR waning. 'The original idea behind call centres was to allow companies to deal with customers in a human way. Then, IVR seemed like the best way of handling a large volume of calls. But it went too far. People become very irritated if they are trapped in an IVR loop demanding more and more responses from them. For most people, 45 seconds exposure to IVR is the limit. After that they hang up.' As calls begin to flow back to the human operator, companies realise that the quality of that agent reflects on their credibility. According to Mr Harris, the time taken to train a call centre agent has risen dramatically as businesses begin to worry about the image that each agent projects. 'Only a few years ago, agents were trained in two or three days. Now, companies will spend four to five weeks preparing a call centre agent to deal with their customers.'   **FT**

Source: 'Can somebody come to the line, please?', by Michael Dempsey, *Financial Times* (3 February 1999).

Questions

1 Search the Internet for other companies that provide similar software or service to PhoneMe. Which Web sites provide such callback functionality?

2 'Not every transaction suits conventional phone contact.' Discuss.

3 Arrange a visit or telephone call to a local call centre. Find out what services are provided in the call centre and what training is required for call centre agents before they are allowed to answer customer queries.

4 How long are you prepared to wait in a telephone queue before you hang up? Time yourself the next time you are held in a telephone-waiting queue.

ASSIGNMENT QUESTIONS

1 Why have call centres grown in popularity for the provision of customer service?

2 Select a mid-sized company that you know well (such as your own bank). Find out how many different points of telephone contact there are for that organisation. Does the size of the resulting number surprise you?

3 What recommendations would you make to companies that have multiple telephone contact points?

4 How is the Internet impacting the way customer service is delivered? Give examples.

References

[1] Wiltshire, M. (1999). 'Vendors of call centre systems share a common vision', *Financial Times*, 3 February.

[2] Shillingford, J. (1999). 'It's not just a question of knowing the language', *Financial Times*, 3 February.

[3] Price, C. (1999). 'Suppliers woo the next generation of PC users', *Financial Times*, 3 February.

[4] www.ida.ie

[5] Moran, N. (1998). 'Turning their heads', *Financial Times survey of Ireland*, 22 September.

[6] Shillingford, J. (1999). 'It's not just a question of knowing the language', *Financial Times*, 3 February.

[7] www.sun.com (1996). 'Integrating computer and telephone technologies'.

[8] Vernon, M. (1999). 'It's still an uphill struggle', *Financial Times*, 3 February 1999.

[9] Moran, N. (1998). 'A leader among PC makers', *Financial Times*, 3 June.

[10] Foremski, T. (1999). 'Fishing gear maker floats a helpful idea', *Financial Times*, 3 February.

[11] Gooding, C. (1995). 'Only speak when you're spoken to', *Financial Times*, 3 May.

[12] Gooding, C. (1996). 'More help to keep the show on the road', *Financial Times*, 6 March.

[13] Williamson, J. (1997). 'Moving into mainstream business', *Financial Times*, 1 October.

[14] Taylor, P. (1996). 'Learning to live together', *Financial Times*, 2 May.

[15] Cleveland, B. and Mayben, J. (1997). *Call Center Management on Fast Forward*. Annapolis, Maryland: Call Center Press.

15

DEVELOPING MARKETING SYSTEMS THAT WORK

SUMMARY

If you have followed each chapter of this book to this point, you may be convinced that information technology has a major, perhaps even a critical, role to play in marketing. We believe this to be true. However, it would be remiss of us not to mention the many problems and difficulties that marketing and business executives have encountered when attempting to design and implement marketing systems. In truth, the design and implementation of any computer system is often characterised by complexity, long elapsed times and project management difficulties.

Designing, developing and managing marketing and IT is a complex business. The research company IDC states that the average company with $3bn in annual revenues and 9,000 employees needs 500 IT professionals to look after the 4,300 desktops and 470 servers, spread over the 40 sites in the typical company.[1] If marketing managers are to tread their way through such complexity, they will need to:

☐ understand some of the common management issues with information technology

☐ understand some specific IT issues in the area of marketing

☐ learn about the trends in IT management and systems development

☐ follow a series of six steps that will help marketing managers get better value from their IT investments.

COMMON MANAGEMENT ISSUES WITH IT

Failure to bridge the business/IT gap

A 1997 study by IDC and Hewlett-Packard found that 46 per cent of chief executives, finance directors and IT directors admit that their IT infrastructure was not adequate to meet business goals.[2] Other commentators support this view. Paul Strassmann is a well-respected author who has studied the issue for many years. In his 1997 book, *The Squandered Computer*,[3] he claims that tens of billions of dollars have been wasted on computer systems in the USA alone and dismisses claims that there is any link between spending on computers and company profitability. Davenport and Prusak (1997)[4] discuss the relationship between technology and the other organisational, behavioural and cultural elements of an organisation and find that information technology, in and of itself, cannot provide solutions to a company's marketing needs. These same themes come through in many other studies. Bensaou and Earl (1998)[5] talk about companies spending millions of dollars on consulting fees trying to resolve IT problems, with little to show for their money. They proceed to provide five separate insights from Japanese management that give a clue as to why these billions of IT dollars have been wasted in the west:

▓ *Strategic instinct versus strategic alignment.* Japanese managers let operational goals drive their IT investments. Western companies strive to align their IT strategies with their business strategies.
▓ *Performance improvement versus value for money.* The Japanese judge investments on the operational improvements they can achieve while western minds use capital budgeting and return on investment (ROI) processes to evaluate IT investments.
▓ *Appropriate technology versus technology solutions.* The Japanese identify performance goals and then select the most appropriate technology to achieve it. Western managers assume that technology offers the smartest means of improving performance.
▓ *Organisational bonding versus IS user relations.* Japanese companies typically rotate employees through the IT function while western companies make their IT specialists more business aware.
▓ *Human design versus systems design.* Japanese systems builders design systems to make use of the knowledge that employees already possess. Western designers go for the most technically elegant solution.

Individually, these distinctions are subtle but, taken together, they amount to a very different mindset on technology. Japanese managers view IT merely as another tool in their armoury with which to defeat the competition. Many western managers have a tendency to fear information technology. They are intimidated by it, step around it and are afraid to manage it. Yet they also view it as a strategic tool and are prepared to spend twice as much as their Japanese counterparts on implementing IT solutions where the probability of failure can often be unacceptably high.

▓ Unrealistic digital age expectations

The digital age is full of companies wanting to buy market share. Amazon.com was valued at more than $30 billion in early 1999, even though it had never generated a profit. In the UK, the Prudential is similarly betting that an estimated £200 million investment in a direct and Internet bank, called Egg, will also be viewed in retrospect as a wise investment (*see* Exhibit 15.1).

Exhibit 15.1

E-COMMERCE EGG   **FT**

In late 1998, Prudential, the UK's leading life assurer, took on the high street and supermarket banks with a direct banking operation called Egg. The service, which relies on the phone and, increasingly, the Internet and digital TV, will extend its reach to younger, more affluent and technology-friendly customers. Prudential named Egg's main competitors as Tesco, J. Sainsbury and Virgin. It also expects to lose up to £200m in the first three years, before entering the black in 2001.

By mid-1999, all the other British banks were pouring money into Internet ventures after waking up to the challenge posed by low-cost online banks like Egg, and to the chance of a higher stock market rating. Abbey National has pledged as much as £100m; NatWest is to plough another £32m into net services; while Barclays has proudly declared itself the largest UK Internet operation with 380,000 online banking customers. Meanwhile, Egg has taken £6.7 billion into its savings accounts in just eight months, thanks to its loss-making interest rates. A third of its 550,000 customers use the Internet for some or all of their transactions.

Source: Financial Times (6 October 1998)[6] and Financial Times (14 August 1999).[7]

Similarly, the cost of providing services such as home shopping cannot always be covered fully, even though they can provide a marketing advantage over the competition. Home shopping has been introduced by supermarkets such as Peapod in the USA, J. Sainsbury in the UK and Albert Heijn in the Netherlands, but there are doubts about whether the typical charge of £5 is enough to cover the cost of selecting the goods from the shelves.[8]

As long as marketing and business managers understand the underlying economics, then the business decisions to provide such services can be assessed realistically. Often, the economics are not fully understood and proper business cases are not produced for such IT-enabled ventures.

■ Subsequent under-delivery against those expectations

The consequence is often a failure of marketing systems, sales systems and IT-enabled services to live up to expectations. Exhibit 15.2 provides an example of the expectations that were made for in-flight entertainment systems in aircraft. While the proposition was solid, the practical difficulties and teething problems of implementing complex systems are nearly always underestimated. The views expressed by Virgin in the Exhibit are interesting and informative. Although there may be a temptation for systems providers to over-sell their products, there is a major obligation on the part of the buyers to understand what it is they are buying. Under-delivery against expectations is as much a function of over-enthusiasm of buyers as it is of over-selling on the part of the systems providers.

Exhibit 15.2

DISAPPOINTMENT IN THE MILE-HIGH CLUB

As the aviation industry gathers at the Farnborough air show in England, a sober realism surrounds the in-flight entertainment industry. It has been a difficult infancy for advanced new in-flight entertainment systems, which were introduced with circus-like hoopla back in 1992 and 1993. The initial difficulties have resulted in supplier–client friction, a lawsuit and at least two companies pulling back from the market. Carriers including British Airways, Northwest Airlines, United Airlines and Virgin Atlantic Airways have had early expectations dashed by the failure of new equipment to live up to its advanced billing. Reliability of the in-flight entertainment systems proved poor in the brutal environment of an airline cabin, and airlines, which had entered complex revenue-sharing deals with device makers, discovered that gambling and pay-per-view movies simply weren't the revenue-spinners they were vaunted to be. British Airways, after three years of 'unsatisfactory' trials, decided in 1997 not to proceed with an interactive entertainment system that it had commissioned. Virgin, an early pioneer, installed a Hughes-Avicom system back in 1993 at a cost of £1 million an aircraft. After finding that some of the gaming functions didn't deliver as expected, it decided in 1996 to install a Matsushita system on its newest aircraft at a cost of £1.7 million per plane. 'It's certainly more reliable,' says Lysette Guana, in-flight entertainment manager at Virgin, 'but it's a few years down the line so you expect that. It's not really a question of Hughes-Avicom versus Matsushita.'

So, with systems costs that can exceed £2 million per plane, the makers need to prove to airlines that the painful part is over. Indeed, the in-flight entertainment industry is in a critical transition period and must demonstrate that the new systems have been fine-tuned to deliver the sort of reliability that carriers insist upon.

Adapted from: Convergence, a Wall Street Journal Europe supplement (Autumn 1998).[9]

▦ Missed deadlines and major cost over-runs

Exhibit 15.2 discusses the three years of unsatisfactory trials experienced by British Airways and Virgin, at the end of which many millions of pounds had been spent without either airline achieving its business objectives. The same problems are routinely encountered by other organisations during the implementation of customer databases, direct marketing systems, sales force automation systems and, more recently, electronic commerce and Internet operations. Managers now commonly expect that systems development efforts will fail to be delivered on time and within the original budget. The impact of such failures is to increase the level of scepticism within the marketing and business community for information systems.

SPECIFIC PROBLEMS WITH IT IN MARKETING

▦ The marketing/IT gap

In many western marketing functions, the same points hold true. IT is rarely taught as a fundamental component of marketing, an indispensable tool that most marketers need to understand. Few marketing professionals can really claim to be fully IT literate or to state that they:

- ▦ appreciate fully the potential of the Internet for marketing
- ▦ can discuss the pros and cons of data warehousing (*see* Exhibit 15.3)
- ▦ have strong views on enterprise resource planning (ERP) systems such as SAP, BaaN or PeopleSoft.

Exhibit 15.3

DATA WHATHOUSING?

Data warehousing remains widely misunderstood by non-IT professionals, according to new research which also shows that marketing teams prefer to tackle customer information problems through market research, rather than improving IT systems. The survey found high levels of dissatisfaction with existing IT systems in servicing marketing needs. Key findings include:

- Almost one in three respondents were totally unaware of the term 'data warehousing'. Only two in five respondents were able to define the term correctly.
- Only 16 per cent of respondents with a data warehouse had measured its return on investment.
- Fewer than one in ten respondents rated IT as 'extremely effective' in creating or improving customer information systems.
- Eleven per cent of respondents blamed the ineffectiveness of their IT systems on a 'lack of information'.
- In all, 46 per cent of respondents did not consider their information systems to be effective in generating information for marketing activities.

Source: Baker and Stone (1998).[10]

There are signs that this is changing. Today, more marketing courses contain modules on information technology. Marketing managers have greater exposure to on-line services for research and are familiar with the capabilities of the Internet. They are beginning to understand the issues associated with using and maintaining customer databases. Future generations of marketing managers will have the required IT skills to operate more effectively than the previous generation.

IT TRENDS IN THE DIGITAL AGE

▨ Increasing use of packaged software

In the past companies tended to design and develop their own marketing systems. Today there are numerous software packages available to support all aspects of sales and marketing. We have mentioned many of them in earlier chapters:

- In Chapter 5, we saw how systems from CACI and Claritas were used for customer segmentation.
- In Chapter 13, we examined customer relationship management (CRM) software from vendors such as Siebel and Vantive.
- In Chapter 14, we saw how there were more than 170 different software solutions for managing telephone call centres.

In the digital age, marketing managers will need to gain a better understanding of the software packages that are available to support their marketing objectives.

■ Outsourcing

The outsourcing of IT underwent phenomenal growth in North America, the UK and Australia throughout the 1990s. Now, the market is taking off in western Europe, South America and parts of south-east Asia, including Japan, which have previously resisted the trend.[11] Table 15.1 shows the scale of some of these outsourcing deals, in a market that is already worth over $100 billion a year.

However, outsourcing of marketing or any other IT operations should not be seen as a solution to an existing problem. Most outsourcing companies will advise their clients to get their systems into shape before they outsource.[13]

One interesting development in recent years has been the increasing use of outsourcing partners to help develop Internet-based marketing solutions. Given that the IT, marketing and Web design skills are unlikely to be present in abundance in most companies, the outsourcing route is seen by many as the natural choice (*see* Exhibit 15.4).

Table 15.1 Top European outsourcing deals, 1998

Lead company	Client	Country	Sector	Value ($m)
IBM	Cable & Wireless	UK/Ireland	Telecoms	3,000
TranSys	London Transport	UK	Transport	1,600
Siemens	National Savings	UK	Banking	1,500
EDS	Banca di Roma	Italy	Banking	1,500
Sema Group	Dept of Social Services	UK	Local government	500
ICL	Dept of Trade and Industry	UK	Government	330
FI Group	First Banking Systems, Bank of Scotland	UK	Banking	246
IBM	IS Consortium Caricentro	Italy	Banking	235

Source: IDC, Financial Times (4 August 1999).[12]

Exhibit 15.4

LEGO OUTSOURCES THE SHOP

Another company to experience the benefits of outsourcing its eCommerce project is Lego, the Danish toy company. When Lego launched Mindstorms and CyberMaster, its first interactive products, it decided it should sell these products on the Web. But the decision brought with it a whole set of business issues that Lego had to face before opening its *World Shop* on the Internet. 'We are manufacturers, not retailers,' says Henrik Loftgaard, marketing manager for the World Shop. It also meant getting outside help. 'We knew we had to outsource the majority of the technical aspects as well as the operational tasks. We could not handle that internally. In the end, Lego chose IBM as its partner. The World Shop opened in March 1999. 'With all the internal and technical challenges inherent in launching the site, it became apparent that having a single partner was the best decision we could have made. Had we to deal with multiple vendors, we would probably not have the site up and running by now,' says Loftgaard.

Source: Financial Times (4 August 1999).[14]

■ The 'computing-defined enterprise'

The Gartner Group,[15] an IT research company, provides an insight into where computing is likely go in the future.[16] Gartner introduces the emerging concept of the 'computing-defined enterprise', which is based on:

- data warehouses
- empowerment of business users
- mobile workers
- Internet/intranet capabilities
- electronic commerce
- speed and flexibility.

The nature of this type of company is significantly different to that of the traditional enterprise. Information technology and information sharing become pervasive throughout the organisation. The implication for marketing managers is clear. Marketers must not only be conversant with the new technologies upon which the computing-defined enterprise is based; they must also be able to lead the discussion on how such technologies can be harnessed to increase shareholder returns. In other words, the marketing function must be capable of leading the rest of the organisation into the digital age.

■ The 'extended enterprise'

The final trend is an even more fundamental change that poses some particularly difficult questions for marketing managers. In the digital age, the enterprise is not simply confined to the company. More and more, firms are opening themselves up to their suppliers and customers, forming networks and sharing information. In some cases, they are even sharing sensitive information with their competitors. The concept of the extended enterprise is particularly common and necessary among Internet companies. Internet-based organisations such as Microsoft HomeAdvisor,[17] iVillage[18] and Third Age[19] typically do not manufacture their own products. They often badge and rebrand other companies' products and services as their own, acting as brokers or 'aggregators' to bring the right combination of products and services to the on-line customer.

If such an extended enterprise is to be created, marketing managers will increasingly be expected to:

- understand the benefits that accrue to each member of the extended enterprise, and the nature of the partnering arrangements to be put in place;
- have a clear view of what product, customer and transactional information they are prepared to share with other companies;
- establish agreed standards for the sharing of such information.

For many companies, this is a difficult concept to implement. The case study at the end of this chapter examines some of the practical difficulties of creating such an extended enterprise.

A POTENTIAL WAY FORWARD

■ Six steps to success

All is not lost, however. If the following six steps are taken, most organisations and marketing departments will stand more than a reasonable chance of getting value for their investments in IT:

- a clearly defined business case
- senior management sponsorship and support
- involvement of marketing and sales users
- adherence to a rigorous systems development methodology
- good project management
- a new attitude and mindset.

A clearly defined business case

While some marketing systems and infrastructural investments may seem intuitively sensible, the discipline of preparing a good, clearly defined business case is important. Unless costs and benefits have been defined up front, it can be difficult to monitor and manage the success of the investment. Without such a business case, it is also often difficult to convince senior management to sponsor and support the investment with the required degree of enthusiasm to see it through successfully to completion. The creation of a business case in support of any marketing system will ensure that costs, revenues and timescales are estimated at the outset, and tracked closely throughout implementation.

Senior management sponsorship and support

While small-scale marketing systems can often be delivered with little senior level involvement or sponsorship, large-scale marketing systems are different because they typically involve re-engineering internal sales and marketing processes and changing the way people go about their day-to-day work. Often, they will also have an impact on the way the company interacts with its suppliers and customers. Without active involvement and support from senior levels within the organisation such large-scale projects will fail to achieve their full objectives. Many organisations will appoint a senior executive or director as the official sponsor of major marketing projects, with full responsibility for the successful implementation of the project. In some cases, the project sponsor will act in this capacity on a full-time basis.

Involvement of marketing and sales users

For any computer system it is important to involve the eventual users of the IT system in its development, and this is particularly true of sales and marketing systems. User involvement in all stages of the development will ensure that the system will meet the needs of the users. All too often, computer systems are developed and 'handed over' to the users without their full involvement or 'buy-in' (*see* Exhibit 15.5). It is also important that users are involved very early on in the process and particularly in the design phase that has a major impact on the rest of the project.

> **Exhibit 15.5**
>
> ### FAILING TO SELL TO THE SALES FORCE
>
> British Columbia Telecom (BC Tel) is one of Canada's largest telephone companies and for many decades held a virtual monopoly on the vast majority of long-distance traffic in Canada's most western province. According to Drew McArthur, BC Tel's business transformation manager, the company recognised that in such a competitive environment, it is the level of relationship with a customer that determines whether or not BC Tel retains the business. To help with the task, McArthur introduced customer relationship management (CRM) software to the BC Tel sales force. 'To increase our advantage in the marketplace, we required the ability to capture and share more customer information,' he adds. But he admits it has not been completely plain sailing – he had not anticipated the initial 'underwhelming' response of the sales force to having such a solution introduced. 'We had expectations that the sales people would have had more of a propensity to learn how to use it,' he adds. 'The challenge is to help sales reps to understand the advantage to themselves if the system is used well.'
>
> *Source: Financial Times* (2 September 1998).[20]

Use of a systems development framework

The design and development of any computer system are major undertakings and require a considerable investment in management time and resources. Successful implementation requires a framework to be adopted and clear stages of development to be addressed in sequence. Such methodologies are built around the concept of a systems development life cycle. Understanding the life cycle and the particular challenges to be faced at each stage is a critical first step in developing successful computer applications. Typically, there are five major phases in this systems development life cycle (*see* Figure 15.1).

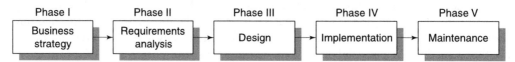

Fig 15.1   Major phases in systems development

Within these major phases there are many lower level steps and tasks. Indeed, a variety of systems development methodologies exist that show how to develop a system in great detail. However, the typical activities in each phase are as follows:

- *Business strategy.* The starting point for any marketing system is a clear understanding of what that computer system is attempting to achieve or to support.
- *Requirements analysis.* Analysis of business requirements involves a number of steps, from analysing existing systems through to interviewing business and marketing managers to identify their issues and objectives.
- *Design.* In this phase, the business requirements are turned into a set of programming specifications for the implementation phase. Nowadays good systems design will often incorporate 'prototypes' for eliciting feedback and response from marketing managers.

■ *Implementation*. Implementation covers programming of new software, configuration of packaged software, testing, training and conversion of existing marketing data to the right format for the new system. Testing and data conversion typically account for the majority of the effort involved in any marketing system, while training is often the area that receives less attention than it deserves.

■ *Maintenance*. Once the marketing system is converted, or commissioned, there is still much development work to do, ranging from fixes to the inevitable 'bugs' in the new system through to the inevitable 'enhancements' or new features that marketing managers want.

Good project management

On an ongoing basis throughout the project, the following management activities will increase the overall chances of success:

■ *Tracking and resolving issues*. During a project, a multitude of different issues will arise. These issues may be technical or may relate to aspects of the business that need to be resolved by marketing managers or general business managers. The technical issues are often the easiest to resolve – issues that require the co-operation of different functions can be more intractable.

■ *Monitoring project progress and risk*. Another integral component of good project management is the ongoing monitoring of progress and project risks. Any project to develop a marketing or customer information system requires a project manager who understands the project management mechanisms of deadlines, milestones, progress reports, progress meetings, escalation procedures for issues that cannot be immediately resolved at this level and steering groups to monitor overall progress.

■ *Establishing a 'project office'*. On large projects, the establishment of a 'project office' is an important consideration. A project office contains all the project plans, files, notes, deliverables and any other relevant material. On smaller projects, a formal project office may not be required.

A new attitude and mindset

However, all these steps will come to nought if marketers themselves do not make a fundamental change in their own perception of what IT can and cannot do for them. On the positive side, there are signs that the gap between marketing and IT is narrowing. First, and perhaps most important, marketing students must gain a solid and practical understanding of computer systems. This is beginning to happen already. Many marketing courses will now include either a module on IT or a practical course on the application of information technology in the field of marketing. Marketing managers have greater exposure to on-line services for research and are familiar with the capabilities of the Internet. They are beginning to understand the issues associated with the use and maintenance of customer databases. Future generations of marketers will have the required IT skills to operate more effectively than the previous generation.

Hopefully, this book can contribute in some way towards this goal. If you feel that it doesn't, e-mail us at the following addresses with suggestions for improvement:

john.oconnor@hotorigin.com
eamonn.galvin@corporate.ge.com

Happy marketing!

Case study

The industry waits four years for retailers and manufacturers to collaborate in the supply chain and then, like buses, three come along at once. Safeway, Tesco and now Sainsbury are all exchanging sales, forecast and promotional information with their key suppliers via the Internet. Safeway was first in November 1997 and Sainsbury went live in May. However, fascinated as the press has been about who was first, it is clear each retailer has built a service appropriate to its business.

The catalyst for these information exchange services was the import to Europe from the USA of Efficient Consumer Response (ECR). ECR is a technique that attempts to get beyond the adversarial relationships that traditionally exist between retailers and manufacturers and encourages them to co-operate in four areas: store assortment, replenishment, promotion and product introductions by sharing data.

While the three retailers have similar goals, they have all gone about the execution in different ways. Safeway launched the Safeway Supplier Information Service (SSIS) at the end of 1997, through which suppliers can tap straight into their EPoS sales data, live and online, enabling them to improve stock levels in Safeway stores, and respond more quickly to demand by customers. Thirty-three suppliers, including both fresh food and packaged goods suppliers, receive scanned sales data for their own products, store by store demand forecasts for the next two weeks, stock level data from stores and depots, promotional data, and product and price files. In the future, they may be given access to data in their particular category, enabling them to manage entire ranges.

Tesco launched the Internet based Tesco Information Exchange (TIE) with seven suppliers in January 1998, sharing seven days' EPoS data, as well as stock, promotions and new product information with suppliers. Suppliers can also get access to a directory of stores, people and news, and give feedback. Sales of a product line are aggregated and are not provided store by store. As Tesco's divisional director, Joe Galloway, explains: 'After all, suppliers are really servicing depots, not stores.'

Sainsbury recently launched Sainsbury's Information Direct (SID) on the Internet as an extension to its existing company Web site. Suppliers are provided with sales, supplier service levels and, soon, stock levels in the depot and stores (by commodity, by department, daily, week to date, and last four weeks). Sainsbury also provides a measure called customer availability, which identifies store stock-outs. For instance, 90 per cent customer availability in any store means 10 per cent of stores are out of stock of the supplier's product.

To get this far has not been easy for the three retailers. Funding for one has been a sore point in many ECR experiments. In the USA, it is said most of the traditional EDI suppliers are funding supplier information networks themselves in a bid to prop up their ailing EDI businesses. In the UK, it is notable that only Tesco is charging its suppliers for the service, or rather suppliers pay EDI provider GE Information Services a fee according to the volume of business they do with Tesco.

Another major issue is the lack of common standards for sharing EPoS data. Bar codes have become the universal currency of modern distribution systems in the 25 years since their introduction. From the raw material to the supplier, goods are marked with the ubiquitous striped rectangles to help each company in the supply chain keep track of stock, invoice customers and monitor sales. Yet there is no common agreement on the value of any particular item of this new currency. Identical bar codes can mean different things to different companies – and in some cases refer to the same products. This has little impact on the customer, who is still likely to marvel at a technology that allows retailers to produce itemised bills, give discounts for special purchases, and run sophisticated loyalty schemes. But it creates confusion in the distribution chain, which costs millions of pounds each year to sort out. An absence of agreement on what bar codes mean makes it harder to develop the ECR approach that is increasingly seen as vital to competitive advantage.

The difficulty arises because the 13-digit bar-code contains very little information. The first two digits are for the country of issue and the next five contain the manufacturer's identity. Then come the five digits that are the manufacturer's product number and the particular item, while the final digit is a check digit that allows the computer to make sure the bar-code is valid. However, when the marketing data research company IRI conducted an examination of the descriptions given to bar code 5000174701678 for a twin pack of Procter & Gamble's Pantene shampoo and conditioner it revealed 11 different product descriptions from 11 UK retailers:

- 50mhair care shampoo
- Pa sh norm/grsy – twin p
- Pntn nm/grs spo/cnd-1/3
- Pantene s/p 250ml + cond n/g
- +Pante shmcn hcmbo rb 450ml
- Pantene shampoo 250ml normal/
- Pantene s/poo&cond norm/grsy 200/2
- Pantene shampoo 250m/cond.200m nm/gy ba
- Pantene twin pk sham/cond.nrm/greas 450m
- Shampoo Pantene shampoo 250ml normal//+cond
- Pantene shampoo 250m/cond.200m.

Some are inaccurate and lack details that would be of value to marketing departments, such as the type of hair for which the product is designed. Only two itemise both elements of the twin pack, the quantity and the hair type. Does it matter? The store that uses the first definition is probably happy, after all. Yet it is losing the opportunity to analyse its sales by missing out essential information. It will be unable to figure out whether twin-pack promotions are popular with its customers, for example, or what sort of hair type they have. If it has a loyalty card scheme, it will know less than it could about what each customer buys.

These inadequacies in its information may have a knock-on effect all along the supply chain if sales data are shared between manufacturers, wholesalers and retailers. All across the industry comparable data are essential for the marketing information companies such as AC Nielsen, which produce the sectoral sales reports that all consumer companies need to run their businesses. The difficulty is increased by growth in cross-border trading in Europe, with companies supplying several countries with products manufactured in one. Over the years some large groups have allowed product item bar codes to be assigned to different products in different countries.

Sources: Financial Times (1 September 1998)[21] and *The Grocer* (2 August 1998).[22]

Questions

1 How do the retailers in this case study exemplify the concept of the 'extended enterprise'?

2 What are the benefits of sharing sales, forecast and promotional information between retailers and their key suppliers?

3 Why has it 'not been easy for the three retailers' to set up their respective collaboration efforts?

4 Use the Internet to research how a company like Tesco can implement electronic links with its suppliers using a service such as GE Information Services' TPN network.

ASSIGNMENT QUESTIONS

1 Choose a company that, in your opinion, employs information technology systems effectively in its marketing function. What distinguishes this company from its competitors?

2 In your opinion, did Amazon.com and Egg.co.uk justify their high market valuations in 1999? Make a case for your answers.

3 Is there really a distinction in the ways that western and Japanese marketing managers view information technology?

4 Visit Third Age's Web site and comment on the range of products and services that Third Age has created as part of its extended enterprise.

References

1 Taylor, P. (1997). 'Management software comes to the rescue', *Financial Times*, 1 October.

2 Shillingford, J. (1997). 'Business goals are often unmet by IT strategies', *Financial Times*, 1 October.

3 Strassmann, P.A. (1997). *The Squandered Computer: Evaluating the Business Alignment of Information Technologies*, New Canaan, Connecticut: The Information Economic Press.

4 Davenport, T.H. and Prusak, L. (1997). *Information Ecology: Mastering the Information and Knowledge Environment*, New York: Oxford University Press.

5 Bensaou, M. and Earl, M. (1998). 'The right mind-set for managing information technology', *Harvard Business Review*, Boston, September–October.

6 Brown-Humes, C. (1998). 'Prudential woos youth with high-tech, high-interest deal', *Financial Times*, 6 October.

7 Mackintosh, J. (1999). 'Banks scramble to follow Egg's lead', *Financial Times*, 14 August.

8 Batchelor, C. (1998). 'Moving up the corporate agenda', *Financial Times*, 1 December.

9 Goldsmith, C. (1998). 'In-flight video and gaming devices aren't so entertaining for airlines', *Wall Street Journal Europe – Convergence Magazine*, Autumn.

10 Baker, P. and Stone, D. (1998). 'A research report into data warehousing', London: KPMG Management Consultants.

11 Moran, N. (1999). 'Change in sentiment over IT outsourcing,' *Financial Times*, 4 August.

12 Moran, N. (1999). 'Change in sentiment over IT outsourcing', *Financial Times*, 4 August.

13 Moran, N. (1997). 'Price is not the main factor', *Financial Times*, 5 November.

14 Nairn, G. (1999). 'Companies can tap into a growing range of services', *Financial Times*, 4 August.

15 www.gartner.com

16 Taylor, P. (1997). 'Farewell to the centralisation of the IT department', *Financial Times*, 5 November.

17 www.homeadvisor.com

18 www.ivillage.com

19 www.thirdage.com

20 Dempsey, M. (1998). 'Sales teams need convincing too', *Financial Times*, 2 September.

21 Willman, J. (1998). 'Advantages slip through a crack in the barcode', *Financial Times*, 1 September.

22 Field, C. (1998). 'Three major food multiples collaborate with suppliers by sharing data across the supply chain', *The Grocer*, 2 August.

INDEX